Content-Based
College ESL Instruction

Content-Based College ESL Instruction

Loretta F. Kasper
Kingsborough Community College/CUNY

With
Marcia Babbitt and Rebecca Williams Mlynarczyk
Donna M. Brinton
Judith W. Rosenthal
Peter Master
Sharon A. Myers
Joy Egbert
David A. Tillyer and Louise S. Wood

LAWRENCE ERLBAUM ASSOCIATES, PUBLISHERS
2000   Mahwah, New Jersey   London

Lawrence Erlbaum Associates, Inc., Publishers
10 Industrial Avenue
Mahwah, NJ 07430

Cover design by Kathryn Houghtaling Lacey

Library of Congress Cataloging-in-Publication Data

Kasper, Loretta F. (Loretta Frances), 1951–
Content-based college ESL instruction / by Loretta F. Kasper ; with
Marcia Babbitt ... [et al.].
    p. cm.
Includes bibliographical references and index.
ISBN 0-8058-3076-6 (pbk. : alk. paper)
1. English language—Study and teaching (Higher)—Foreign speak-
ers. 2. English language—Study and teaching (Higher)—United
States. 3. Interdisciplinary approach in education. I. Title.
PE1128.A2K376 1999
428'.0071'173—dc21   99-31397
                                                          CIP

Books published by Lawrence Erlbaum Associates are printed on
acid-free paper, and their bindings are chosen for strength and dura-
bility.

Printed in the United States of America
10 9 8 7 6 5 4 3 2 1

Contents

III
Incorporating Technology Into Content-Based Instruction

Preface

Content-Based College ESL Instruction: An Overview

Loretta F. Kasper

Kingsborough Community College/CUNY

Khalid had gone through a four-course ESL sequence, getting straight As in every course. After passing the English as a Second Language (ESL) exit exam with a high score, Khalid entered the mainstream college curriculum. One of his first mainstream courses was business administration, a requirement for his major. Several weeks into the semester, Khalid was in a state of panic. He had thought he knew English, but was unable to understand the lectures and the readings in his business class. When Khalid went to the business professor to ask for help, the professor told him that if he could not understand the work, he would not pass the course. Khalid was so frustrated that he wanted to drop the course. He felt he would never be able to succeed in college.

Veronica was in her fourth semester of college ESL. She was a conscientious student who had started at the beginning level of English and had progressed to the advanced level. Despite the progress she had made in English, Veronica's academic status was now in jeopardy. College rules restricted to four the number of semesters a student could remain in developmental English classes. If Veronica did not pass the institutional reading and writing examinations by the end of her fourth semester, she would have to leave college. Although Veronica studied hard and practiced English every day, she was unable to pass these examinations. As a result, her dream of earning a college degree was cut short.

Khalid's and Veronica's stories unfortunately are typical of the experiences of many college ESL students. Some of these students have achieved passing grades in ESL courses, yet remain painfully underprepared to deal successfully with the linguistic and academic demands of mainstream college courses. Others never get the opportunity to fulfill their academic goals because they are unable to progress rapidly enough to meet prescribed levels of English language proficiency within set time limits.

ESL students, like Khalid and Veronica, now comprise a substantial portion of the college population, and their numbers continue to increase dramatically (Crandall, 1993). This dramatic increase in the college ESL population, coupled with the pressure of institutional time limitations on developmental instruction, presents a critical challenge to ESL educators. This challenge is twofold and demands pedagogy that addresses both the linguistic and the academic needs of ESL students in college. College ESL students need instruction that will facilitate the development of their English language skills to enable them to meet quickly the requisite levels of linguistic proficiency. This instruction must also prepare these students to enter and to succeed in mainstream college courses. Yet, for ESL students to succeed in the academic mainstream, they must be able to do more than identify a vocabulary item, hold a simple conversation, or find the main idea of a reading passage. They must be able to use the English language as a means for acquiring knowledge, in the process engaging in the active analysis, interpretation, critique, and synthesis of information presented in English (Kasper, 1996; Pally, 1997).

THE CONTENT-BASED MODEL OF ESL INSTRUCTION

Recent studies (Benesch, 1988; Brinton, Snow, & Wesche, 1989; Crandall, 1995; CUNY Language Forum and CUNY ESL Council, 1992; Kasper, 1994, 1997) have provided both empirical and anecdotal evidence demonstrating that content-based college ESL instruction effectively increases students' English language proficiency, teaches them the skills necessary for success in mainstream college courses, and helps to ease their transition from the sheltered ESL program to the academic mainstream. In a content-based course, ESL students use English to expand their existing knowledge bases (Kasper, 1998), as they are presented with interdisciplinary material in a meaningful, contextualized form in which the primary focus is on the acquisition of content area information (Brinton et al., 1989). The result of this type of instruction is that ESL students gradually acquire greater control of the English language, enabling them to participate more fully in an increasingly complex academic and social environment (Kasper & Singer, 1997).

AN OVERVIEW OF THIS VOLUME

This book is meant to inform and to train readers, be they graduate students in MATESOL (Master of Arts In Teaching English to Speakers of Other Languages) programs, ESL faculty, or college administrators, in the techniques of content-based instruction (CBI). The goal of each of the chapters in the book is to offer information, suggestions, and instructional tools grounded in theory and practice that will assist readers' efforts to develop content-based materials and programs appropriate to their educational institutions and situations.

The essays in this volume speak to the many and varied issues in content-based college ESL instruction, and as such are divided among three sections: Laying the Groundwork for a Content-Based Pedagogy; Building English Language Skills through Content-Based Instruction; and Incorporating Technology into Content-Based Instruction.

One of the key concerns in college ESL instruction involves how to assess students' progress. This is especially true in a CBI context where assessment becomes a multifaceted task that involves the evaluation of both linguistic and content knowledge. Because assessment is a critical factor in determining both instructional design and student performance, each chapter in this book addresses assessment issues as they apply to the particular methodology described therein.

PART I: LAYING THE GROUNDWORK
FOR A CONTENT-BASED PEDAGOGY

The four chapters in this section offer a foundation for the design and implementation of content-based college ESL instruction as they speak to various issues of educational theory and practice and address the concerns of ESL students and faculty. Chapter 1, "Content-Based College ESL Instruction: Theoretical Foundations and Pedagogical Applications," responds to the question most critical to the focus of this volume: Why content-based college ESL instruction? In this chapter, I offer an answer that is grounded within the framework of second language acquisition research and cognitive theory. I also discuss practical considerations that must be addressed when designing and implementing content-based programs, such as choosing an appropriate CBI model, training faculty, and developing reliable and valid assessments.

Chapter 1 describes several different CBI models, and the success of any of these models is dependent on effective administration. In chapter 2, "Keys to Successful Content-Based Programs: Administrative Perspectives," Marcia Babbitt and Rebecca Mlynarczyk provide a detailed treatment of the many and varied administrative issues inherent in content-based college ESL programs. They maintain that developing an effective content-based program requires a great deal of planning, cooperation, and coordination. Drawing on their experience as codirectors of the ESL program at Kingsborough Community College/CUNY, Babbitt and Mlynarczyk make suggestions for how to deal with issues such as student recruitment, curriculum development, and program evaluation and fine-tuning.

With the spread of CBI as a paradigm in second and foreign language instruction, it has become increasingly important to build exposure to this paradigm into teacher training programs. In chapter 3, "Out of the Mouths of Babes: Novice Teacher Insights into Content-Based Instruction," Donna Brinton discusses the hands-on experience with CBI that is built into the master's in applied linguistics program at the University of California, Los Angeles in the introductory Teaching English as a Second Language (TESL) methods course and the field practicum in TESL. As a component of both courses, students participate in e-mail dialogue journal exchanges with the course instructor and their peers. Brinton's chapter examines these dialog journal interchanges as they pertain to the novice teachers' reactions to CBI and the light that these comments shed on the challenges of preparing teachers to effectively implement CBI.

The first three chapters are written from the perspective of ESL faculty committed to a CBI paradigm. In chapter 4, "ESL Students in the Mainstream: Observations From Content-Area Faculty," Judith Rosenthal, a Kean University biology professor, speaks from the perspective of a mainstream instructor and takes the position that all faculty, whatever their academic discipline, must contribute to the development of English language proficiency by nonnative speakers. As she describes how CBI instruction facilitates ESL students' transition into the mainstream, Rosenthal seeks to raise readers' awareness of the types of classroom activities and practices that fail to take into consideration the linguistic needs of ESL students and makes specific suggestions for how mainstream faculty may assist the ESL students in their classes.

PART II: BUILDING ENGLISH LANGUAGE SKILLS THROUGH CONTENT-BASED INSTRUCTION

The four chapters in the second section of the book each offer concrete suggestions for content-based pedagogical activities that may be used to build English language skills and prepare ESL students for the demands of the college mainstream. The activities described in these chapters are directed toward ESL students from the lower levels to the more advanced, and target a variety of skills, each essential to students' linguistic and academic progress.

The development of grammatical proficiency is a major linguistic concern for both teachers and ESL students at all levels of instruction. In chapter 5,

"Grammar in Content-Based Instruction," Peter Master maintains that attention to grammar within the areas of content being studied is necessary if ESL students are to acquire the cognitive academic language proficiency necessary for college level work. He believes that because CBI focuses on the use of language to convey thoughts and ideas, it offers many meaningful contexts within which students can develop grammatical competence. Master discusses some of these content-based contexts and provides examples of how to teach the grammatical system through them.

As we attempt to prepare ESL students for the academic mainstream through content-based programs, we must remember that course materials need to be made accessible to all students. Because many colleges and universities have begun to strictly limit the number of semesters a student may remain in developmental courses, accessibility is an especially critical issue for lower level ESL students who need to develop English language proficiency more rapidly than ever before. In spite of this fact, all too often CBI is not made available to lower level ESL students because the language generally found in content-based materials is deemed too difficult for these students. However, topical short stories can provide an excellent foundation for introducing content-based topics, and subsequently academic texts themselves, into lower level ESL courses. In chapter 6, "The Short Story as a Bridge to Content in the Lower Level ESL Course," I offer a blueprint for how to use short stories to introduce academic content into lower level courses.

Visual media such as film also offer unique benefits to ESL students endeavoring to become proficient readers, writers, listeners, and speakers of the English language. Film imagery, integrated into the content-based college ESL course, may be used to provide reinforcement and clarification of concepts presented in related print texts. Whether viewing the complete film or excerpted sequences, ESL students benefit from a graphic, visual illustration of key critical thinking concepts, thus making subject matter more concrete (Kasper & Singer, 1997). The structure and content of film can also serve as a visual model for various modes of written discourse. In chapter 7, "Film Imagery: A Visual Resource for Clarifying Content and Developing Academic Writing Skill," I describe how film may be used to clarify content, and I discuss how it may also be used to teach various forms of academic writing, such as comparison–contrast, cause–effect, and argumentation.

Finally, although there are a relatively large number of content-based materials that target the development of reading and writing skills, there are few that address listening and speaking skills. This is unfortunate because academic success requires competence not only in reading and writing, but also in listening and speaking. Sharon Myers believes that because commercially produced materials do not often meet student needs, teacher-prepared materials are essential to fill the gap. In chapter 8, "Speaking Science: Developing ESL

Materials for University Students in Academic Disciplines," Myers illustrates how ESL students' listening and speaking skills may be effectively developed through teacher-created audio recordings that are designed with students' level of English, content area interest(s), and background knowledge in mind.

PART III: INCORPORATING TECHNOLOGY INTO CONTENT-BASED INSTRUCTION

Modern computer applications have expanded the body of instructional resources available to faculty and students, and the four chapters included in this section each describe how CBI may be enhanced through computer-based activities. Hypertext applications incorporated in e-mail, the Internet, and the World Wide Web offer powerful tools for integrating language and content. Using the computer provides students with increased possibilities for cooperative learning contexts in which all participants benefit from improved language and content skills as they gather information and share knowledge.

Although ESL students may study within an English-speaking environment, few classes or assignments encourage or require their active interaction with native speakers. Joy Egbert believes that CBI incorporating community-based field experience can create a learning context that supports real-world language use and that promotes intercultural understanding. She further believes that this experience may be broadened and strengthened through computer-based activities. In chapter 9, "Computers as Content and Context in a Cross-Cultural Language Field Experience," Egbert describes her "Kids and Computers" course, which brought together college ESL and local elementary school students in an intercultural exchange that addressed the issues of cultural diversity, technology use, and authentic English language practice through both face-to-face interaction and e-mail communication.

ESL students, in particular, can benefit greatly from e-mail exchanges that provide the opportunity for students to practice both writing and reading skills in the process of sharing knowledge, experience, and culture with other students who may live across the country or even the world. In chapter 10, "*The Keyboard to Success: An ESL/Basic Writing Internet Partnership*," David Tillyer and Louise Wood describe their experiences working together for three semesters on an intercultural e-mail exchange that paired nonnative speakers from an ESL class in New York with native speakers from a Basic Writing (BW) class in South Carolina. Tillyer and Wood explain their reasons for participating in the exchange, describe the process of conducting one, consider problems encountered, enumerate positive outcomes, and offer guidelines for a productive e-mail intercultural exchange.

The Internet contains the largest body of content-based resources in history, and incorporating Internet technology into ESL courses can provide students with a richer and more valuable educational experience as they are encouraged to interact with language in new and varied ways (Pennington, 1996). In chapter 11, "The Internet and Content-Based College ESL Instruction: Reading, Writing, and Research," I offer a rationale and provide concrete guidelines for using the Internet to teach and refine English language, critical literacy, and academic skills through a content-based activity I call *focus discipline research*.

The first three chapters in this section describe how technology may be used to enrich CBI. Although enriching instruction is important, incorporating technology into content-based courses fulfills an educational need far more critical to ESL students' future progress.

Technological literacy now counts among the basic skills necessary for success not only in college, but also in the workplace. This means that to be prepared for the demands of the academic mainstream, and subsequently for the workforce, students must be able to use technology to gather and manage information. I conclude the book with chapter 12, "The Role of Information Technology in the Future of Content-Based ESL Instruction," which discusses why and how information technology should be made an integral component of content-based ESL courses, taking into account the needs and concerns of college faculty, administrators, and students.

A FINAL NOTE

The 12 chapters in this volume seek to provide readers with a broad view of the growing field of content-based ESL instruction. Each of the authors has drawn from his or her personal and classroom experiences with this instructional methodology to offer a comprehensive treatment of issues key to the success of ESL students in college, as well as concrete suggestions for how to implement CBI most effectively. We hope that our readers will find this information useful and call on it in their efforts to empower college ESL students to become full members of the English-speaking academic community.

* * *

Loretta F. Kasper is the owner and moderator of Content-ESL, an e-mail listserv that provides a forum for discussion of issues in Content-Based ESL and an avenue of communication for students and faculty participating in content-based projects. If you wish to subscribe to this list, please send an empty e-mail message to: content-esl-subscribe@egroups.com

Additional information on this list may be found at: http://members.aol.com/Drlfk/Content-ESL.html

REFERENCES

Benesch, S. (1988). *Ending remediation: Linking ESL and content in higher education*. Washington, DC: TESOL.

Brinton, D. M., Snow, M. A., & Wesche, M. B. (1989). *Content-based second language instruction*. Boston: Heinle & Heinle.

Crandall, J. (1993). Diversity as challenge and resource. In P. Zadra & N. D. Lay (Eds.), *Proceedings on the conference on ESL students in the CUNY classroom: Faculty strategies for success* (pp. 4–19). New York: CUNY.

Crandall, J. (1995). *ESL through content-area instruction*. McHenry, IL: Delta Systems.

CUNY Language Forum and CUNY ESL Council. (1992). *Into the academic mainstream: Guidelines for teaching language minority students*. New York: Author.

Kasper, L. F. (1994). Improved reading performance for ESL students through academic course pairing. *Journal of Reading, 37*, 376–384.

Kasper, L. F. (1996). Writing to read: Enhancing ESL students' reading proficiency through written response to text. *Teaching English in the Two-Year College, 23*(1), 25–33.

Kasper, L. F. (1997). The impact of content-based instructional programs on the academic progress of ESL students. *English for Specific Purposes, 16*(4), 309–320.

Kasper, L. F. (1998). Meeting ESL students' academic needs through discipline-based instructional programs. In T. Smoke (Ed.), *Adult ESL: Politics, pedagogy, and participation in classroom and community programs* (pp. 147–157). Hillsdale, NJ: Lawrence Erlbaum Associates.

Kasper, L. F., & Singer, R. (1997). Reading, language acquisition, and film strategies. *Post Script, 15*, 5–17.

Pally, M. (1997). Critical thinking in ESL: An argument for sustained content. *Journal of Second Language Writing, 6*(3), 293–311.

Pennington, M. C. (1996). The power of the computer in language education. In M. C. Pennington, (Ed.), *The power of CALL* (pp. 1–14). Houston: Athelstan.

ACKNOWLEDGMENTS

I thank each of the contributing authors for sharing their expertise in the field and for providing readers with insights gained through their experiences using CBI. I also thank them for getting manuscripts in on time and for taking the time to edit and revise their work.

I join with the contributing authors in thanking all of the ESL students who worked with us in our efforts to promote CBI. They provided each of us with valuable insights and helpful feedback on this pedagogical method.

I thank my husband, Howard, for his support and patience during the many hours I spent writing this book.

Finally, I thank Naomi Silverman for her belief in this project and for all of the advice and support she provided during its development.

I

Laying the Groundwork
for a Content-Based Pedagogy

1

Content-Based
College ESL Instruction

Theoretical Foundations
and Pedagogical Applications

Loretta F. Kasper
Kingsborough Community College/CUNY

Being successful in an English-speaking academic environment requires that ESL students be both functionally and academically literate, that they be able to use English to access, understand, articulate, and critically analyze conceptual relationships within, between, and among a wide variety of content areas. It is the basic premise of this volume of essays that content-based instruction (CBI) enables college English as a Second Language (ESL) students to develop and refine these necessary literacy skills. Through planned, purposeful, and academically based activities that target linguistic and critical thinking skills and engage students in meaningful and authentic language processing, CBI fosters a functional language learning environment that goes beyond simply presenting information in the second language. This functional language-learning environment offers ample opportunities for students to use English to gather, synthesize, and evaluate information (Pally, 1997) as it teaches them appropriate patterns of academic discourse and sociolinguistic conventions relating to audience and purpose (Soter, 1990).

This chapter describes the theoretical foundations and pedagogical applications of CBI in college ESL programs. The theoretical foundations of CBI, as well as the method itself, are interdisciplinary in nature, deriving from second language acquisition research and cognitive learning theory. The pedagogical applications of these theories result in meaningful and relevant contexts for language use, enabling students to develop the functional and academic literacy skills necessary for success in college.

THEORETICAL FOUNDATIONS

The linguistic and cognitive theories that provide the foundation for CBI each emphasize the importance of providing multiple opportunities for ESL learners to interact with authentic, contextualized, linguistically challenging materials in a communicative and academic context. These theories view second language acquisition (SLA) as a complex cognitive act, in which prior knowledge and strategy use are both critical to success.

Krashen's Comprehensible Input Hypothesis

In his SLA theory, Krashen (1985) posited that two factors, learning and acquisition, are involved in the development of second language skill. Learning refers to the process of gaining formal knowledge about language through explicit instruction in linguistic forms and structures. Acquisition is a process similar to that which occurs with a first language—language is acquired as it is used as the medium for learning other things. Because Krashen (1982, 1985) believed that similar processes underlie first (L1) and second (L2) language acquisition, he asserted that the focus of SL instruction should be on meaning rather than on form.

Krashen (1982, 1985) stated that language structures are most efficiently acquired when presented through comprehensible input that is just beyond the learner's current proficiency level, thereby forcing him or her to reach beyond the linguistic input and use previous knowledge and communicative context to glean the meaning of unfamiliar structures. Thus, Krashen's model provides a theoretical foundation for content-based ESL courses that offer students contextualized language curricula built around meaningful, comprehensible input through which not only language, but also information, is acquired (Brinton, Snow, & Wesche, 1989). Language acquisition is further facilitated and motivation increased if the information acquired is highly relevant to students' personal and educational goals (Snow, Met, & Genesee, 1989).

Cummins' Two-Tiered Skill Model

Whereas Krashen emphasized meaningful, comprehensible input as key to effective SLA, Cummins (1981) asserted that becoming proficient in a second language involves a two-tiered model of skill acquisition. At the first tier, the learner acquires what Cummins called *basic interpersonal language skills.* These basic interpersonal, or functional literacy, skills involve the ability to converse with others and to articulate needs in the L2, and according to Cummins, can be developed within 1 to 2 years. In contrast, the second tier, called *cognitive academic language proficiency*, involves the acquisition of academic literacy skills, that is, the ability to use the L2 both to understand complex, often decontextualized linguistic structures, and to analyze, explore, and deconstruct the concepts presented in academic texts. Cummins stated that it may take as many as 5 to 7 years to fully master cognitive academic language proficiency.

The distinction between proficiency in basic interpersonal communication and cognitive academic language is critical to the needs of the college ESL student, who must become not only functionally, but also academically literate, and who must be able to use English not just as a means to converse and communicate, but also as a vehicle for learning, articulating, and analyzing information from a variety of academic disciplines (Clair, 1994). Cummins argued that learners cannot acquire cognitive academic language skills from everyday conversation; developing these cognitive skills requires task-based, experiential learning typified by students' interactions with contexts, tasks, and texts that present them with complex interdisciplinary content. Thus Cummins' model provided another theoretical foundation for the type of task-based experiential learning that is such an integral part of content-based college ESL instruction.

Cognitive Learning Theory

Both Krashen's and Cummins' theories suggest that SLA is a complex cognitive task. If SLA is viewed as such, the principles of cognitive learning theory should be applied when developing ESL instructional methodology. Although a full discussion of cognitive learning theory is beyond the scope of this chapter, its basic principles may be considered as offering support for the CBI model.

Basic to cognitive learning theory is the belief that learning is developed through a series of stages (Anderson, 1983, 1985). Learning begins with an instructional or study phase, called the *cognitive stage*, in which the learner gradually develops a rough mental representation of task requirements. The learner refines and strengthens this representation in the second *associative stage* of learning but still consciously attends to rules and sometimes needs outside support when performing the task. In the third stage of learning, the *autonomous stage*, the task representation is increasingly refined, and the learner is now able to perform the task automatically and autonomously. Cognitive learning theory maintains that for students to progress through these stages, they require extensive practice and feedback, as well as instruction in the use of various learning strategies. Only when these conditions are met will learners develop sufficient proficiency to be able to function on an autonomous level in the learning environment.

O'Malley and Chamot (1990) applied the principles of cognitive learning theory to L2 pedagogy. Their learning model, the Cognitive Academic Language Learning Approach (CALLA), relies heavily on a cognitive principle called *scaffolding*, "the provision of extensive instructional supports when concepts and skills are being first introduced and the gradual removal of supports when students begin to develop greater proficiency skills, or knowledge" (Chamot & O'Malley, 1994, p. 10). These researchers advocate using materials drawn from major content areas (e.g., science, history) to develop academic language skills and to provide direct instruction in learning strategies. Chamot and O'Malley believe that this type of instructional program maximizes ESL students' acquisition of both language and content knowledge.

Content-based assignments lend themselves well to scaffolding (see e.g., Kasper, chap. 11, this volume). Students begin with structured tasks that guide them step-by-step through the process of gathering, evaluating, and synthesizing information. These tasks are designed to provide challenging linguistic input and to teach various learning strategies. As students become familiar with effective learning strategies and techniques, they are encouraged to explore topics in a less structured and more self-directed manner. Thus content-based learning tasks that incorporate scaffolding provide the context for students to progress naturally through the cognitive, associative, and autonomous stages of learning.

READING AND WRITING AS COGNITIVE CONSTRUCTS

When SLA is viewed as a cognitive act, and the principles of cognitive learning theory are applied to it, linguistic skills such as reading and writing become cognitive constructs. Viewing them this way implies that both are selective, active, and strategic acts. Furthermore, this view suggests that reading and writing interact to build knowledge that can then be used to facilitate performance in future reading and writing tasks.

Reading as a Cognitive Task

A cognitive view of reading holds that readers do not receive information from individual texts; rather, they approach reading in the context of the entire world of their experience. This view of reading implies that information does not create comprehension; instead comprehension depends on prior knowledge. As a cognitive function, reading requires the activation of strategies for how to approach text content, along with appropriate relevant schemata, or background knowledge, for how to interpret that content. Comprehension takes place through the process of elaborating and integrating new information into the existing knowledge network. The cognitive act of reading is therefore a dynamic, recursive, integrated process through which the reader continuously constructs the world and then continuously verifies and/or modifies that construct on the basis of new incoming information.

In terms of a cognitive theory of reading, readers use preexisting knowledge to create a cognitive map that guides their construction of meaning. ESL students may experience comprehension problems either because they lack the schemata that native speakers fluently use to make meaning out of text, or because they apply inappropriate schemata and misunderstand the text (Bransford & Johnson, 1972). Thus, a faulty cognitive map for constructing meaning may cause L2 learners to lose their way in their attempts to comprehend English language texts. Helping students develop appropriate and varied schemata can solve this problem and increase comprehension.

From a cognitive point of view, academic content is a critical factor in increasing reading comprehension because such content builds and activates domain-related knowledge, or schemata, from which the reader may draw to aid in constructing meaning from text (Anderson & Pearson, 1984). Practically speaking, each time ESL students read content-based texts, they learn something new about both the English language and the subject area under study. When this new information is introduced into the cognitive system, students must either elaborate on or modify their existing network of schemata to fit new information into what they already know (Kasper, 1995/96). Assimilating new information, therefore, requires both that students form new schemata and that they accommodate existing schemata, further building the overall knowledge base.

Content-based texts develop overall reading skill because every text read and processed in this way further builds and reinforces the student's network of schemata. The resulting expanded schematic knowledge base then facilitates meaning construction and aids in comprehension of future texts. In fact, a study by Nelson and Schmid (1989) found that the effect of the schematic network created by content-based texts and activities generalizes to enhance ESL students' comprehension even of unrelated texts.

Writing as a Cognitive Task

In a cognitive model, reading and writing interact to build knowledge and improve comprehension. Content-based materials take advantage of this interaction by promoting meaning construction through activities that require the ESL reader to engage in, to interact with, and to synthesize information from texts (Zamel, 1992). Writing focuses the learner's attention on key features of text and encourages deep processing and extended analysis (Grow, 1996). Therefore, viewed as a cognitive task, writing helps students elaborate new knowledge so that it becomes interconnected and useful.

To compose an appropriate written response to a text, students must first transform the information presented into knowledge that they can use. As described in the previous section, this transformation results when the reader connects new information to prior knowledge, which may include personal experience and other texts read. This newly gained knowledge can then be used to analyze, interpret, and synthesize subsequent information presented.

Producing written responses to content-based texts builds and reinforces a student's network of schemata by offering a means for working out and considering readings from several different perspectives. In this way, writing provides insights into text that may not have been obvious at the initial reading (Zamel, 1992). When students compose a written response to text, that text becomes a richer and more meaningful experience through the interactive effects of reading and writing, as reading builds knowledge to use in writing, and writing consolidates knowledge and builds schemata with which to read (Kasper, 1996). As students process and produce texts, they refine functional and academic literacy skills (Johns, 1997), with not only knowledge of language and content enhanced, but higher order critical thinking skills also developed (Pally, 1997).

DEVELOPMENT OF CRITICAL THINKING SKILLS

The ability to think critically about information is a higher order cognitive skill that students must develop if they are to succeed in college. In their mainstream courses, students will be asked to discuss issues, pose questions, and evaluate differing viewpoints. They may be asked to describe interdisciplinary or intertextual relationships. To carry out these tasks, students must be able to function on an autonomous level, synthesizing information from a variety of sources and weighing the importance of the different pieces of information they have found. By providing various contexts for students to accrue information and by asking them to question, synthesize, and evaluate that information across various modes of discourse, CBI activities support learning in two ways. They give students the opportunity to practice, in the ESL course, the critical thinking skills they will need outside it, and they allow students to become familiar with rhetorical conventions as they apply across disciplines (Pally, 1997). Through purposeful, goal-directed writing assignments, which involve planning, organizing, reading, and editing and which span such rhetorical modes as description, definition, comparison–contrast, cause–effect, and argumentation, students practice and refine critical thinking skills (Bensley & Haynes, 1995; Langer & Applebee, 1987) as they expand knowledge, generate ideas, and develop their own thinking styles (de Sanchez, 1995). By providing numerous contexts that require students to define problems, examine evidence collected from a variety of sources, and make objective judgments on the basis of extended study (Wade,

1995), CBI activities help to facilitate students' progress from the cognitive to the associative to the autonomous stage of language acquisition.

INCREASING THE COGNITIVE ACCESSIBILITY OF CONTENT-BASED MATERIALS

The content-based reading and writing activities suggested by these theoretical models involve complex texts and tasks that are linguistically and cognitively demanding. If content-based materials are to be effective in helping ESL students build language and academic skills, allowing them to progress from the cognitive and associative to the autonomous stage of skill development, these materials must be made as accessible as possible to these students. This can be accomplished by presenting information in both verbal and visual forms, thereby promoting dual coding in the cognitive system (Paivio, 1979).

By providing multiple paths for both encoding and retrieval, dual coding leads to a stronger representation of information in the cognitive system. This dually coded cognitive representation, consisting of both visual and verbal items, improves comprehension (Chun & Plass, 1997) and enables information to quickly become part of the overall knowledge base, so that it may then be used to facilitate the acquisition and comprehension of subsequent information (Kosslyn, 1988).

Visual aids, such as graphic organizers, films and videos, and hypermedia technology, help to enhance comprehension and so provide dual support for ESL students' interaction with content-based textual materials. Graphic organizers are schematics that illustrate the knowledge structure of text and thus clarify complex text by visually representing important points and relationships between concepts. Film, through its clear, visual depiction of complex, often abstract content area concepts, offers an additional powerful aid to text comprehension, language development, and content learning (Kasper & Singer, 1997; see also Kasper, chap. 7, this volume). Internet technology also fosters dual coding of information through textual material supplemented by strong hypermedia reinforcement (Kasper, 1998; Warschauer, 1996).

Thus, the use of visual aids as supplied by graphic organizers, film, and hypermedia technology transforms complex content-based material into comprehensible input and leads to a deeper level of information processing and hence greater understanding of the material presented. As students develop a deeper understanding of interdisciplinary information, they are better able to interact with that information autonomously on an intellectual and critical thinking level.

PEDAGOGICAL APPLICATIONS

The philosophy put forth in this volume of essays is that students' academic and cognitive needs should drive curricular design. Stoller and Grabe (1997) proposed a model for language learning that reflects this philosophy and bridges linguistic and cognitive theory and L2 pedagogical practice. According to Stoller and Grabe (p. 78), to maximize linguistic and cognitive development, content-based approaches should (a) "view language as a medium for learning content, and content as a resource for learning language," (b) support "purposeful and meaningful language use," and (c) make a distinction between "social and academic language." In addition, content-based courses should aim to meet ESL students' academic needs by offering a curriculum of "predetermined content as specified in institutional guidelines or existing course offerings."

For SLA and cognitive theories to translate into an ESL pedagogy that provides abundant opportunities for relevant language use, meaningful communication, and strategy instruction, a number of practical considerations must be addressed when designing and implementing content-based programs. These include choosing an appropriate instructional model, training ESL faculty to deliver effective CBI, and developing reliable and valid assessments through which to measure students' progress.

INSTRUCTIONAL MODELS

Content-based courses may be designed around a variety of instructional models. Content-based courses that focus on developing the overall skills necessary for success in an English-speaking academic environment are referred to as English for Academic Purposes (EAP). These courses may involve interdisciplinary collaborations or be self-contained within the ESL program, focusing on themes taken from one or more content areas. ESL students may also study the content of a specific discipline in English for Specific Purposes (ESP) courses, with the goal not only of developing linguistic and academic skills, but also of preparing for the needs of a particular workplace environment. Finally, ESL programs can align with programs in Writing Across the Curriculum/Writing In the Disciplines (WAC/WID) to offer further support to students as they continue to learn and practice the conventions of academic discourse in a variety of educational contexts in the college mainstream.

The specific model chosen depends on the instructional situation and resources, the requirements of the institution, and the needs of the ESL students in the program and/or college. However, no matter which program model is chosen, each derives from the principles of SLA and cognitive learning theory discussed previously and fulfills students' needs through instructional activities aimed at developing and refining the linguistic and academic skills necessary for a successful college experience.

ENGLISH FOR ACADEMIC PURPOSES (EAP)

The instructional models described in this section are each designed to meet a variety of needs common to all college-level ESL students by teaching the general study, language, and content skills necessary for these students to function and be successful in an English-speaking academic environment. Thus content-based courses, or programs referred to as intensive, linked, and self-contained, all fall under the umbrella term, English for Academic Purposes (EAP).

Intensive Content-Based ESL Programs

An intensive content-based ESL program is an EAP model that involves a highly structured interdisciplinary collaboration among faculty representing ESL and several mainstream disciplines. Courses are block programmed, so that students remain together for the entire day and all students in the program attend the same classes. An intensive content-based ESL program requires that students be able to devote the entire day to their course work, and so there is little flexibility in scheduling. However, intensive content-based programs offer ESL students the opportunity to take several credit-bearing courses along with the ESL course. Thus, students may take ESL, sociology, speech, and history, receiving full academic credit for each of the three mainstream course components of the intensive program.

Instruction in intensive content-based ESL programs is a truly inter- and multidisciplinary experience. Effective intensive programs are like tightly knit chains—all course components are interconnected. As a result, there is strong reinforcement of learning as thematic concepts are considered from several different interdisciplinary perspectives. Thus, students may read, in their ESL class, an article or a book about a historical event. They may then debate the causes and effects of that historical event in their speech class. Finally, they may consider the effects of that historical event on society in their sociology class. The history class lays the groundwork for instruction by providing the students with the background knowledge necessary to complete each of the subsequent tasks in their other courses.

One of the greatest advantages of intensive content-based ESL programs is the spirit of community that they foster. The fact that students and faculty spend many hours together daily leads to the formation of strong communal bonds. This sense of community within the intensive program not only gives ESL students many varied opportunities for communication in English, thereby improving language skills (Ullman, 1997), but also helps these students feel that they are a part of the greater academic environment at the college (see Babbitt & Mlynarczyk, chap. 2, this volume).

Linked Courses

Like intensive content-based ESL programs, linked courses are EAP models that involve interdisciplinary collaborations. However, whereas intensive content-based programs require that an entire schedule of mainstream courses be integrated into the ESL sequence, linked courses pair an ESL course with one specific mainstream course, such as psychology or biology, with students enrolled simultaneously in each. To be most effective, instruction in both components should be completely coordinated, so that the ESL and the content area instructor develop parallel materials and share ideas for course assignments.

Linked courses offer college ESL students a number of advantages. These courses provide the opportunity to focus on complex and enduring content over the course of a full semester. This sustained content study offers multiple opportunities to review and practice linguistic forms and structures, as it develops critical thinking skills and fosters cognitive academic language proficiency (Pally, 1997). Linked courses present academic material in multiple contexts, which allows instruction in the mainstream discipline to be reinforced through the activities in the ESL course, and linguistic skills to be strengthened through the activities in the mainstream course (Kasper, 1994). Like intensive content-based programs, linked courses enable students to improve their English language skills while earning some degree credits; however, linked courses provide greater flexibility in scheduling and course selection than do intensive programs because the entire program is not prearranged.

Potential Problems in Implementing Interdisciplinary Collaborations

Although linked courses and intensive programs offer many benefits to both ESL students and faculty, there are a number of potential problems that may arise when implementing these programs. Because of administrative and financial concerns, it is often difficult to schedule and offer these interdisciplinary collaborations. Faculty schedules must be set up to allow instructors to meet and to attend each other's classes. Additionally, coordinating instruction often requires that funds be made available for released time as well as for faculty development workshops. For these programs to work most effectively, both faculty and students must commit the time and the energy necessary to produce a strong interdisciplinary collaboration (see Babbitt & Mlynarczyk, chap. 2, this volume, for a detailed discussion of administrative issues in CBI programs).

Self-Contained Content-Based ESL Courses

Often, despite good intentions and diligent efforts, it is not possible to implement interdisciplinary collaborations, and so an equally effective alternative is needed. When circumstances preclude offering linked courses and/or intensive programs, self-contained content-based ESL courses (sometimes referred to as theme courses) offer a viable instructional option because research (Kasper, 1995/96) has demonstrated that students enrolled in highly structured, self-contained courses experience the same kinds of linguistic gains as those enrolled in interdisciplinary collaborations.

The self-contained content-based ESL course follows an EAP model and may be designed around any mainstream subject area(s), with the course focus being unidisciplinary or multidisciplinary. A unidisciplinary self-contained course presents a variety topics drawn from one focus discipline, such as psychology or biology, and so offers opportunities for sustained content area study. It is essentially identical to the ESL component of a linked course because it covers the topics that would normally be presented in the corresponding mainstream course. The difference between the unidisciplinary ESL course and the linked course is that students are not simultaneously enrolled in that mainstream course. The multidisciplinary self-contained ESL course is designed to expose ESL students to academic material in several different mainstream disciplines and may include subject areas as diverse as linguistics, computer science, business, psychology, and biology. Following the principles of CBI, the specific subject areas represented in the multidisciplinary course should be chosen based on students' interests and the mainstream courses they are most likely to take in college.

Although scheduling and faculty collaboration are not concerns in the self-contained content-based ESL course, these courses do have some disadvantages. First, they offer no degree credit to the ESL student. Second, teaching an effective self-contained content-based course requires that the ESL instructor become sufficiently familiar with the content of the subject area(s) covered in the course. Additionally, the ESL instructor is solely responsible for choosing and/or developing appropriate interdisciplinary materials. As a result, designing and teaching an effective self-contained content-based ESL course requires a significant time commitment without the benefit of the released time that is often available to instructors participating in interdisciplinary collaborations. However, when circumstances preclude offering linked courses or intensive programs, the self-contained content-based ESL course represents an effective educational alternative.

Effects of EAP Models on Student Performance

Several studies of the effects of each of the EAP models discussed have found that a common benefit is enhanced linguistic growth and transfer of knowledge and skill to other instructional contexts (Babbitt & Mlynarczyk, chap. 2, this volume; Kasper, 1994, 1995/96; Pally, 1997, 1998). Learning enhancement appears to result from multiple exposure to language and content (Kasper, 1994) and an interdisciplinary approach to learning that teaches students to consider information from a variety of different perspectives (Pally, 1997). By providing students with opportunities for extended interaction with one or a variety of subject areas, EAP courses help to build and develop schemata, which according to the principles of cognitive learning theory, can then be used as a framework within which to fit, interpret, and understand subsequent information (Anderson, 1985), promoting transfer of knowledge and skill to new learning contexts (Nelson & Schmid, 1989).

ENGLISH FOR SPECIFIC PURPOSES (ESP)

Although English for Specific Purposes (ESP) and English for Academic Purposes are sometimes noted as subdivisions of each other (Jordan, 1997), the needs of the students served by each model are somewhat different. Whereas EAP programs target the general needs of college level students, ESP programs target the immediate, identifiable, and specific needs of adult students (Johns, 1997). Because ESP programs emphasize the language and academic conventions needed for study and/or work in a particular discipline (Jordan, 1997), courses are structured around highly focused content determined by "the learner's specific and apparent reason for learning" (Hutchinson & Waters, 1987, p. 19).

Hutchinson and Waters noted that although adult learners may be "conceptually and cognitively mature" (p. 129) with a high level of subject area knowledge, they often lack the second language skills necessary to express this knowledge effectively. The activities used in ESP courses are therefore highly specific and simulate discipline-based tasks through which students practice using appropriate vocabulary and discourse patterns (see Myers, chap. 6, this volume). For example, students studying business need to be able to interpret trends in data and to explain the causes and effects of various events, and an ESP course in English for Business would focus on developing students' ability to carry out each of these tasks effectively. To meet the demands of the business environment, students must be able to communicate ideas in an understandable way, which requires that they master basic conversational language and bottom-up linguistic features, such as basic grammar and mechanics (Arani et al., 1998). In addition, interpreting trends and explaining causes and effects requires critical thinking skills because students must be able to articulate and to analyze relationships among various issues and principles in the discipline and present their findings in a coherent, expository report. This demands mastery of top-down linguistic features, such as organization and appropriate discourse patterns. Thus, succeeding in business requires proficiency in both basic conversational and cognitive academic language, as well as a mastery of both bottom-up and top-down linguistic features.

Effects of ESP on Student Performance

ESP programs can be very effective in helping students develop familiarity with task demands as they vary from one discipline to the next and even from one course to another within the same discipline (Prior, 1992). Moreover, because these programs recognize that students come to them not as empty vessels, but with some degree of knowledge of subject area content, ESP programs are able to capitalize on and further develop the often rich schemata that students bring to the course. In fact, Myers (1995) found that ESP materials significantly improved both language and academic skills by taking advantage of already existing schemata that were activated simultaneously and multimodally by engaging students actively in the interpretation and analysis of reading, writing, and audiovisual texts.

WRITING ACROSS THE CURRICULUM/WRITING IN THE DISCIPLINES

According to a report published by the Language and Learning Across the Curriculum Committee (LALAC) of the National Council of Teachers of English, people who read and write about a subject are the ones who learn it best (LALAC, 1997, p. 1). This report went on to say that students are most likely to become engaged, independent, critical thinkers when their learning is viewed as an opportunity for significant investigation, individual application, and personal reflection (LALAC, 1997, p. 3).

The theoretical foundations for programs in Writing Across the Curriculum/Writing In the Disciplines (WAC/WID) are similar to those for EAP and ESP programs. Central to EAP, ESP, and WAC/WID pedagogical philosophy is the question, *"How do students learn the conventions of academic discourse?"* According to Cooke (1991), if writing is to become a natural and effective skill for students, they must be offered practice and instruction in a great variety of academic settings. They must learn to write "for different readers and in many contexts" (p. 9). Although Cooke's statement applies to all college students, offering interdisciplinary contexts for writing and general language use is especially important for ESL students. Many elements of both academic discourse and vocabulary are field-specific in nature, and so must be learned in contexts particular to the discipline in question (Arani et al., 1998; Myers, chap. 6, this volume).

Mainstream programs in WAC/WID extend the scope of student writing beyond the confines of the ESL course to improve content learning and to familiarize students with discourse conventions as they differ across disciplines. Aligned with content-based ESL instruction, WAC/WID programs represent strong mainstream supports that reinforce and enhance the development of students' linguistic and academic skills. Content area courses that follow a WAC/WID instructional model have a strong writing component, with assignments designed to contribute toward the learning goals of the course by providing students with extensive practice in writing and familiarizing them with discipline-specific patterns of discourse. WAC/WID instruction is therefore geared to promote thinking and learning, as well as to develop fluency in writing about the subject. When students explore interdisciplinary issues through writing, they are engaged in a cognitively demanding process that both requires and fosters a higher level of abstraction. This creates a learning context in which students must consciously put ideas into words, and in so doing, gives them the opportunity to understand thoughts that might otherwise remain inaccessible. WAC/WID helps ESL students learn better because it encourages active engagement with subject matter, and thereby, helps students "to see patterns, connect ideas, and make meanings" (Cooke, 1991, p. 6).

There are several differences between the focus of WAC and WID programs, and it is important to note these differences. Programs in WAC usually focus on teaching rhetorical skills that are necessary in all sorts of courses and so tend to emphasize the rhetorical modes, definition, comparison–contrast, and cause–effect (Arani et al., 1998). WAC programs target the development of students' ability to define and solve problems, their ability to examine ideas carefully and support them with evidence, and their ability to incorporate and synthesize information (Sully, 1995). Thus the types of writing taught in WAC programs would be similar to those taught in many EAP programs.

In contrast, WID programs tend to focus on rhetorical conventions as they are specific to given disciplines; thus, the types of writing taught in WID programs would be similar to those taught in many ESP programs. Because the particular rhetorical needs and practices of the discipline dictate the types of writing assigned, programs in WID tend not to separate writing process from content (Kaufer & Young, 1993). Let us consider business and the discourse modes important in this discipline. Although definition, comparison–contrast, and cause–effect are each important discourse modes in business; memo writing is also considered a mode of discourse in business. For this reason, teaching the rhetorical and discourse features of a good memo (e.g., format, headings) would be a central component of a WID program in business writing (Arani et al., 1998).

WAC/WID programs offer much needed mainstream support to content-based ESL programs because they teach students to be flexible when writing for different disciplines. WAC/WID instruction is an integral component of the interdisciplinary collaborations discussed previously and provides ESL students with multiple cross-disciplinary support for learning both language and discourse patterns. The multiple writing contexts afforded by WAC/WID instruction teach students to read a content area or an English assignment and determine how best to articulate knowledge based on those rhetorical conventions specific to the discipline under study. Most importantly, WAC/WID instruction teaches students that writing is more than just a language learning exercise; it is a valuable tool that can be used to develop thinking, to explore issues, and to increase understanding of any and all subject matter.

Effects of WAC/WID on Student Performance

In her study of the experiences of ESL students with writing across the curriculum, Leki (1995) found that students' knowledge of appropriate rhetorical strategies is key to helping them develop more effective academic writing skills. Strategy knowledge and use occurs on both a conscious and an unconscious level. Leki suggests that writing skills can be developed by building on strategy knowledge at the conscious level and by incorporating activities that will make students conscious of strategies that they may use but not be aware of using. Finally, she advocates specific strategy instruction to introduce students to and give them practice in strategies that they had not thought of before.

In addition to instruction and practice in effective rhetorical strategies, content-based writing assignments should be designed to encourage a deep level of processing and the use of higher order critical thinking skills. Leki & Carson (1994) suggested that simply asking ESL students to produce written responses to content-based texts is insufficient for developing academic writing skills. In keeping with WAC/WID philosophy, these researchers stated that content-based "ESL programs need to move away from writing tasks that require students only to tap their own opinions and experiences and toward work that encourages them to integrate those opinions and experiences with external sources of information and argument" (p. 95). In this way, CBI students will be able to move toward the goal of producing "knowledge transforming" (Bereiter & Scardamalia, 1987) forms of writing, in which they engage intellectually and critically with outside sources of information.

TRAINING FACULTY

No matter which of the previously described program models is chosen, for CBI to be most effective, faculty must be trained in the method and must be confident in its pedagogical efficacy. Faculty designing or participating in content-based programs often express a number of significant, and legitimate, concerns regarding how to implement it most effectively (Brinton, 1998).

Each of these concerns must be addressed if students are to derive the desired results from content-based courses.

Because CBI represents a major departure from traditional skills-based approaches to language instruction, teachers are concerned about how to justify the method to the many students who come to ESL courses primarily interested in improving grammar, writing, and speaking skills. These students often expect instruction that individually addresses each of these skills. CBI models do not specifically focus on grammar, writing, or vocabulary exercises, but rather present these linguistic points in the context of learning about something else. For this reason, some ESL students may need to be convinced of the effectiveness of this method and of its relevance to their immediate language learning goals. Justifying CBI to students is easier if course content reflects their needs and interests, as well as the requirements of the institution. Here teachers need to point out the advantages of teaching language through content, offering examples to demonstrate the effectiveness of this type of instruction.

Teachers often raise the question of how to select content so that instruction will be most appropriate to student needs. Content-based courses may cover a variety of subject areas or may focus on the sustained study of one specific subject area. ESL programs and faculty must decide which content-based model best suits their specific student population and the requirements of their institution, and then design course content appropriately.

Once content is selected, instructors may express trepidation that their knowledge of the content area may be inadequate. Teaching content-based courses requires that faculty develop a degree of expertise in the subject area, and as with decisions regarding course content, the level of expertise required depends on the individual teaching situation. ESL faculty in interdisciplinary collaborations have the advantage of the support of mainstream teachers in delivering content information to students because these collaborations provide the context for teachers to work together to integrate materials and to develop a connected thematic curriculum. In contrast, teaching self-contained content-based courses requires that ESL faculty develop sufficient expertise to deliver instruction based on one or several content areas. In this case, ESL teachers may research a subject area, networking with mainstream faculty to clarify and/or elaborate on information (see for example, Myers, chap. 6, this volume). ESL faculty may also choose to focus on a subject area in which they have expertise, for example, language acquisition. I have found that, no matter what their major, ESL students all find studying the principles and theories of language acquisition both interesting and relevant, and instruction may be broadened and these principles discussed within the contexts of several other disciplines, such as psychology or sociology.

Faculty involved in CBI also wonder about how best to balance language and content instruction, so that students acquire not only content area knowledge, but also basic language skills. To take their place in the college mainstream, ESL students must be able to read and comprehend the salient points in an academic text; they must be able to ask and answer questions in class; they must be able to write at an acceptable level of grammatical accuracy. This means that a balance must be struck between instruction in content information and instruction in linguistic skills. However, this is a natural balance, for as a body of recent research demonstrates, language skills are most effectively developed when taught in the context of acquiring information (Blakely, 1997; Brinton, Snow, & Wesche, 1989; Kamhi-Stein, 1997; Larsen-Freeman, 1997; Master, chap. 5, this volume, May-Landy, 1998; Zuengler & Brinton, 1997).

Finally, instruction that integrates the teaching of language and content raises the question of how to appropriately assess student performance. Because the goal of CBI is to develop linguistic and cognitive skills through a process in which information is acquired, articulated, and analyzed, measuring student achievement involves addressing not only linguistic proficiency, but also higher order thinking skills. The issue of assessment in content-based ESL courses is discussed next.

ASSESSMENT OF LANGUAGE AND CONTENT

Assessment is a critical component of any college course, but it is especially so in a content-based ESL course. If we accept the notion that a second language can be acquired most efficiently when presented in meaningful contexts where the primary focus is on acquiring information (Brinton, Snow, & Wesche, 1989), then we must devise assessments that reflect this goal. The assessment tasks we choose and the way in which we carry out assessment define for students what counts as success in the program (Auerbach, 1992). In addition, instructors themselves sometimes view assessment as the product of learning, perceiving a test score as an indication of how much a student has learned in the course.

Therefore, because students and their teachers often view assessment tasks as reflecting the real objectives of the course, ideally assessment should derive from instructional practice (May-Landy, 1998). Unfortunately, individual faculty and ESL programs may not be solely responsible for choosing assessment measures because these measures may be dictated by the college or university administration. In these cases, assessments often consist of standardized multiple-choice tests, in which linguistic structures and content information may be presented in a highly decontextualized format. Yet because the test may be part of an institutional requirement that students must meet if they are to continue in their studies, it often becomes the main force in shaping student (and teacher) motivation, which in this case is extrinsic in nature and derived from factors outside the classroom. In this situation, it becomes important for ESL programs to strive to develop alternate modes of assessment that more appropriately reflect the goals of the content-based curriculum.

Weigle and Jensen (1997) believe that for tests to reflect the goals of CBI—the concurrent teaching of academic subject matter and L2 skills—they should present a balance between language and content and should engage students in higher order thinking tasks. These authors stated that "authenticity and interactiveness are paramount considerations" (p. 211) in test design. They borrowed these terms from Bachman and Palmer (1996), who defined an authentic task as one that simulates a real-world language task and an interactive task as one that requires the learner to actively apply linguistic, topical, and strategy knowledge.

Designing authentic and interactive content-based assessments means that students should be required to complete discourse level tasks, rather than discrete, decontextualized tasks. Content-based assessment should therefore target the skills that students actually need to use in an academic setting. The comprehension of academic texts does not require that students simply deal with discrete points of language, nor that they simply consume and regurgitate information. To interact successfully with academic material, students must be able to analyze and critically evaluate information, and they must be able to connect new information with what they already know, synthesizing knowledge. Therefore content-based assessments should not simply target isolated elements of language nor factual information, but should provide tasks that require students to integrate information and to form and articulate their own opinions about the subject matter.

May-Landy (1998) suggested that instructors and college and university administrators adopt a broader view of assessment as a multifaceted construct, one that describes the process of learning and that includes not only one discrete test score, but all types of feedback occurring over the course of the semester. Moreover, she stated that it is important to communicate this broad definition of assessment to students, so that they will come to gauge their progress through intrinsic factors (i.e., the ability to interact with language and information), rather than through extrinsic factors (i.e., the number of correct answers on a discrete-item test).

May-Landy (1998) also stressed the importance of extraordinarily frequent assessment, which is closely tied to the curriculum and which may take several forms. For example, a student may be asked to read an article and then to report on it to the class, summarizing, critically evaluating, and comparing the information presented to other material studied. The assessment may be based on how accurately and coherently the student is able to convey and interpret information. Assessment may also take the form of corrective feedback—is the information correct and the language accurate? May-Landy stated that discrete points of language can be taught by using them within the context of the content area being discussed (see also Larsen-Freeman, 1997; Master, chap. 5, this volume) and assessed in the same manner. For example, as they respond to the issues within a content area, students might be required to hypothesize and imagine what would happen "*If . . .* " Done in this way, language is never viewed as separate from context and content. Students learn the language feature (the conditional) by using it within a content-based context, and they are assessed on how accurately they are able to use the language feature to convey content-based contextualized information.

In keeping with a broader view of assessment, Short (1993) believes that because a wide variety of language and cognitive skills, including communicative competence, appropriate use of academic language, problem solving, and concept comprehension, are developed in the context of CBI, assessment of these skills should be wide and varied as well. Short stated that assessment measures must mirror instructional practice, and that students must be given the opportunity both "to demonstrate ability, skill, and knowledge through the medium that suits them best" and "to take some responsibility for their own evaluation" (p. 653). She suggested using a number of alternative assessment measures, such as skill checklists and reading–writing inventories, anecdotal records and teacher observations, portfolios, performance-based tasks, essay writing, oral reports, and interviews. Short recognizes that the accountability, validity, and reliability of these alternative assessments may be questioned. However, studies (Blanche, 1990; Heilenmann, 1990; Peirce, Swain, & Hart, 1993; Yap, 1993) have shown that involving the L2 learner in the assessment process is not only recommended, but yields a measure of language proficiency that is both valid and reliable.

Content-based assessment, then, should be viewed as an interactive process that engages both teacher and student in monitoring the student's performance (Hancock, 1994). By designing highly contextualized assessment tasks that challenge higher order thinking skills as well as develop proficiency in language features, we not only help students acquire the skills they need to be successful at learning a new language, but also teach them to measure progress in terms of cognitive skill development as well as linguistic accuracy. Meaningful, authentic assessments provide a wider range of evidence on which to judge whether students are becoming competent, purposeful language users and instills in students lifelong skills related to critical thinking. Assessments of this type then become a basis for future learning, as they teach students how to evaluate what they have learned both in and outside of the language class (Hancock, 1994).

Because students (and their teachers) view curriculum and assessment as inextricably linked, the what, how, and why of assessment define a program's view of language, literacy, and learning (Wrigley, 1992). If we want our students to engage in reflective learning and to understand that language acquisition is more than perfecting grammar, more than ingesting information, we must design tests that support this educational position. Assessment tasks that derive from the principles of CBI should measure language acquisition as a cognitive, higher order learning task, one that requires not only bottom-up, but also top-down processing.

CONCLUSION

The need to meet the linguistic, cognitive, and social demands present at various levels of the academic hierarchy (Benesch, 1997) requires that college ESL students become competent users of English as a means not only of communicating, but also of acquiring, interacting with, and transforming knowledge. We can empower students to meet these demands by designing and implementing ESL instruction that facilitates and hastens linguistic proficiency development, familiarizes students with the requirements and conventions of academic discourse, and supports the use of critical thinking and higher order cognitive processes.

This volume of essays contends that a content-based pedagogy meets each of these requirements. In this first chapter, I have described the theoretical foundations for content-based college ESL instruction and suggested a number of instructional models through which this theory may be put into classroom practice. The chapters that follow provide specific and detailed discussions of the many and varied issues that must be considered in the design and implementation of content-based programs and activities so that ESL students may more effectively develop the wide range of skills they need to be successful in college.

REFERENCES

Anderson, J. (1983). *The architecture of cognition.* Cambridge, MA: Harvard University Press.

Anderson, J. (1985). *Cognitive psychology and its implications.* 2nd ed. New York: Freeman.

Anderson, R. C., & Pearson, P. D. (1984). A schema-theoretic view of the basic processes in reading comprehension. In P. D. Pearson (Ed.), *Handbook of Reading Research* (pp. 255–291). New York: Longman.

Arani, M., Bauer-Ramazani, C., Deutsch, L., Doto, L., Russikoff, K., Smith, B., & Velasco-Martin, C. (1998). *Preparing ESL students for academic content courses.* Colloquium presented at the 32nd annual meeting of TESOL. Seattle, WA.

Auerbach, E. R. (1992). *Making meaning, making change: Participatory curriculum development for adult ESL literacy.* Washington, DC and McHenry, IL: Center for Applied Linguistics and Delta Systems, Inc.

Bachman, L. F., & Palmer, A. S. (1996). *Language testing in practice: Designing and developing useful language tests.* Oxford: Oxford UP.

Benesch, S. (1997). *Critical needs analysis and curriculum development in English for Academic Purposes* (EAP). Paper presented at Discipline-Based Instruction: Benefits and Implementation: A CUNY Faculty Development Colloquium. Brooklyn, NY: Kingsborough Community College.

Bensley, D. A., & Haynes, C. (1995). The acquisition of general purpose strategic knowledge for argumentation. *Teaching of Psychology, 22*(1), 41–45.

Bereiter, C., & Scardamalia, M. (1987). *The psychology of written composition.* Hillsdale, NJ: Lawrence Erlbaum Associates.

Blakely, R. (1997). The English Language Fellows Program: Using peer tutors to integrate language and content. In M.A. Snow & D.M. Brinton (Eds.), *The content-based classroom: Perspectives on integrating language and content* (pp. 274–289). New York: Longman.

Blanche, P. (1990). Using standardized achievement and oral proficiency tests for self-assessment: The DLIFLC study. *Language Testing, 7*, 202–229.

Bransford, J. D., & Johnson, M. K. (1972). Contextual prerequisites for understanding: Some investigations of comprehension and recall. *Journal of Verbal Learning and Verbal Behavior, 61*, 717–726.

Brinton, D. M. (1998). *Novice teacher reactions to content-based instruction.* Paper presented at the 32nd annual meeting of TESOL. Seattle, WA.

Brinton, D. M., Snow, M. A., & Wesche, M. B. (1989). *Content-based second language instruction.* Boston: Heinle & Heinle.

Chamot, A. U., & O'Malley, J. M. (1994). *The CALLA handbook: Implementing the cognitive academic language learning approach.* Reading, MA: Addison-Wesley.

Chun, D. M., & Plass, J. L. (1997). Research on text comprehension in multimedia environments. *Language Learning and Technology, 1*(1), 60–81.

Clair, N. (1994). Informed choices: Articulating assumptions for language minority students (Content-based ESL). *ERIC/CAL News Bulletin, 18*(1). [Online]. Available May 31, 1998: http://www.cal.org/ericcal/news/

Cooke, V. (1991). *Writing across the curriculum: A faculty handbook.* Victoria, Canada: Centre for Curriculum and Professional Development.

Cummins, J. (1981). The role of primary language development in promoting educational success for language minority students. In J. Cummins (Ed.), *Schooling and language minority students: A theoretical framework* (pp. 1–50). Los Angeles: Evaluation, Dissemination, and Assessment Center.

de Sanchez, M. A. (1995). Using critical-thinking principles as a guide to college-level instruction. *Teaching of Psychology, 22*(1), 72–74.

Grow, G. O. (1996). *Serving the strategic reader: Reader response theory and its implications for the teaching of writing.* An expanded version of a paper presented to the Qualitative Division of the Association for Educators in Journalism and Mass Communication. Atlanta, August, 1994. [Online]. Available: http://www.famu.edu/sjmga/ggrow. Original paper available as ERIC Documentation Reproduction Service No. ED 406 644.

Hancock, C.R. (1994). Alternative assessment and second language study: What and why? *ERIC Digest.* [Online]. Available: http://www.cal.org/ericcll/digest/Hancoc01.htm

Heilenmann, K. L. (1990). Self-assessment of second language ability: The role of response effects. *Language Testing, 7*, 174–201.

Hutchinson, T., & Waters, A. (1987). *English for specific purposes: A learning-centered approach.* Cambridge: Cambridge University Press.

Johns, A. M. (1997). *Text, role, and context: Developing academic literacies.* Cambridge: Cambridge University Press.

Jordan, R. R. (1997). *English for academic purposes: A guide and resource for teachers.* Cambridge: Cambridge University Press.

Kamhi-Stein, L. D. (1997). Enhancing student performance through discipline-based summarization-strategy instruction. In M. A. Snow & D. M. Brinton (Eds.), *The content-based classroom: Perspectives on integrating language and content* (pp. 248–262). New York: Longman.

Kasper, L. F. (1994). Improved reading performance for ESL students through academic course pairing. *Journal of Reading, 37*(5), 376–384.

Kasper, L. F. (1995/96). Using discipline-based texts to boost college ESL reading instruction. *Journal of Adolescent and Adult Literacy, 39*(4), 298–306.

Kasper, L. F. (1996). Writing to read: Enhancing ESL students' reading proficiency through written response to text. *Teaching English in the Two-Year College, 23*(1), 25–33.

Kasper, L. F. (1998). *Interdisciplinary English and the Internet: Technology meets content in the ESL course.* Paper presented at the 3rd Annual Teaching in the Community Colleges Online Conference. 7–9 April. Available: http://leahi.kcc.hawaii.edu/Papers/Kasper.html

Kasper, L., & Singer, R. (1997). Reading, language acquisition, and film strategies. *Post-Script, 16*(2), 5–17.

Kaufer, D., & Young. R. (1993). Writing in the content areas: Some theoretical complexities. In L. Odell (Ed.), *Theory and practice in the teaching of writing: Rethinking the discipline,* (pp. 71–104). Carbondale & Edwardsville, IL: Southern Illinois University Press.

Kosslyn, S. M. (1988). Imagery in learning. In M.S. Gazzaniga (Ed.), *Perspectives in memory research* (pp. 245–273). Cambridge, MA: MIT Press.

Krashen, S. (1982). *Principles and practice in second language acquisition.* Oxford: Pergamon.

Krashen, S. (1985). *Input hypothesis: Issues and implications.* New York: Longman.

LALAC. (1997). *Learning through language: A call for action in all disciplines.* [Online]. Available: http://www.sfasu.edu/lalac/brochure.html [19 May 1998].

Langer, J. A., & Applebee, A. N. (1987). *How writing shapes thinking: A study of teaching and learning.* Urbana, IL: National Council of Teachers of English.

Larsen-Freeman, D. (1997). Grammar and its teaching: Challenging the myths. *ERIC Digest (March).* (Online). Available: http://www.cal.org/ericcll/digest/Larsen01.htm [July 25 1998].

Leki, I. (1995). Coping strategies of ESL students in writing tasks across the curriculum. *TESOL Quarterly, 29*(2), 235–260.

Leki, I., & Carson, J. G. (1994). Students' perceptions of EAP writing instruction and writing needs across the disciplines. *TESOL Quarterly, 28*(1), 81–101.

May-Landy, L. (1998). *Linking assessment to the content-based curriculum.* Paper presented at the 32nd annual meeting of TESOL. Seattle, WA.

Myers, S. A. (1995). Using written text to teach oral skills: An ITA training class using field-specific materials. *English for Specific Purposes, 14*(3), 231–245.

Nelson, G., & Schmid, T. (1989). ESL reading: Schema theory and standardized tests. *TESOL Quarterly, 23,* 539–543.

O'Malley, J. M., & Chamot, A. U. (1990). *Learning strategies in second language acquisition.* Cambridge: Cambridge University Press.

Paivio, A. (1979). *Imagery and verbal processes.* Hillsdale, NJ: Lawrence Erlbaum Associates.

Pally, M. (1997). Critical thinking in ESL: An argument for sustained content. *Journal of Second Language Writing, 6*(3), 293–311.

Pally, M. (1998). Film studies drive literacy development for ESL university students. *Journal of Adolescent and Adult Literacy, 41*(8), 620–628.

Peirce, B. N., Swain, M., & Hart, D. (1993). Self-assessment in two French immersion programs. *Applied Linguistics, 14*, 25–42.

Prior, P. (1992). *Redefining task: Academic writing in six graduate courses.* Paper presented at the 23rd Annual TESOL Conference, Vancouver, Canada.

Short, D. J. (1993). Assessing integrated language and content instruction. *TESOL Quarterly, 27*(4), 627–656.

Snow, M. A., Met, M., & Genesee, F. (1989). A conceptual framework for the integration of language and content in second/foreign language instruction. *TESOL Quarterly, 23*, 201–217.

Soter, A. O. (1990). The English teacher and the non-English-speaking student: Facing the multicultural/multilingual challenge. In G. E. Hawisher & A. O. Soter (Eds.) *On literacy and its teaching: Issues in English education* (pp. 224–242). Albany, NY: SUNY Press.

Stoller, F. L., & Grabe, W. (1997). The six-t's approach to content-based instruction. In M.A. Snow & D. M. Brinton (Eds.) *The content-based classroom: Perspectives on integrating language and content* (pp. 78–94). New York: Longman.

Sully, B. (1995). *Malaspina University-College's writing-across-the-curriculum project.* [Online]. Available: http://www.mala.bc.ca/www/wac/proj.htm [19 May 1998].

Ullman, C. (1997). Social identity and the adult ESL classroom. *ERIC Digest, EDO-LE-98-01.* [Online]. Available: http://www.cal.org/ncle/digests/Socident.htm [19 June 1998].

Wade, C. (1995). Using writing to develop and assess critical thinking. *Teaching of Psychology, 22*(1), 24–28.

Warschauer, M. (1996). Computer-assisted language learning: An introduction. In S. Fotos (Ed.), *Multimedia language teaching* (pp. 3–20). Tokyo: Logos International.

Weigle, S. C., & Jensen, L. (1997). Issues in assessment for content-based instruction. In M. A. Snow & D. M. Brinton (Eds.) *The content-based classroom: Perspectives on integrating language and content* (pp. 201–212). New York: Longman.

Wrigley, H. S. (1992). Learner assessment and ESL literacy. *ERIC Digest.* [Online] Available: http://www.cal.org/ncle/Digests/AssessQA.htm [8 June 1998].

Yap, K. O. (1993). Integrating assessment with instruction in ABE/ESL programs. *ERIC Document ED 359210.*

Zamel, V. (1992). Writing one's way into reading. *TESOL Quarterly, 26*, 463–485. New York: Longman.

Zuengler, J., & Brinton, D. M. (1997). Linguistic form, pragmatic function: Relevant research from content-based instruction. In M. A. Snow & D. M. Brinton (Eds.), *The content-based classroom: Perspectives on integrating language and content* (pp. 263–273).

2

Keys to Successful Content–Based Programs

Administrative Perspectives

Marcia Babbitt
Rebecca Williams Mlynarczyk
Kingsborough Community College/CUNY

No matter how innovative the program design, how dedicated the faculty, or how motivated the students, a content-based English as a Second Language (ESL) program will not succeed unless administrative issues are dealt with effectively on a day-to-day basis. Lines of communication among everyone involved in the program—college administrators, program directors, participating faculty members, support staff such as tutors and counselors, and students—must be kept open at all times. We hope that readers keep in mind the overriding importance of communication while considering the four major areas discussed in this chapter: program design and planning, recruitment of students, curriculum development and pedagogy, and program evaluation and fine tuning.

PROGRAM DESIGN AND PLANNING

The first step in planning a content-based ESL program should be considering the overall purpose of the new program. Colleges and universities across the United States report an increase in the population of second language (L2) students. For example, in the mid 1990s, the City University of New York

(CUNY) ESL Task Force reported that by the year 2000 approximately 50% of students in CUNY senior and community colleges would be foreign-born (City University of New York, 1994). The presence of large numbers of second-language (L2) students is not unique to CUNY, and it is clear that if these students are to achieve their dream of getting a higher education, they need to master academic English as quickly as possible. Research shows that content-based programs can effectively meet this need (see, e.g., Kasper, 1995, 1997). And experience, both within the CUNY system and elsewhere, has shown that following certain important principles will enhance the success of such programs.

Course Design

One of the most important decisions that must be made when designing a content-based program relates to the instructional model that will be adopted. In an influential book entitled *Content-Based Second Language Instruction*, Brinton, Snow, & Wesche (1989) described three possible approaches: theme-based courses, sheltered courses, and adjunct courses.[1] Theme-based courses are taught by language professionals but focus on content from other disciplines in their teaching of language. Brinton et al. (1989) defined sheltered courses as "content area courses taught by content specialists, but that integrate appropriate language and study skills into the curriculum" (p. 15). We define sheltered courses more broadly to include ESL courses that follow the syllabus of a particular mainstream course. In both theme-based and sheltered courses, ESL students are taught in separate classes that include no non-ESL students. Adjunct courses link a language course and a content course and are designed to help ESL students learn appropriate language and study skills while also mastering academic content. Content courses that are part of a linked program may include non-ESL students.

All three models have been shown to be effective in developing students' language skills and in improving pass rates in ESL courses (Brinton et al.; Kasper, 1995, 1997). Theme-based and sheltered courses are both self-contained, and the major administrative concerns in these two content-based models are student needs assessment and faculty development. Faculty need to be trained in how best to integrate language and content and in how to use content-area materials most effectively to develop basic language skills. Because the theme-based and sheltered models involve only ESL stu-

---

[1]These course labels are those proposed by Brinton, Snow, and Wesche in their 1989 work. Since that time, other researchers in the field have used other labels to refer to these same course models. For example, the uni- and multidisciplinary (i.e., single/multiple content) courses described by Kasper (1995, 1997; chap. 2, this volume) follow a sheltered and a theme-based model, respectively. In addition, the paired/linked courses described by Babbitt and Mlynarczyk (1997) and by Kasper (1994; 1995/96) follow an adjunct model.

dents, it is easier to adapt course content to the needs of the particular students enrolled in the program in any given semester.

Although theme-based and sheltered courses may be a more viable option in specific learning situations (e.g., in an English Language Institute), these content-based models sometimes do not give ESL students the opportunity to earn academic credit while improving English language skills. In contrast, the adjunct model, which pairs the ESL course with one or more content courses, offers students a learning experience that not only closely links language and content, but that also guarantees them the opportunity to earn credits toward a college degree. Because the adjunct model involves an interdisciplinary collaboration with courses outside the ESL program, it requires more extensive planning and administrative support and so is subject to problems and concerns that do not occur in self-contained content-based courses. We therefore focus extensively on the adjunct model of content-based college ESL instruction, using examples drawn from our experiences in the ESL program at Kingsborough Community College of the City University of New York. At Kingsborough, we have offered ESL students two content-based, adjunct model options—the Intensive Program and the Linked Program. The Intensive ESL Program is highly structured and offers students a blocked program schedule of one noncredit ESL course and four credit-bearing content-area courses (e.g., Speech, Sociology, Psychology). The Linked Program pairs an ESL course with one content course (e.g., Psychology). Instructors and tutors involved in the two courses work closely together to plan the curriculum for both courses.

Assessing Student Needs

In designing a content-based ESL program, it is essential to begin with an assessment of student needs. Needs assessment in most English for academic purposes (EAP) programs (see Kasper, chap. 1, this volume, for a full discussion of EAP) is primarily descriptive in nature. In other words, it focuses on students' and professors' perceptions of what students need to succeed within the existing situation. On a pragmatic level, college level ESL students share certain obvious needs: they need to improve English language skills, to pass skills assessment tests, to be able to understand lectures and take effective notes on their content-area courses, and to be able to understand and answer test questions in both ESL and content-area courses. While other researchers (e.g., Benesch, 1996) have advocated a "critical approach" to needs assessment that recognizes the "political and subjective" (p. 736) nature of the process and that is open to ways in which the existing situation might be transformed to improve education; this chapter focuses on describing how well-designed content-based programs go a long way toward meeting the pragmatic needs of college ESL students.

Enlisting Support from Administrators

Content-based adjunct programs like the one at Kingsborough are heavily inter-disciplinary in nature, and thus it is crucial to seek administrative support early in the planning stages. Because many people will be involved in the program and because budget requests often do not coincide with preexisting categories, it is important that administrators be informed about program development. Our ESL Program was fortunate to have the enthusiastic support of high level administrators from the beginning. Both the Dean of Academic Programs and the Provost, himself an immigrant educated in the United States, strongly advocated a program that would provide students with needed language skills while they were taking academic courses in other disciplines.

Effective communication with college administrators is key to keeping the program running smoothly. This means not only sending timely written reports but also acquainting administrators with the program's day-to-day operations by inviting them to visit classes, come along on field trips, or speak at faculty development workshops.

Choosing the Director or Codirectors

Because of the amount of coordination involved in implementing a program involving faculty members from several different departments, the choice of the right program director is extremely important. According to Brinton (1997), the job requirements of a program director involve many talents—the diplomatic skills of an ambassador, the facility with numbers of an accountant, and the technical skills of a computer expert, to name just a few. In fact, a survey reported by Matthies (1984) found that the skills required of directors of intensive English programs could be categorized as either educational or managerial and that the most successful directors were the ones who were best able to combine the two roles. Nonetheless, most of the respondents to Matthies' survey indicated that they felt more comfortable with the parts of the job that tapped their skills as educators and less comfortable with the managerial tasks.

Because no one person is likely to possess such a wide range of skills, it may be advisable to appoint codirectors for the program. In our own experience as Codirectors of Kingsborough's ESL program, the two of us have found that working in tandem reduces the strain of being responsible for a complex program; we also feel that our decision making is more solid because we have a chance to talk things through with each other and discuss many options before making a decision.

In any case, it is the directors who are responsible for maintaining strong communication among all involved in the program. A regular stream of meetings, phone calls, e-mail messages, and memos is essential to make sure that everyone knows what is going on and has a chance to communicate concerns and suggestions. The key requirements for this position are a high energy level and an understanding of and commitment to the principles of content-based language learning and to the specific institution's program. Because of the considerable work involved in this job, the director(s) should be granted adequate compensation in the form of released time from teaching (usually preferable for full-time instructors) or additional remuneration (for part-time instructors).

Connecting with Other Departments

During the planning process, it is important for the program director(s) to make contact with other departments to explore courses that might effectively be linked with ESL. From the point of view of the chairperson of another department, there are pros and cons involved in joining a collaborative program. Because smaller class sizes are often regarded as necessary for effective teaching of L2 students, department chairs may have to seek permission from college administrators to lower the cap on class size. There is also the possibility that some program segments may not attract enough ESL students, and then both the ESL and the content course will have to be canceled. However, many chairs are excited by the idea of working collaboratively with another department, which often enhances collegiality. In addition, participating instructors benefit from faculty development activities and often become more effective teachers for all of their students. Another plus relates to the ESL students themselves. Faculty in other departments often find L2 students to be highly motivated and hard working; in many cases these students' enthusiasm for learning compensates for their limited knowledge of English. Most importantly, if college administrators strongly support the collaborative program, this offers an incentive for other departments to lend their assistance. All of these points should be discussed when recruiting members of other departments to participate in a content linked program.

In choosing appropriate courses to link with ESL, it is important to keep the students' needs firmly in mind. Courses that not only serve to develop the students' linguistic abilities, but that are also required for graduation are good candidates for linking. If many of the ESL students in the program have the same major, it may be advisable to link with a course in that major. At Kingsborough, we have successfully linked ESL courses with those in a variety of disciplines including sociology, psychology, history, health, business, and computer science.

Selecting Faculty

Although all the factors discussed so far are extremely important, the program will succeed only if it is effectively implemented in the classroom. This depends largely on the commitment and expertise of participating faculty, as well as on sufficient administrative support (Brinton et al., (1989, p. 71). Selecting the right teachers for a collaborative program is crucial to its success; therefore, it makes sense to seek out people who enjoy working with others. It is important that content-area faculty be "particularly sensitive to the needs and abilities of second language learners" (Brinton et al., 1989, p. 21). Department chairs may be able to recommend instructors who have these qualities or who have an interest in participating in the program. In any case, it is wise for the ESL director to speak with each faculty member being considered for the program in order to assess his or her suitability. At times, ESL faculty may not feel comfortable teaching in a collaborative setting. Although in time these teachers may find that they do enjoy working as part of a team, if they do not, they can still participate in a CBI program by adopting a theme-based model in their individual ESL courses.

Faculty Development

Teaching in a content-based ESL program does not constitute "business as usual" either for the ESL professors or for faculty in other departments. It is, therefore, essential to offer enough support to help participating teachers implement the program effectively. This faculty development has two major purposes: providing the collaborating teachers (and tutors) with the necessary time to discuss and thoughtfully plan how they will coordinate and interrelate course material, and acquainting faculty members with pedagogical techniques appropriate for use in content-based programs. Brinton, Snow, and Wesche pointed out what inevitably happens when faculty are not given the support they need to adapt their teaching:

> Unless adequately prepared for their new teaching duties, teachers will invariably have to fight the urge to rely on their traditional teaching techniques as well as on materials and lesson plans developed over the years for a different audience—many of which may be inconsistent with the goals of the content-based program. (1989, pp. 74–75)

Curriculum Development Workshops

In the Kingsborough program, we have found it extremely useful to offer a series of curriculum development workshops for participating faculty, tutors, and counselors before the semester begins. These workshops provide an opportunity to acquaint people with the rationale for content linking and to introduce them to effective pedagogical techniques. In the initial workshops, we sometimes invite outside consultants to work with teachers who are new to the program. We also ask participants to do some background reading related to the goals and pedagogical assumptions of the program (see Benesch,; Bruffee, 1993; MacGowan-Gilhooly, 1996a, 1996b; Smoke, 1994; Tillyer, 1994; Tinto, Goodsell Love, & Russo, 1993, Tinto, Goodsell Love, & Russo, 1994; Van Slyck, 1997).

Team Meetings

As the workshop series continues, it is important to allot more time for team meetings in which participants work out specific plans for the new courses. One area that is essential to discuss before classes begin is how to assess student progress. Team members should be clear on how students' work will be evaluated in each of the courses (for example, multiple choice exams, essay exams, research papers). If possible, the assessments should reflect the program's values. For example, if the program hopes to develop students' fluency in speaking and writing, they should not be assessed solely on the basis of multiple choice tests. Team members should also try to avoid assigning several tests or papers during the same week. Finally, linguistic correctness is an important issue that needs to be discussed openly. When ESL students are encouraged to speak and write freely, they often deviate from standard English, and participating faculty need to decide how to deal with student errors. Usually it is the ESL professors (and perhaps the tutors) who assume the major responsibility for helping students move toward standard English; instructors in the other disciplines are often satisfied simply to comment (and grade) primarily on content.

On-Going Communication

Once classes begin, it is essential that participating faculty members continue to communicate regularly. Brinton, Snow, and Wesche (1989) recommended weekly meetings. At Kingsborough, the professors in one of our most successful teams (who were friends before their involvement in this program) talk several times a week and exchange weekly lesson plans. Other teams try to meet for lunch once a week or stay in touch through phone calls and e-mail. Another way of staying informed is by an occasional visit to the partner-professor's classes. Such visits lead to improved communication within the program because teachers gain a firsthand understanding of the requirements in other courses. In addition, teachers can learn from observing another teaching style and may, as a result, make subtle changes in their own pedagogy.

Support Services

In addition to selecting an appropriate model of instruction and effective teaching methods, designers of content-based ESL programs must also decide what types of support services are needed to help students succeed. If possible, tutors should be hired to help students cope with difficult academic content and to serve a counseling function. Tutors occupy a kind of middle ground between teachers and students, and students often feel more comfortable discussing problems with them than with their instructors. Such a tutoring component can improve communication with students and help instructors deal with problems early on.

The tutors have proved to be an invaluable part of our program. Because they both observe and participate in the various courses, the tutors have the most complete sense of what is going on in all of the courses and what is expected of students. In order to work effectively, however, tutors require the same kind of professional development activities as instructors do. This professional development may consist of a special course or seminar for tutors involved in the content-based program or of weekly meetings (with compensation) between tutors and professors.

Ideally, a counseling component should also be incorporated into a content-based program. Counselors are trained professionals who are available to talk with students about personal or academic problems. In our program, counselors teach two one-credit courses, SD 10 and SD 11, which provide valuable information about the college's resources, adjustment to college life, study habits, and future career possibilities.

Practical Suggestions

One piece of advice we would offer to those who are in the early stages of program design is to start small, perhaps with just with one level of ESL or with one other academic department. Once the program is under way, problems inevitably arise, but they will not be overwhelming if the number of teachers and students involved is small. After these initial problems have been resolved, the program can be expanded.

Another word of advice is to think of unanticipated situations not as problems but as opportunities. For example, in our program's third semester, the number of entering students at the intermediate level of ESL was unexpectedly small, and so a second section of the intermediate level Intensive Program had to be canceled. However, the number of entering students at the high intermediate level was larger than expected, so a new high-intermediate level was created. Even though the students and faculty were recruited at the last minute, this new segment was highly successful and has been continued ever since.

Low registration numbers sometimes lead to other problems that may have creative solutions. For example, the number of students enrolled in the content course may be too low, and as a result, the department chair may be forced to open up the course to native speakers of English. On the surface, this appears to be a problem, but it is one that is counterbalanced by the valuable learning opportunities it can provide. The ESL and content teachers can devise assignments that require collaboration between the ESL students and the native speakers. These collaborations often lead to friendships between native speakers and ESL students and encourage them to spend time outside of class talking about the course.

One aspect of Kingsborough's program design that has proved to be even more powerful than we originally expected is the strong sense of community that develops among students when they spend their first semester in college working closely for many hours a week with the same group of students. It is significant that this community is primarily of an academic nature, although the social elements of student friendship and solidarity are also extremely important. Tinto et al. (1994) stressed the importance of a sense of academic community to increasing student retention. In explaining why most programs designed to increase student retention are not very successful, Tinto et al. (1994) pointed out that they are "largely nonacademic in nature" (p. 5). He believes programs that help students to create their own academic support system are crucial, especially for commuter students. In a more recent article, Tinto (1997) elaborated on why learning communities are so effective:

> ... participation in a shared learning experience enabled new college students to bridge the academic-social divide that typically confronts students in these settings. It allowed them to meet two needs, social and academic, without having to sacrifice one in order to meet the other. But more than simply allowing the social and academic worlds to exist side by side, the learning communities provided a vehicle for each to enhance the other. Students spoke of a learning experience that was different and richer than that with which they were typically acquainted. (p. 611)

We believe that a content-based program should include both factors Tinto advocated in his research: shared learning, in which students develop a strong bond with students who are taking two or more of the same courses, and connected learning, in which the shared courses are organized around a connecting theme. The importance of both shared and connected learning has been apparent in the feedback we have received from professors and tutors in our program. As one of the ESL professors reported,

> Almost all the students have formed a bond with each other. They were working closely and efficiently in class and out of class; they were helping each other with the homework and other assignments; they bonded with tutors and felt comfortable asking them and me for help; they created relationships and friendships, in most cases beyond the ethnic culture and language. In order to do that, they had to use English in a meaningful and purposeful, emotionally positive way. All these factors, underlying a learning community, created a gen-

eral atmosphere of ease, comfort, and home, especially important to facilitate second language learning.

Additionally a tutor reported,

> The strategic 'link' to the other academic fields ... has created an elaborate safety net for students. By safety net I mean a valuable tight knit community of hardworking students where each helps the other. In my opinion, these students would have experienced serious difficulties on their own. ... As someone who has been through the school system 'alone,' I am now able to understand and appreciate the vast difference team work makes and the rewards it produces.

We believe that this strong learning community is the most important feature of our program and that it contributes significantly to student performance (see Appendix). Follow-up research documents many positive results of students' participation in this content-based program: high retention and pass rates, frequent skipping of one or more of the required ESL courses (determined by regular departmental assessments graded by professors other than the classroom teacher), and extremely high grade point averages as the programs "graduates" continue in the college and eventually transfer to 4-year institutions (Babbitt & Mlynarczyk, 1997; Fox, 1996; Kasper, 1997).

Budgeting

To run successfully, content-based programs require money. There are two avenues for providing funding for a content-based program: internally through the regular college budget and externally through grant funding. Grants are an excellent way of meeting budgetary needs for the short term, and depending on the grant, funds may be provided for only one semester or for several years. Funding through grants can help initiate a small pilot program that, after one or two semesters, may be institutionalized. Grant monies can also be used to supplement an already existing college funded program budget by financing, in part or totally, activities such as in and out-of-class tutoring, tutor training, faculty development workshops, and faculty–tutor team meetings, which are ongoing throughout the semester.

During the fifth semester of our Intensive English program, we received an Innovative ESL Programs Grant awarded by the CUNY Office of Academic Affairs. We used this grant to fund four 4-hour faculty development workshops. The grant allowed us to compensate adjunct faculty, full-time faculty, and tutors for attending these workshops. It also enabled us to create a new content-based linked program, which paired each ESL course with one content-area course. In addition, the grant provided the funds we needed to include additional tutoring hours, peer counselors, a computer consultant, clerical services, and materials as part of our new program.

Grants can also be used to finance extracurricular events that enhance the content-based learning experiences. These extracurricular events may include talks and/or discussions by invited guest speakers, trips related to topics studied in content courses, or informal get-togethers for all students, faculty, and tutors in the program.

Although grant funding is certainly helpful, the major portion of long-term budgetary needs should be met internally through college funds. The program functions best if driven by the college administration, which tends to lend stronger support to a program to which it has committed itself financially. If administrators are sympathetic to the situation of ESL students in the college environment, or if the success or retention rates for ESL students are low, administrators will probably be willing to support a small content-based program and compare content-based and regular program outcomes at the end of the first semester. If administrators are less than enthusiastic initially, ESL faculty can attract their attention by showing them reports of other programs that have positively affected acceleration and retention of ESL students. Administrators, then, might be willing to support a small pilot or experimental program, but would probably predicate future support on outcomes of 1 or 2 semesters. Nevertheless, once the program has demonstrated clear success as compared to the existing program, it is likely that administrative support will continue.

Starting small and slowly is advisable not only to enlist initial administrative support but also to ensure continued support. A small content-based program gives team members the ability to work out problems, make decisions, and implement changes on an ongoing basis. In a small program, team members can give close attention to issues of curriculum, coordination, tutoring, pedagogy, individual and collective student problems, and student reactions.

It is also essential for administrators to recognize the need to provide compensation to faculty participating in content-based linked programs for the time required to plan curriculum and coordinate coursework. This compensation may be made either through released time or through payment for attendance at faculty development workshops. In either case, monthly faculty development sessions and weekly team meetings should continue throughout the semester.

Any expansion of ESL course hours and inclusion or expansion of tutoring hours will need to continue beyond the first semester. The college will need to agree to fund these extra hours not only for the original number of linked sections, but also for added sections as the program expands. If the program continues to be successful, administrators may be willing to institutionalize these extra hours for all content-based linked sections and to expand the total number of sections so that more ESL students can reap the benefits of content linking. We have been fortunate at Kingsborough in that extra class and tutoring hours continue to be supported by our administration.

Administrators will also need to approve other measures that require allocation of funds; for example, limiting class size for ESL and content courses and providing funds for adjunct (and perhaps full-time) faculty to conduct orientation and recruitment sessions. At Kingsborough, our orientation sessions for ESL students have become a standard part of the general college orientation, with ESL counselors, as well as speech and ESL faculty, on hand to help recruit and preregister students for our Intensive and Linked Programs. At these orientations, we explain the programs to the students, show them program schedules, place those students whose placement results are not complete, and pre-register students for their chosen program.

Scheduling of Courses

As with other administrative aspects of an adjunct program, successful scheduling depends in large part on careful attention to detail both in the presemester planning stages and throughout the semester. Scheduling is an important and complex component of an adjunct program and requires that planning begin one semester to one year ahead of program implementation. Schedule planning begins within the ESL Program itself at the beginning of the previous semester, then widens to include other departments and the registrar's office for assignment of rooms and final coordination of all linked classes.

Directors must first assess needs in terms of how many students they expect to register for the semester and how many sections of each level they will create. Directors must be able to dovetail hours for all linked classes in the program in order to meet student and faculty scheduling needs and room requirements. Directors should meet with chairs of other departments, and for sections that have been running, should try to retain the same schedules and faculty teams. Occasionally, however, changes in staffing may be necessary. People may leave the program, take on new positions in the college, or simply not work out. It is sometimes necessary to cancel or postpone a component of the program that doesn't work well even after attempts have been made to resolve problems inherent in it. We discontinued one paired section in our Linked Program after only one semester because of several problems with the linking. Problems ranged from scheduling difficulties for tutors in both courses, to less-than-effective integration of course materials, to content course materials being too difficult for the students.

Location of Classrooms

Location of classrooms is also an important consideration because it can have an effect on how ESL students see themselves in relation to the rest of the college and to each other. If rooms are located in a remote or isolated section of the college campus, students and faculty feel separated from the college community. To enhance ESL students' sense of being an integral part of the college, rooms should be located near campus offices and the cafeteria. If possible, these classrooms should be allocated for the exclusive use of the ESL students in the program. Students enjoy having rooms available to them where they can socialize and work together on assignments. Faculty and tutors can also come to these rooms to meet with each other. This space can add a dimension to the sense of community that is created among students, faculty, and tutors in a content-based adjunct program.

Extracurricular Activities

We believe that extracurricular activities are an important component of a content-based program. They help forge the language experience (Burkart & Sheppard, 1996) aspect of CBI as they bring ESL students together with others in their program and integrate them into the college community at large. Intermediate level students in our program participated in a college-wide African American Read-In, a program in which students and faculty read works of various genres written by African Americans. One of the highlights of this program came when a Russian woman and a Haitian man read a dialogue from Toni Morrison's *The Bluest Eye*. This joint participation represents how students from diverse backgrounds may be brought together to form the strong academic—social learning community necessary for their successful integration into college life. Other extracurricular activities scheduled in our program include an informal lunch held during the third week of the semester, visits to historical immigration sites, such as Ellis Island or the Lower East Side Tenement Museum, and a visit by E. R. Braithwaite, author of *To Sir, With Love*, a book read by the intermediate students in the program. We have found that involving students in these types of extracurricular activities provides them not only with enjoyable experiences, but also with a feeling of belonging to a college community that cares about their future and that wants them to succeed.

RECRUITMENT OF STUDENTS

Whichever content model an ESL program follows, finding the students and registering them in appropriate courses and levels is of utmost importance. If the total institutional enrollment of ESL students is low, it can become a struggle to fill linked, theme-based, or sheltered sections, although the greatest number of difficulties may arise in recruiting for linked sections. Brinton et al. (1989, p. 74) suggested that in this case it is important to address whether there is incentive among students to take linked courses. Students usually have a strong incentive for taking courses that are of high interest and/or that fulfill requirements and provide credit toward graduation. Students may think they don't need linked courses if these courses are not in their major areas; program directors and advisers must convince them that content courses linked with ESL courses fulfill requirements for graduation or carry elective credits for all major areas. Most linked courses in our program fulfill graduation requirements (e.g., Introductory Psychology or Speech). One course, Introduction to the Internet, is an exception in that although it has a high interest level, it offers elective credits only.

Where recruitment is concerned, program directors and faculty must become more than advisers; they must become salespersons and even telemarketers. This helps to increase the number of students in linked courses and reduce the number of misplaced students. We often phone students who have applied for admission and taken assessment tests, but who have not come in to register. We also phone those students who have come to an orientation session, but who have either not taken assessment tests or have failed to register. The third group we phone are those who register for inappropriate courses.

One important step in recruiting students for content-based programs is to attach ESL recruitment to institutional recruitment and orientation efforts. Orientation is critical to the success of content-based ESL programs for several reasons. The learning communities that are the backbone of content-based programs begin to develop at orientation. ESL students become aware that they are special and important, and they begin to feel comfortable in their new environment—a first step to becoming an integral part of the college community. At Kingsborough, orientation for incoming students is run by the Department of Student Development, which invites students to a 3 to 4 hour orientation session. The ESL directors invite prospective ESL students (those who have applied and been tested) by separate letter to attend the orientation. All students check in at tables for their chosen majors, and all ESL students, regardless of major, check in at the ESL table. After a plenary session, students meet separately with others from their field. At our ESL orientation, we familiarize students with our programs, place them when initial placements are incomplete, and preregister them for the appropriate Linked or Intensive program of their choice. Students have the opportunity to meet faculty, discuss issues of concern to them, be grouped with others at their level, and decide on courses. We also make students aware of program success rates. We tell them that when they take a linked program, their chances of passing non-ESL courses dramatically increase and their chances of skipping an ESL level also increase.

Orientation sessions are essential to the recruitment process, and on-site registration is also important. At Kingsborough, the orientation sessions take place on nonregistration days; therefore, on-site registration is sometimes difficult because there are many aspects of the registration procedure, such as tuition payment, financial aid processing, and certification of immunization, that cannot be handled on nonregistration days. However, whenever possible, on-site registration should be implemented because by including registration with orientation, an institution reduces the chances of student misadvisement and facilitates the entire registration process for new students.

CURRICULUM DEVELOPMENT AND PEDAGOGY

In developing the curriculum for a content-based program, it is important to consider what teaching methods are most appropriate. In a section of the *C-ESL Guide No. 2* entitled "Designing, Implementing, and Sustaining Content-ESL Programs," Burkart and Sheppard (1996) discussed four commonly used methods: cooperative learning activities, whole-language activities, the language experience approach, and interdisciplinary learning. Cooperative learning activities engage small groups of students in tasks where they exchange knowledge and experiences, making their own connections with the content and the language. Whole language closely integrates listening, speaking, reading, and writing, asking students to use language in natural ways for clearly defined purposes. The language experience approach asks students to draw on relevant experiences and language acquired both inside and outside the classroom. Interdisciplinary learning combines content and language in meaningful contexts and develops critical thinking skills needed for various academic tasks.

We make use of all four of these approaches in the Kingsborough program. The overall educational philosophy is based on the principles of whole language, which assumes that learning is a social activity and proceeds from the whole to the parts. So, instead of starting with small bits of language such as words or sentences, learners in whole language programs—from a fairly early stage of language acquisition—read and write whole texts in the form of stories and even books.

In devising the Kingsborough program we were greatly influenced by another whole-language program, the Fluency First approach to teaching ESL, developed at City College of New York by MacGowan-Gilhooly and Rorschach (MacGowan-Gilhooly, 1991a, 1991b). This approach is based on the idea that language is acquired most efficiently when students progress from the development of fluency to clarity to correctness. Therefore, in the earlier stages of language acquisition, teaching should emphasize the development of fluency, then move to a concern with clarity, and finally, after students have reached a more advanced level, to a focus on correctness. In the City College program, students in the first level read and write whole books. In the next level, their reading and writing are focused on more "academic" subjects, and in the highest level, students work with regular college textbooks and strive to make their writing as correct as possible. At Kingsborough, we adapted the Fluency First approach and teaching methods to help students improve their English proficiency while also mastering other academic content such as that encountered in introductory history and sociology courses (Mlynarczyk, 1998).

Although our overall educational philosophy is based on whole language, within the classroom we also rely heavily on the other three learning approaches mentioned: cooperative learning, the language experience approach, and interdisciplinary learning. Most content-based programs recognize that L2 students need to actively process academic material for themselves in order to master it (Pally, 1997). This is partly because ESL students often lack the background information needed to contextualize the content of their professors' lectures. Therefore, we constantly provide opportunities in the ESL and speech courses for students to work in small groups on content-related activities that are basically cooperative in nature. Examples of such activities include working together to answer questions about content-course readings, reading aloud and discussing students' weekly reading journals, or working together to anticipate—and later to answer—possible exam questions.

Our classroom methodology also emphasizes a language-experience approach to learning. We believe that students will understand and retain academic material more completely if they are given opportunities to construct the mental schemata essential to true learning by connecting what they are studying in class with their own experiences outside the classroom. Kasper (1997) pointed out that it is important for students in content-based programs to "assimilate ... new information to their existing knowledge base, requiring them to form new schemata and to accommodate existing schemata" (p. 318). For this reason, teachers in our program work hard to create experiential learning situations for students. These activities may range from field trips (e.g., visiting Ellis Island or the Lower East Side Tenement Museum to enhance understanding of immigration in the early part of the century) to interviews (e.g., interviewing a person currently active in a union to better understand the growth of the labor movement in the United States).

Even within the classroom, students are constantly encouraged to connect their experience outside of school with what they are learning in school. One effective way of doing this is through what we refer to as point-of-view writing, in which students are asked to take on an imaginary persona and write in the first person from that character's perspective. For instance, students who are studying the deplorable conditions in Native American boarding schools in the 19th century might be asked to write a letter or journal entry from the point of view of one of the following characters: a 10-year-old girl attending the school, the child's mother or father, one of the teachers in the school, the principal of the school, or a government official working in the Bureau of Indian Affairs.

Here we incorporate the principle of scaffolding (Chamot & O'Malley, 1994; see also Kasper, chap. 1, this volume). To demonstrate point-of-view writing, teachers model a sample response on the board before students actually begin to write. Once students catch on to the idea of adopting someone else's point of view, they enjoy this type of writing and are eager to hear what other students have written. At the same time, the activity enables them to experience vicariously some of the issues they are encountering in their academic courses.

Finally, an interdisciplinary approach is an essential feature of our program. As a result of careful planning by professors and tutors, cross-disciplinary concepts and content are interrelated in a way that reinforces classroom work and makes it more meaningful than is usually the case when courses are taught as discrete and unrelated subjects. The following example of the program's interdisciplinary approach to content is drawn from the high-intermediate level in which students study the U.S. Depression of the 1930s. In the history course, students read primary sources detailing the lives of Americans during this period. This content is reinforced in the ESL class, where most of the reading and writing is related to what the students are studying in the history course. For example, students read *Jews Without Money*, Michael Gold's (1930) autobiographical novel describing his childhood and adolescence in the Jewish immigrant community of New York's Lower East Side in the early part of the twentieth century, as well as *Growing Up*, Russell Baker's (1982) memoir about life in the United States during the Depression and World War II. Students develop their composition skills by writing and revising essays related to important themes covered in the history course, and they enhance their fluency by keeping journals about both the history reading and the related books they are reading for their ESL course. Toward the end of their work on the Great Depression, students interview an older American who remembers what life was like during this period and write an essay about what they have learned. Before conducting the interview, students practice interviewing techniques and conduct mock interviews in their speech course and in tutorial sessions.

PROGRAM EVALUATION AND FINE TUNING

Evaluation of a content-based program is necessary to its survival. If quantitative and qualitative evaluation measures are initiated and positive academic results can be documented, the program will be more likely to continue. Evaluation should be multifaceted and should include data gathering from diverse sectors of the institution both central and ancillary to the program's operation: faculty, tutors, students, tutoring center directors, counselors, department chairs, and administrators. Evaluative data should be both formative, gathered throughout the semester, and summative, collected at the end of the semester (see Brinton et al., 1989, pp. 75–76).

Faculty should be encouraged to evaluate and refine components of the program in order to implement changes during the course of the semester and to plan for innovations in subsequent semesters. Monthly program meetings provide a forum for presenting, discussing, and deciding how to implement new ideas. At these meetings, all team members should feel free to address any problems or potential problems so that solutions can be explored. Moreover, faculty should be asked to submit midsemester and final evaluative program reports to be used to assess the program and fine-tune any aspects that require adjustment.

Qualitative evaluative data from administrators and department chairs can be gathered informally through meetings, phone conversations, and other discussions both during the semester and again when the semester is completed and results are known. Suggestions and ideas should be considered, and if an idea appears to have the potential of enhancing the learning experience for students in the program, it should be implemented. Some changes can be made during a semester in progress, for example, the setting up of extra review or note-taking tutorials for students who may be having difficulty with a particular course.

Although feedback from both faculty and administrators is important, much of the qualitative data should come from the students themselves. During the semester, students can provide formative evaluation through responses to certain aspects of the program that they have been experiencing. Students should also be asked to provide summative evaluation at the end of the semester by responding to a comprehensive evaluation form, in which they rate components of the program on a numerical scale and answer open-ended questions. We have asked students to provide feedback on the most important ways in which their English improved during the semester, which of the activities they found most helpful, how they felt about course linking and its effect on their English skills, whether the tutoring component was helpful to them, and, finally, what suggestions they could offer for improving the effectiveness of the program.

An end-of-semester 3- to 4-hour faculty development workshop is useful for assessing the progress of the students and the effectiveness of many components of the program such as tutoring, collaboration among team members, student projects, and collaboration among students. Qualitative evaluation data about various components of the program can be presented at the final meeting so that successes can be lauded, problems analyzed, and solutions considered. Quantitative data involving the end-of-term progress of students in the program should also be reported at the final workshop. These quantitative results may be based on grades, pass rates, acceleration rates, comparison of pass rates of ESL and non-ESL students for the same content courses, and comparison of nonlinked and linked ESL students in ESL and other courses. If student success and retention rates in a content-based program exceed the rates in a noncontent-based program, as has been the case at Kingsborough (see Appendix for recent ESL results and Kasper, 1995 for retention data), the program will be more likely to grow and flourish.

Evaluation should include not only determining short-term student success rates, but also long term success rates. This may be done by comparing pass rates in comparable courses for ESL students in and out of the program and comparison of grade point averages (GPAs, or other course averages) for ESL and non-ESL students over a period of time. Research of a longitudinal nature, which involves the tracking of students, can be done by the school's Office of Institutional Research or perhaps through grant funding (see for example Kasper, 1997, which reported on a follow-up study of the possible long term effects of CBI). As we continue to build our program at Kingsborough and to learn more about how a well-functioning intensive or linked program is designed and composed, we continue to implement new features, fortify proven features, research the results, learn from our mistakes, and keep the interest and future of our students as the bottom line.

Finally, if the results of a content-based linked ESL program show promise, even after only one or two semesters, it is important to disseminate the results. Dissemination begins inside the institution itself, with reports of results to administrators, department chairs, faculty, and tutors. Then participants in the program can begin to inform other institutions of the results of the program through conference presentations and journal articles. At Kingsborough, we began by presenting our program's first and second semester's results to colleagues at other institutions at conferences in fall of 1995 and spring of 1996.

CONCLUSION

Developing an effective content-based ESL program requires a great deal of planning and coordination. The chances for success will be maximized if program developers work carefully to create a coherent program, beginning with preplanning and following through with student recruitment, curriculum development, and program evaluation and fine tuning. Maintaining good communication among all who are involved in the program is crucial.

Program design will inevitably be shaped by individual circumstances at a particular college or university. These circumstances must be kept in mind when making basic decisions such as whether to use a theme-based, sheltered, or adjunct approach. Whatever model is ultimately adopted, we feel it is important to develop a program in which an academic–social learning community will take root and thrive. In a content-based ESL program that is well designed and thoughtfully implemented, students develop the ability to listen and learn from one another as well as from their instructors and textbooks.

When learning is shared in a linked or theme-based environment, ESL students begin to feel connected to one another, to the subject matter, and to the institution in which they are studying. They are no longer passive students absorbing information, but they are actively constructing knowledge and defining their own connections to and roles in the institution.

REFERENCES

Babbitt, M., & Mlynarczyk, R. (1997). Final report. Campus-based English as a second language (ESL) innovative programs: Spring 1997. Unpublished report. Brooklyn, NY: Kingsborough Community College.

Baker, R. (1982). Growing up. New York: Penguin.

Benesch, S. (1996). Needs analysis and curriculum development in EAP: An example of a critical approach. TESOL Quarterly, 30(4), 723–738.

Brinton, D. M. (1997). The challenges of administering content-based programs. In Snow, M. A., & Brinton, D. M. (Eds.), The content-based classroom: Perspectives on integrating language and content. (pp. 340–346). White Plains, NY: Addison Wesley Longman.

Brinton, D. M., Snow, M. A., & Wesche, M. B. (1989). Content-based second language instruction. Boston: Heinle & Heinle.

Bruffee, K. A. (1993). Collaboration, conversation, and reacculturation. In K. A. Bruffee, (Ed.), Collaborative Learning: Higher education, interdependence, and the authority of knowledge (pp. 15–27). Baltimore: Johns Hopkins University Press.

Burkart, G. S., & Sheppard, K. (1996). Designing, implementing, and sustaining content-ESL programs. C-ESL Guide No. 2. [Online]. Available: http://www.ncbe. gwu.edu/miscpubs/cal/contentesl/c-esl2html [April 17, 1998]

Chamot, A. U., & O'Malley, J. M. (1994). The CALLA handbook: Implementing the cognitive academic language learning approach. Reading, MA: Addison-Wesley.

City University of New York. (1994). Report of the CUNY ESL Task Force. New York: The Instructional Resource Center, CUNY.

Fox, R. N. (1996). Intensive ESL Program: Spring 1996 outcomes. Institutional Research Report No. 114. Unpublished report. Brooklyn, NY: Kingsborough Community College.

Gold, M. (1930). Jews without money. Emeryville, CA: Publisher Group West.

Kasper, L. F. (1994). Improved reading performance for ESL students through academic course pairing. Journal of Reading, 37(5), 376–384.

Kasper, L. F. (1995). Theory and practice in content-based ESL reading instruction. English for Specific Purposes 14(3), 223–230.

Kasper, L. F. (1995/96). Using discipline-based texts to boost college ESL reading instruction. Journal of Adolescent and Adult Literacy, 39(4), 298–306.

Kasper, L. F. (1997). The impact of content-based instructional programs on the academic progress of ESL students. English for Specific Purposes, 16(4), 309–320.

MacGowan-Gilhooly, A. (1991a). Fluency before correctness: A whole language experiment in college ESL. College ESL, 1(1), 37–47.

MacGowan-Gilhooly, A. (1991b). Fluency first: Reversing the traditional ESL sequence. Journal of Basic Writing, 10, 73–87.

MacGowan-Gilhooly, A. (1996a). Achieving clarity in English: A whole-language book (3rd ed.). Dubuque, IA: Kendall/Hunt.

MacGowan-Gilhooly, A. (1996b). *Achieving fluency in English: A whole-language book* (3rd ed.). Dubuque, IA: Kendall/Hunt.

Matthies, B. F. (1984). The director's job skills in intensive English programs. *The American Language Journal, 2,* 5–16.

Mlynarczyk, R. W. (1998). Fluency first in the ESL Class: An integrated approach. In T. Smoke (Ed.), *Adult ESL: Politics, pedagogy, and participation in classroom and community programs.* Mahwah, NJ: Lawrence Erlbaum Associates.

Pally, M. (1997). Critical thinking in ESL: An argument for sustained content. *Journal of Second Language Writing, 6*(3), 293–311.

Smoke, T. (1994). Writing as a means of learning. *College ESL, 4*(2), 1–11.

Tillyer, D. (1994). High tech/Low monitor: An ESL writing course at City College of NY meets multicultural needs with e-mail. *APEX-J, 1*(1) May 3 1999. [Online]. Available: http://leahi.kcc.hawaii.edu/pub/apexj/

Tinto, V. (1997). Classrooms as communities: Exploring the educational character of student persistence. *The Journal of Higher Education, 68*(6), 599–623.

Tinto, V., Goodsell Love, A., & Russo, P. (1993). Building community. *Liberal Education*, Fall, 16–21.

Tinto, V., Goodsell Love, A., & Russo, P. (1994). *Building learning communities for new college students: A summary of research findings of the collaborative learning project.* Unpublished report. National Center on Post-secondary Teaching, Learning and Assessment. Syracuse University School of Education, Syracuse, NY.

Van Slyck, P. (1997). Repositioning ourselves in the contact zone. *College English, 59*(2), 149–170.

APPENDIX:
RESULTS OF THE SPRING, 1998 SEMESTER
FOR THREE INTENSIVE ESL PROGRAM LEVELS:

Low-Intermediate (ESL 07); Intermediate (ESL 09); And High-Intermediate (ESL 91)[2]

ESL 07

Of the 11 students enrolled, 63.63% (7 students) passed, with 27.27% (3 students) skipping one level (the intermediate ESL 09 level) and moving directly into ESL 91; 36.36% (4 students) advancing to ESL 09; and 36.36% (4 students) repeating. Generally, passing rates for noncontent-linked ESL 07 courses range between 60-65% with virtually no skipping of levels.

---

[2]The levels of ESL at Kingsborough are as follows from lowest to highest: ESL 07; ESL 09; ESL 91. After students exit from ESL 91, they go on to either ENG 92 or ENG 93, which are developmental courses within the regular English department sequence. Students who pass either ENG 92 or ENG 93 exit from the developmental sequence and progress to ENG 12, mainstream freshman composition.

ESL 09

There were 17 students enrolled in the ESL 09 course. Of these, 88.23% (15 students) passed. 5.88% (1 student) skipped 2 levels and moved into Eng. 93; 23.53% (4 students) skipped the next level, ESL 91, and moved into Eng. 92; 58.82% (10 students) advanced one level into ESL 91; and 11.76% (2 students) repeated. Passing rates for noncontent-linked ESL 09 courses range between 65% and 70% with virtually no skipping.

ESL 91

Of the 16 students who completed the ESL 91 course, 87.5% (14 students) passed. 12.5% (2 students) skipped two levels and went directly into Eng. 12 (freshman English); 56.25% (9 students) skipped one level (Eng. 92) and moved into Eng. 93; 17.64 (3 students) advanced one level into Eng. 92; and 12.5% (2 students) repeated. Passing rates for noncontent-linked ESL 91 courses are similar to those for noncontent-linked ESL 09 courses (65% to 70%).

3

Out of the Mouths of Babes

Novice Teacher Insights
Into Content-Based Instruction[1]

Donna M. Brinton
University of California, Los Angeles

I t is difficult to trace the exact appearance of content-based instruction (CBI) on the second/foreign language scene. However, it is safe to say that this approach has been gaining popular acceptance since the mid to late 1980s (see, e.g., early volumes devoted to this approach by Cantoni-Harvey, 1987; Crandall, 1987; and Mohan, 1986) and that today, it constitutes a major instructional paradigm in virtually all second/foreign language instructional settings.[2]

Early accounts of CBI (e.g., Benesch, 1988; Brinton, Snow, & Wesche, 1989; Short, 1991a, 1991b; Snow & Brinton, 1992) were primarily descriptive in nature, devoting the bulk of their discussion to issues such as curriculum and materials development, testing, program assessment, student reactions, and the like. This exclusionary focus on issues of implementation led Johns (1992) to note the lack of an established research tradition within the paradigm and to encourage CBI practitioners to emulate the types of research being done in the field of English for Specific Purposes (ESP).

---

[1]This article is a revised version of a paper delivered at the colloquium on Challenges of Content-Based Instruction for Teacher Education (Dorit Kaufman, organizer) at TESOL '98, Seattle, WA.

[2]At the 32nd Annual Conference of Teachers of English to Speakers of Other Languages held in Seattle, Washington (March, 1998), for example, 97 sessions were listed under this topic heading.

THE NEED FOR TEACHER EDUCATION IN CBI

Paralleling this lack of a research focus in the early works on CBI is a lack of guidance in the area of CBI teacher education. Brinton, Snow, & Wesche (1989) noted the need for approach-specific training in order for teachers to effectively deliver CBI:

> The very notion of converting to content-based teaching involves re-educating teachers to view their instructional domain and responsibilities quite differently than they might previously have. Unless adequately prepared for their new teaching duties, teachers will invariably have to fight the urge to rely on their traditional teaching techniques as well as on materials and lesson plans developed over the years for a different audience—many of which may be inconsistent with the goals of the content-based program. (pp. 74–75)

The authors also called for both preservice and inservice training programs to orient teachers to the approach. However, they made no concrete suggestions as to the scope or content of such training programs.

As experience with this model of instruction evolved, however, it clearly became necessary to more specifically address teacher education for CBI. Snow and Brinton, in their 1992 guest-edited issue of *The CATESOL Journal*, prevailed on Peter Master to contribute a piece devoted to this topic. In this article, Master echoed Snow and Brinton's concern, noting:

> CBI requires an adjustment on the part of the ESL teacher, who may be intimidated by the prospect of having to teach subject matter with which he or she may not be familiar. This fear of subject matter is well known to English for Specific Purposes (ESP) practitioners, who have long had to deal with the same issue, but for ESL it raises questions about teacher training for new teachers and teacher development for those who have been teaching ESL for some time. (Master, 1992, p. 77)

Master then sketched out the components of an inservice training program for CBI instructors. With respect to those delivering theme-based instruction, for example, he noted the special need for training in needs assessment and curriculum and materials development. For instructors delivering sheltered content instruction, he emphasized that content-area instructors should receive training in adjusting their speech and delivery to the needs of English language learners. Finally, Master notes that the most critical components of a training program for instructors involved in adjunct language instruction are the discussion of the relationship between language and content faculty[3] and training in collaborative curriculum and materials development to

---

[3]One suggestion he makes for better preparing faculty involves having them role play situations in which differences of opinion regarding instructional issues must be resolved.

promote students' language development. He also noted that, like the content faculty delivering sheltered instruction, adjunct content faculty require training in how to accommodate their speech so that the concepts are easily accessible to English language learners.

Although Master's article addressed training for only one type of CBI (i.e., adjunct instruction) and in its scope is not intended as an all-inclusive treatment of CBI teacher training, it set the scene for subsequent works in this area. As we embark on the third decade of CBI practice, those who educate teachers to do CBI can avail themselves of a great deal of additional material on this topic. For an overview of the competencies that a CBI teacher preparation program should address, for example, they can find excellent guidance in Peterson (1997). Similarly, for a description of a collaborative teacher training efforts, teacher educators are well advised to consult Kaufman (1997) and Crandall (1998). To better prepare content-area instructors to teach English language learners, they can refer to any one of the many recent handbooks (e.g., Adamson, 1993; Echevarria & Graves, 1998; Peitzman & Gadda, 1994; Peregoy & Boyle, 1993; Rosenthal, 1996). Finally, to supplement the literature on teaching English language learners, these teacher educators can look to the wealth of training literature in first language instruction intended to prepare teachers for language across the curriculum.[4]

RESEARCH IN CBI TEACHER EDUCATION

Unfortunately, much the same complaint that Johns (1992) leveled at the literature on CBI practice can today be lodged against the literature on CBI teacher education—it lacks a well established or systematic research base. Little, in fact, is documented about the actual difficulties of novice teachers who embark on the venture of CBI or the problems of experienced teachers who are being retrained to do CBI (and are, therefore, experiencing a radical shift in instructional paradigms).

Clearly, much is to be learned by focusing the lens of CBI research on this critical area of investigation. Several avenues offer themselves up for such research. The first, as proposed by Crandall (1998), involves having those involved in CBI carry out action research, either individually or collaboratively with colleagues across the disciplines. As Crandall noted:

> Action research engages teachers in collecting and analyzing data from a variety of sources that both describes what happens in classes and helps improve prac-

---

[4]These works are too numerous to mention here. Some excellent examples are: Farrell-Childers, Gere, & Young, 1994; Fathman, Quinn, & Kessler, 1992; Hein & Price, 1994; Lemke, 1990; Lindquist, 1995; Saul, Reardon, Schmidt, Pearce, Blackwood, & Bird, 1993; Scott, 1992; Tschudi & Lafer, 1996.

tice. Student interviews, analysis of student writings, audio- or videotaping of classes, dialogue journal writing with students or other teachers are all possible means of addressing and analyzing instructional questions … Action research projects can focus on one or many students and involve a variety of data-gathering procedures … [They] can engage a number of teachers in a common research question, such as promoting greater thematic integration across the curriculum for students or engage individual teachers in research projects which collectively help address instructional questions … Reflecting on these case studies and sharing them with each other [helps] promote greater understanding of the challenges and possible strategies for meeting these in English language and other classrooms." (p. 5)

Crandall cites several examples of collaborative research involving ESL and content-area specialists, such as that of a high school chemistry teacher and an ESL teacher-in-training seeking to identify what learning strategies are most useful for the English language learners in the chemistry classroom or that of an ESOL and a middle school mathematics teacher collaborating to analyze the problems students had with mathematical and algebraic language.

A second (perhaps more conventionally recognized) avenue for research in CBI teacher education involves conducting interviews with or administering questionnaires to the teachers involved. As an example of such research, Goodwin and Jensen (1996) conducted an investigation of novice and experienced teaching assistants at the University of California, Los Angeles (UCLA) who were using CBI as an instructional approach. As their primary research questions, Goodwin and Jensen cited the following:

1. Which issues are of most concern to instructors using CBI for the first time?
2. Which issues are they most comfortable with after having used CBI?
3. Which training methods are most effective?

To answer these questions, the researchers administered a prequarter questionnaire to the novice instructors (i.e., teaching assistants in their first quarter of teaching) about their concerns with using the CBI model (e.g., justifying the model to students, determining how and what to evaluate, extracting the language and teaching points from the content materials). They also administered a similar postquarter questionnaire to both the novice and experienced instructors ascertaining their comfort level with various issues in CBI (e.g., being knowledgeable in the content area, justifying the model to students, balancing the content with the language and skills focus of the course). Finally, they conducted postquarter videotaped group interviews with the novice and experienced populations to further define their concerns and to obtain feedback on the training they had received.

The results from the two populations shed a great deal of light on training issues in CBI. In the prequarter questionnaire, the novice teaching assistants indicated their primary areas of concern as being knowledgeable in the content areas, extracting the language and teaching points from the content, and integrating language skills within the CBI framework. In the open-ended section of the questionnaire, the subjects noted the need for more theoretical background and an expanded explanation of CBI, a discussion of how the approach differs from a traditional ESL class, and a synopsis of its strengths and weaknesses as an instructional approach. In the postquarter questionnaire, interesting differences in the two populations emerged, with the experienced teaching assistants indicating that they were least comfortable with determining how and what to evaluate, integrating the skills within the content-based framework, and being knowledgeable in the content area. The novice teaching assistants, on the other hand, indicated their least comfortable areas as balancing the content as a vehicle with the language and skills focus of the course, determining how and what to evaluate, and working without traditional textbooks. In the videotaped postquarter group interviews, both populations indicated that in terms of training and supervision, the most helpful components had been the weekly level meetings with their course supervisor, experience with the model, the sample lesson plans provided, and the observation/feedback sessions with their supervisor.

A third research paradigm that can inform CBI teacher preparation programs is case study research such as that carried out by Adamson (1993) and his students enrolled in an applied linguistics graduate course. The subjects of this study were 34 nonnative speakers of English, all of whom were enrolled in content-area courses at the high school or university level. The research, geared to finding out how ESL students accomplish academic tasks in content courses, involved the graduate students' tutoring an ESL student, then subsequently writing up the experience in the form of field notes. In most cases, the tutoring sessions were also audiotaped, and portions of the tapes were transcribed to better capture insights. The student researchers also carried out observations of their subjects in their content-area classes, interviewed their instructors, and made copies of relevant documents (e.g., their tests, course papers, class notes). These data were then analyzed and written up by the student researchers in case study format. In the aggregate, these 34 case studies provide important background about the academic skills required of English language learners in their content-area classes and form a information base for CBI training programs.

A final research tool that can provide useful insights into teacher training issues are dialogue journal exchanges between teacher trainers and their trainees. As described variously (see, for example, Porter, Goldstein, Leatherman, & Conrad, 1990), dialogue journals allow participants in Teaching English as a

Second Language (TESL) preparation programs to "reflect on discussions, lectures, readings, and field experiences and obtain feedback on these reflections from a knowledgeable mentor" (Holten & Brinton, 1989, p. 23). By reading and responding to the participants' journal entries, the teacher educator gains an open window into their issues of primary concern, thus receiving valuable information on issues that should be included in future such training programs. Brinton and Holten (1989), for example, compared the dialogue journal commentaries of native speaker and non-native speaker practicum participants to chart their growing awareness of pedagogical issues over a 10-week period. Their findings, i.e., that novice teachers wrestle most with the issues of methods and activities, techniques, and lesson organization, can inform TESL program design and help to better structure the curriculum of teaching practica. Similarly, Holten, and Brinton (1995) examined the dialogue journal exchanges of three ESL student teachers, making recommendations that the practice teaching curriculum include more of a focus on the assessment of learner's language proficiency, classroom management, lesson organization, and lesson delivery. They supported the use of dialogue journals as a research tool, claiming that in this manner TESL "preparation programs can craft more supportive programs to assist new teachers in maturing and achieving their ultimate goal as effective, confident teachers in their own right" (p. 26).

BACKGROUND OF THE PRESENT STUDY

Given the dearth of research into CBI teacher preparation, there is an urgent need for studies that inform CBI preservice and inservice education efforts. The study described here makes use of the final research tool mentioned, that is, its research base is formed by the dialogue journal exchanges between participating students, their peers, and their course instructor or supervisor.[5]

In the initial phase of the study, the dialogue journals of 19 participants who had aided, student taught, or worked as a teaching assistant in a university-level ESL course using CBI as its approach were examined for comments specifically relating to the approach. Of these, only 13 of the journals were found to contain comments relevant to the research focus and were selected for further analysis. These participants were all enrolled in one of two graduate-level courses at UCLA: the basic TESL methods course (Applied Linguistics 210—Theories of Language Education and Learning) and the ESL field practicum (Applied Linguistics 380—Supervised Teaching: English as a Second Language), and were required to complete the dialogue journal as part of the course requirement. The majority of the participants were enrolled in the

---

[5]I was both the graduate course instructor/supervisor and the researcher in the study being reported here.

TABLE 3.1

Breakdown of Participants by Native Language, Gender, Program, and Status

Participant[6]	Native Language	Gender	Program	Status
BS	English	M	MA	Teaching Assistant
HC	English	F	Staff	Classroom Aide
HP	English	M	MA	Classroom Aide
HS	Cantonese	F	MA	Classroom Aide
HT	Japanese	M	Ph.D.	Teaching Assistant
JH	Korean	F	MA	Classroom Aide
KM	Korean	F	MA	Classroom Aide
KS	Korean	F	MA	Student Teacher
LT	Mandarin	F	MA	Classroom Aide
PD	English	M	MA	Classroom Aide
PT	English	F	Undergraduate	Classroom Aide
SJ	English	F	MA	Classroom Aide
SK	Japanese	M	MA	Classroom Aide

university's master's in TESL program. Six were native speakers of English and seven were nonnative speakers. The breakdown of participants by native language, gender, program, and status is shown in Table 3.1.

As a key component of the dialogue journal requirement, the participants were placed under the supervision of an experienced mentor teacher (i.e., a teacher well versed in CBI as an approach) in either the on-campus ESL courses for matriculated students at UCLA or in parallel credit-bearing courses offered through UCLA Extension's American Language Center.[7] Both programs employed what is known as a simulated adjunct model of CBI (Valentine & Repath-Martos, 1997), in which authentic content is imported into an ESL class via authentic video lectures from undergraduate content-area classes. These video lectures form the core of the content unit and are supplemented by authentic content-area reading and writing assignments along with

---

[6]To preserve anonymity, each subject has been identified by a two-letter identifier (not the subject's initials).

[7]Students enrolled in the basic methods course served as teacher aides for a total of 20 courses/term; students enrolled in the TESL practicum served as student teachers for a total of 40 courses/term. In two cases, enrolled graduate students were serving as teaching assistants and were thus allowed to use this teaching assignment to fulfill the aiding/student teaching requirement.

related readings (e.g., excerpts from popular sources and from literature), language and skill-area instruction, related discussion activities, visuals, etc.[8]

In the unstructured format of the dialogue journal, the participants regularly recorded observations and questions about their experience with CBI. They then sent these journals to both the course instructor or supervisor and a peer via e-mail and received responses to their journals from both correspondents. (See Appendix A for instructions to participants concerning the dialogue journal exchanges). In this manner, a lively "conversation" about the course and issues of immediate interest transpired that could later be used by the teacher–researcher to pinpoint the major issues that these teachers-in-training experienced vis-à-vis CBI. (See Appendix B for a sample dialogue journal exchange between instructor, participant, and peer).

PROCEDURES

To inform CBI teacher preparation programs, the participants' dialogue journal exchanges were examined and relevant passages commenting on any aspect of CBI were highlighted and extracted.[9] The passages were then collected, and the individual comments were coded by participant and categorized under the following headings:

1. Importance of content or theme selection: the journal respondent's, course instructor's, or students' responses to the content or theme of the instructional unit
2. Coming to terms with the instructional paradigm: general assessment of the use of CBI as an instructional approach
3. Authenticity of the approach: the authenticity of course materials, tasks, or the instructional approach itself
4. Need for content expertise: the requirement for content expertise on the part of the language instructor and the demand by students for content knowledge
5. Appropriateness of the paradigm to the student population and setting: Relevance of CBI to the student population, instructional setting, and type of course
6. Problems in the curriculum: Other perceived problems in the CBI curriculum

---

[8]See Weigle & Jensen (1997) and Holten (1997) for further information on the simulated adjunct approach.

[9]For the purpose of this study, the instructor and peer responses to the original dialogue journal entry were not analyzed.

RESULTS

In this section, selected participant comments are examined for the light they can shed on the ways in which instructors new to the CBI paradigm grapple with key instructional issues. Before proceeding to this section, however, it should be noted that although the participants had varying degrees of prior teaching experience, they were all new to working with CBI and were, therefore, defined as "novices" for the purpose of this study. In this respect, it is interesting to note the participants' initial impressions of CBI, as it is in their initial dialogue journal entries describing the course and its approach that they attempt to define for themselves and their readers what CBI entails. In the following two comments, note the clear definition and description of the approach as recorded by SJ and HC:

> I like this approach, content-based instruction, teaching language skills in a way that is very relevant to these college students. I particularly liked the authenticity of one of their activities. They watched a segment of an actual UCLA history lecture as a listening exercise. The first time they watched it, they were told to listen for a series of adjectives describing the new American; the second time, they listened for the main points of his lecture. In this activity, they were required to use first their bottom-up language processing, and then their top-down, both of which are necessary to properly digest an academic lecture. [SJ, ns][10]

> The curriculum in this course is content-based. It uses materials from various academic disciplines in the form of real UCLA reading assignments and lectures. A typical exercise is to have the students watch a videotape of a real university lecture by a professor and use the lecture to carry out various learning exercises. The first academic subject used in the course is folklore and folk culture, which is a good one as students can relate the topic to their own cultures' particular folk experiences. In one exercise students are asked to watch a videotape of a segment of a lecture on folk objects and answer content questions afterward. As they watch, they fill in answers in a chart in the textbook that asks both general comprehension and detail-oriented content questions about the lecture. In this case the professor is talking about a cemetery he visited in East Los Angeles and the differences he noticed between the tombstones of three different ethnic groups. The students watch the tape and jot down their responses. Then [mentor teacher] plays the tape a second time, and they continue to jot down answers in the chart in the textbook. She then has them discuss their answers. [HC, ns]

---

[10]All dialogue journal entries indicate author (refer to Table 3.1 for the subject identifiers) and native speaker (ns) or nonnative speaker (nns) status.

In their subsequent journal entries, however, the subjects move beyond simple description and definition, that is, they quickly assume a more objective stance in which they begin to evaluate the strengths and weaknesses of the approach.

Importance of Content or Theme Selection

By far the most numerous comments regarding CBI from the dialogue journals centered around the content or themes selected for a given instructional unit. HP, for example, begins by simply questioning the choice of Sociology as a content area. However, in a later entry, on having received input from students regarding their reactions, he begins to question the appropriateness of this choice of content:

> I forgot to ask [mentor teacher] why the subject was Sociology. Had the students expressed an interest in that subject? Were these all students interested in the social sciences and humanities? [HP, ns]

> On my way down the hallway after class, I was lucky enough to get some comments about the class from some students. [A female Spanish student] had two lines of comment. First, it is simply a class, a required one, for her. It's not something she would have signed up for if given a choice. Second, the class doesn't fit her needs exactly, since she's studying interior design. However, she went on to say, on second thought, that learning to write better would be helpful for the history class she wants to take next quarter and possibly for theory-oriented interior design classes in the future. She seemed clear that the main purpose of this class is to learn to write better academic English. [HP, ns]

Yet a more obvious example of the onset of an evaluative stance in the journal entries is provided by SK, who clearly notes student dissatisfaction with the history content of the course in which he is aiding:

> During the coffee break, I talked with a couple of students (one Italian man and one French lady) about how they feel about dealing with one content area for five weeks. They lost no time in responding as if they have been waiting for the opportunity to speak about this, saying that they don't want to learn the theory of History 160 but just want to be able to write and speak better. They also said because they are tired of the content they can't keep their motivation high. [SK, nns]

These participant observers, despite their "novice" status as CBI practitioners, find themselves quite literally confronted with all the same issues as their more experienced mentor teachers in the CBI class. And in some cases, (as with SK and HP) they are privy to reactions that the enrolled students may not feel comfortable sharing with the mentor teacher. In the following comment, SJ notes an improvement in class atmosphere and student motivation due to the midquarter change in topic:

The class I'm observing seems to be getting more and more interactive as the quarter progresses. Or perhaps the higher degree of participation is due to the topic of families. Because of its personal nature, this topic has the potential to create lots of discussion. Each student is, in a sense, an "expert" with a lot of contextual knowledge … [SJ, ns]

Note here that SJ, like her peers SK and JP, displays extreme sensitivity to student reaction to the theme and pinpoints relevant theme or topic selection in her journal as one of the key ingredients for success in a CBI program.

Coming to Terms With the Instructional Paradigm

A second common area of commentary involves the participants coming to terms with CBI in general, that is, specifically weighing the advantages or disadvantages it may offer to ESL students. In the following comments, we see a range of reactions to CBI, from SK's highly enthusiastic response to HP's neutral one to LT's initial skepticism:

> I didn't know that the content based teaching approach would be this wonderful … [SK, nns]

> This was the first time I've actually seen content-based learning in action. Before I had only read about it and basically agreed with most of the principles behind it. [HP, ns]

> As for the video lecture, I think it's a good way to drill the students in listening comprehension and notetaking skills. The students can organize their thinking and concentrate their minds on the lecture. At that time, I thought that the lecture he selected (Sociology) was somewhat a boring topic for the students and they might not be so responsive to it. However, I realize that since the majority of the students are undergrads, for sure they will be contacting with a variety of lectures in their own fields. [LT, nns]

In general, the comments in this category avoid being overjudgmental, no doubt in keeping with the fact that the participants are still in the process of sorting out their own reactions to CBI practice and attempting to match these with what they have read or heard about this approach from a more theoretical perspective.

Authenticity of the Approach

At the very foundation of CBI (and ESP, for that matter) is the claim of relevance to students' needs across the curriculum. Like Valentine & Repath-Martos (1997), the participants in this study carefully measured this claim against the actuality of practice, arriving at a range of conclusions. PD, for instance, measures what he sees in his mentor's class against concepts being discussed that week in the methods course, arriving at a globally positive evaluation of CBI with respect to the issue of authenticity:

> In [mentor teacher's] class I got to look at a paper that was returned to the students that day. As a test of their abilities, I think it is both interactionally and situationally authentic. The class exercises are very similar to what the test requires and the future in class requirements they may face. [PD, ns]

Similarly, BS (one of the two teaching assistants in the study) agrees with the principle of using authentic lecture segments in the CBI class but notes the practical difficulties that occur when such lectures are delivered via video rather than live (thus significantly reducing the authenticity quotient of this practice):

> I think the use of videos of Professor Laslett's class is an excellent idea—I do think sometimes though that because he's often referring to information on handouts (or other materials) which the students in the real class have, he treats important points almost nonchalantly, reducing them to mumbled ramblings at breakneck speed. Unfortunately, these are often the points that the ESL students are meant to catch. On one hand, I can reason that it is good practice for the students to experience such a lecture delivery, but on the other hand, they are handicapped in a way, because they don't have all the handouts, and they can't stop the prof for repetition or clarification. [BS, ns]

HT (the second teaching assistant in the study and by far the most experienced teacher), measures practice against theory even more critically, as can be seen in the two comments that follow:

> I am at a loss how to make speaking activities authentic. What I am doing now is to have [students] discuss the video they have watched and the reading in groups. But the contents of the discussion as well as their questions are superficial and far from authentic. This comes partly from the fact that ESL teachers are not experts of the content. (I could make my class discussion more authentic if the content were about interlanguage phonology). [HT, nns]

> I would like to see how speaking functions at a university level, focusing on undergraduates ... in reality, they have to register for discussion sections, in which participation counts part of a grade. In terms of authenticity, we should train students to speak as if they were in the discussion section. To develop teaching strategies I would observe some discussion sections to see how they are going. [HT, nns]

Although critical vis-à-vis the types of speaking activities he is having his own students do, HT's comment can be seen as more directed to his own teaching than at the method itself. Rather than conclude that authenticity of speaking activities is not possible within this method, HT continues to explore ways in which CBI practice can be improved to include authentic academic speaking activities.

Need for Content Expertise

Long documented as a problematic issue in Language for Specific Purposes, the extent to which CBI instructors need to be experts in the content area chosen for a given instructional unit sparks lively debate, even among those well versed in CBI practice. The students in this study were quick to identify this as a problematic issue. SK, based on his observational experience, notes:

> [Mentor teacher]'s knowledge and his insight to the immigration issue are deep enough to let students give a deeper thought to an issue … a teacher who can offer only linguistics knowledge might not be able to draw full attention from students. In this sense, in my opinion, a language teacher needs to be more than he sells only linguistics information. I would like to buy more intellectual information as well as language when I am a student. [SK, nns]

Similarly, BS relates an early incident in his first experience using CBI in which his content knowledge is challenged by one of his students:

> On the other hand, content-based instruction demands a great deal of comprehension on the part of the instructor, in order to guide discussions and to be able to respond to students' questions. The other night in my class, I was, with all the confidence I could muster, assuring the students that in the assimilation model, intermarriage takes place between immigrants and members of the host culture. Then, a student pointed out that the professor on the video (who teaches the history class) highlighted, as an example of marital assimilation, Irish marrying Jewish people. Faced with this blatant contradiction, I broke down and admitted that I didn't have an answer for him. I just felt completely false pretending to be an expert on immigration. [BS, ns]

By nominating this topic, these subjects probe the limits of the CBI teacher's authority and seek to identify the role of the teacher (and conversely that of the student) within this approach.

Appropriateness of the Paradigm to the Student Population and Setting

One limitation of this study was that all the ESL courses in which participants were placed were university level, with the only variable being the student population enrolled (i.e., regular matriculated students in the daytime university ESL classes and community members or students seeking a part-time professional degree in the evening parallel Extension classes). Despite this limitation, the participants were able to identify a crucial difference in the appropriateness of the simulated adjunct model to the two populations involved. HT, for example, notes general satisfaction with the simulated adjunct model in the type of setting where matriculated students are studying English for academic purposes:

> My impression after four weeks have passed is that at a university or advanced level English should be taught in an authentic context. Of course, the best way is to attend lectures in order to master academic English, but in terms of teaching language, I believe that there is no better way than the content-based approach … Those students taking at least ESL 33C have all reached a certain satisfactory level of what [Widdowson] calls "usage." The problem is whether they can use their English appropriately on the use level in an academic context. I have found that although their general English ability, such as speaking, is satisfactory the English ability required of their campus life is still desired. It would be silly to use general ESL textbooks even for academic purposes because they have almost no problem with the knowledge (usage) of English. [HT, nns]

PD, on the other hand, notes one example of an Extension student's dissatisfaction with the instructional model based on the perceived lack of relevance of the content being covered to her needs and interests:

> While I could see the importance of assessing learner needs and goals in theory, the lesson of such was driven home by a conversation with a student I had just the other day. While the topics and skills of the simulated adjunct were most likely relevant to the majority of the students, this particular student was on a one year exchange. For her, it was just too much American stuff that she wasn't really interested in. I assume she would desire a more theme based approach with greater topic variety … Of course, the issues of authenticity and relevance of the studied material is intimately linked to student goals, and the benefit of the majority can not be discounted by the unfortunate mismatch of a few. [PD, ns]

In the same vein, BS notes his own difficulty as instructor of "buying in" to this model given the obvious mismatch of the curriculum's focus to his students' interests:

> Well, we've started Module 2 in 33C. The content is "kinship systems," from Anthropology 9. So far, so good. [The professor] who is featured on the video portion of this module is much clearer than the professor in Module 1. That's a relief. The terms are once again highly specialized (e.g. "uxorilocal") and while I can see the value for the students in the ESL Service Courses to learn field-specific terms, there's at least one Extension instructor who's less than

thrilled about teaching them … I don't quite know how to justify completely the content for Extension students. [BS, ns]

Had the participants in fact had more of a chance to experience a variety of CBI courses in a range of settings (e.g., theme-based CBI courses in intensive language institutes, sheltered content classes at the high school level, etc.), there is no doubt that the comments in this category would have yielded even richer insights for curriculum planners.

Problems in the Curriculum

Throughout the journals, students tended to critically view practice through the lens of theory—often relating the classroom routines and procedures they were observing to concepts or issues which were addressed in the course readings. HT, in the comment below, relates CBI instructional practice to the concepts of top-down vs. bottom-up information processing, noting the tendency of CBI to rely more heavily on the former:

> My teaching as well as [supervising instructor]'s has tended to be a top-down approach, in which the content-based approach can be more easily conducted. But we must not forget that there is a big pitfall here. As a learner of English as well as a teacher, no matter how advanced level we have reached, we sometimes have difficulty with a bottom-up process, which results in the failure to understand text or speech. [HT, nns]

Similarly, HP chooses to focus on concepts contained in the assigned course readings on sheltered English and relate these to the class he is observing:

> Something about cognitive/academic language proficiency vs. basic interpersonal communicative skills and sheltered English … seems paradoxical. We're supposed to provide a context-rich environment to help students understand content in an academic, relatively context-poor environment. Isn't there a danger that students will become too dependent on a teacher providing so much additional context? If so, could this hinder cognitive development down the line. … How much contextualization is too much, if there is such a thing as too much? These are all merely questions that float in and out of my head, nothing I expect any sort of answer to. [HP, ns]

Finally, HT notes the difficulty of CBI to allow a systematic focus on grammar instruction (see Eskey, 1997):

> I have found that through this approach it is very difficult to deal with language items. I have to confess that I do not know yet what language items should be taught in my class. … I have found it hard to teach grammar in a systematic way

through the content-based approach. Fortunately, the students seem to enjoy this approach and not to like to be told about grammar. But this fact makes the teaching of language items more difficult. [HT, nns]

CONCLUSIONS

The findings of the study reported in this chapter underscore the need for a CBI-specific training component in the MA in TESL curriculum. Despite the relative dominance of CBI on the second and foreign language instructional scene, MA in TESL programs have been slow to develop courses that specifically address this approach. Stoller (1998) made a convincing case for reconceptualizing the MA in TESL curriculum to make CBI a more prominent feature in the TESL methods course as well as courses on curriculum, syllabus and materials design, program administration, and skills-specific courses (e.g., L2 reading and writing). As critical components to include, she suggested that such courses cover the foundations and rationale for CBI, an overview of the different CBI models and their salient characteristics, the settings in which the various models are most applicable, sound instructional practices that are in concordance with the CBI approach, an analysis of commercially available CBI materials, and finally the development of thematic units to integrate language and content.

As a teacher educator with a long-standing interest in CBI theory and practice, I strongly concur with Master's (1997) call for training institutions to develop courses that better prepare future teachers to practice current approaches such as Language for Specific Purposes (and by extension, CBI).[11] I also agree with Stoller's call to include CBI across the training curriculum.

However, in addition to the suggestions made by Stoller, I believe that such CBI training should aim beyond the graduate methods classroom to include practical, hands-on experience with a CBI program in action. Specifically, I would argue the following:

1. Aiding and/or student teaching[12] are critical components of the basic TESL methods and practicum courses, particularly for those students who enter an MA training program with little or no prior teaching experience. However, even for students who *are* experienced teachers, these

---

[11]As an adjunct faculty member, I teach graduate-level courses in CBI at two Los Angeles area universities. However, my home institution, UCLA, has no such course in its MA curriculum despite the fact that the resident faculty expertise to teach such a course is available and our ESL program for matriculated students, in which our graduate teaching assistants instruct, has adopted a content-based curriculum.

[12]Our MA program at UCLA includes both—that is, students taking a basic TESL methods course in their first quarter of study have the option to serve as aides in an ESL class and in their third quarter of study have the option to student teach in an ESL setting. In both cases, they are teamed with an experienced mentor teacher and receive additional supervision and guidance from the TESL graduate instructor or supervisor.

course components can be of benefit if the student wishes to receive hands-on experience with a particular approach (e.g., CBI).

2. There is a clear value in teacher education programs to include a multi-faceted mentoring component of the type experienced by the participants in the study reported here. In other words, in addition to the guidance and supervision provided by the experienced ESL teacher with whom the graduate student is paired, the scaffolding of experience that is provided by the graduate instructor and the sharing of similar concerns or classroom experiences by a peer all conspire to make the learning experience a more meaningful one.

3. Novices to CBI should be encouraged to go beyond experiencing the approach and to truly reflect on the teaching practice. To some extent, such reflective teaching (Richards & Lockhart, 1994) can be achieved in class discussion. However, as can be seen from the quality of teacher commentary cited in this study, the journal format (e.g., double-entry journals, dialogue journals) is particularly conducive to such practice.

The participants in this study have sharply focused their "lens" on the day-to-day realities of CBI practice, noting in vivid detail and with keen analysis the strengths and weaknesses of the approach. As both the teacher educator and researcher in this study, I was repeatedly struck by the ways in which these "novices" to the approach were able to pinpoint and critique those areas where theory and practice were not in total harmony. Out of the mouths of babes, as it were, came wisdom that could serve to truly inform CBI classroom practice as well as graduate training curricula.

In closing, I encourage teacher educators, and specifically those involved in CBI teacher training, to fill the gaps in teacher education research alluded to at the outset of this article and to make use of the identified research avenues. Granted, studies such as the one reported here are small-scale in size and provide only very limited insights into the types of issues that most perplex practitioners new to a particular instructional approach such as CBI. But collectively, such small-scale studies provide an important source of guidance for those conducting the preservice and inservice training of instructors.

REFERENCES

Adamson, H. D. (1993). *Academic competence—Theory and classroom practice: Preparing ESL students for content courses.* New York: Longman.

Benesch, S. (Ed.). (1988). *Ending remediation: Linking ESL and content in higher education.* Washington, DC: Teachers of English to Speakers of Other Languages.

Brinton, D. M., & Holten, C. (1989). What novice teachers focus on: The practicum in TESOL. *TESOL Quarterly 23*(2), 343–350.

Brinton, D. M., Snow, M. A., & Wesche, M. B. (1989). *Content-based second language instruction.* Boston: Heinle & Heinle.

Cantoni-Harvey, G. (1987). *Content-area language instruction: Approaches and strategies.* Reading, MA: Addison Wesley.

Crandall, J. (1987). *ESL through content-area instruction: Mathematics, science, and social studies.* New York: Prentice Hall.

Crandall, J. (1998). Collaborate and cooperate: Teacher education for integrating language and content instruction. *English Teaching Forum, 36*(1), 2–9.

Echevarria, J., & Graves, A. (1998). *Sheltered content instruction: Teaching English-language learners with diverse abilities.* Boston: Allyn & Bacon.

Eskey, D. (1997). Syllabus design in content-based instruction. In M. A. Snow & D. M. Brinton (Eds.), *The content-based classroom: Perspectives on integrating language and content* (pp. 132–141). White Plains, NY: Longman.

Farrell-Childers, P., Gere, A. R., & Young, A. (1994). *Programs and practices: Writing across the secondary school curriculum.* Portsmouth, NH: Boynton/Cook.

Fathman, A. K., Quinn, M. E., & Kessler, C. (1992). *Teaching science to English learners, grades 4–8.* Washington, DC: National Clearinghouse for Bilingual Education.

Goodwin, J., & Jensen, L. (1996, March). *Becoming a content-based ESL instructor: Training and supervision.* Paper delivered at the annual convention of Teachers of English to Speakers of Other Languages, Chicago, IL.

Hein, G. E., & Price, S. (1994). *Active assessment for active science: A guide for elementary school teachers.* Portsmouth, NH: Heinemann.

Holten, C. (1997). Literature: A quintessential content. In M. A. Snow & D. M Brinton (Eds.), *The content-based classroom: Perspectives on integrating language and content* (pp. 377–387). White Plains, NY: Longman.

Holten, C. A., & Brinton, D. M. (1989). "You shoulda been there": Charting novice teacher growth using dialogue journals. *TESOL Journal, 4*(4), 23–26.

Johns, A. (1992). What is the relationship between content-based instruction and English for specific purposes? *The CATESOL Journal, 5*(1), 71–75.

Kaufman, D. (1997). Collaborative approaches in preparing teachers for content-based and language-enhanced settings. In M. A. Snow & D. M. Brinton (Eds.), *The content-based classroom: Perspectives on integrating language and content* (pp. 175–186). White Plains, NY: Longman.

Lemke, J. L. (1990). *Talking science: Language, learning, and values.* Norwood, NJ: Ablex.

Lindquist, T. (1995). *Seeing the whole through social studies.* Portsmouth, NH: Heinemann.

Master, P. (1992). What are some considerations for teacher training in content-based instruction? *The CATESOL Journal, 5*(1), 77–84.

Master, P. (1997). ESP teacher education in the USA. In Brown, G. & Howard, R. (Eds.), *Teacher education for LSP (Languages for Specific Purposes,* pp. 22–40). Clevedon, UK: Multilingual Matters.

Mohan, B. A. (1986). *Language and content.* Reading, MA: Addison-Wesley.

Peitzman, F., & Gadda, G. (1994). *With different eyes: Insights into teaching language minority students across the disciplines.* White Plains, NY: Longman.

Peregoy, S. F., & Boyle, O. F. (1993). *Reading, writing, and learning in ESL.* White Plains, NY: Longman.

Peterson, P. W. (1997). Knowledge, skills, and attitudes in teacher preparation for content-based instruction. In M. A. Snow & D. M Brinton (Eds.), *The content-based classroom: Perspectives on integrating language and content* (pp. 158–174). White Plains, NY: Longman.

Porter, P., Goldstein, L., Leatherman, J., & Conrad, S. (1990). An ongoing dialogue: Learning logs for teacher training. In J. C. Richards & D. Nunan (Eds.), *Second language teacher education* (pp. 227–240). Cambridge: Cambridge University Press.

Richards, J. C., & Lockhart, C. (1994). *Reflective teaching in second language classrooms*. Cambridge: Cambridge University Press.

Rosenthal, J. W. (1996). *Teaching science to language minority students*. Philadelphia, PA: Multilingual Matters.

Saul, W., Reardon, J., Schmidt, A., Pearce, C., Blackwood, D., & Bird, M. D. (1993). *Science workshop: A whole language approach*. Portsmouth, NH: Heinemann.

Scott, J. (Ed.). (1992). *Science and language links: Classroom implications*. Portsmouth, NH: Heinemann.

Short, D. (1991a). *Integrating language and content instruction: Strategies and techniques*. National Clearinghouse for Bilingual Education Program Information Guide Series 7. Rosslyn, VA.

Short, D. (Ed.). (1991b). *How to integrate language and content instruction: A training manual* (2nd ed.). Washington, DC: Center for Applied Linguistics.

Snow, M. A., & Brinton, D. M. (Eds.). (1992). Special theme issue: Content-based instruction. *The CATESOL Journal, 5*(1).

Stoller, F. L. (1998). *The challenges of training teachers in content-based instruction in a small community*. Paper delivered at the annual convention of Teachers of English to Speakers of Other Languages, Seattle, WA.

Tchudi, S., & Lafer, S. (1996). *The interdisciplinary teacher's handbook: Integrated teaching across the curriculum*. Portsmouth, NH: Boynton/Cook.

Valentine, J. F. Jr., & Repath-Martos, L. M. (1997). How relevant is relevance? In M. A. Snow & D. M. Brinton (Eds.), *The content-based classroom: Perspectives on integrating language and context* (pp. 233–247). White Plains, NY: Longman.

Weigle, S. C., & Jensen, L. (1997). Issues in assessment for content-based instruction. In M. A. Snow & D. M. Brinton (Eds.), *The content-based classroom: Perspectives on integrating language and content* (pp. 201–212). White Plains, NY: Longman.

APPENDIX A:
INSTRUCTIONS TO PARTICIPANTS REGARDING
THE DIALOGUE JOURNAL EXCHANGE

Applied Linguistics 210
(Theories of Language Education and Learning)

Classroom aiding: You may choose to aide 2 hours a week during weeks 2 through 10 of an on-campus ESL course. This option is highly recommended for those who will be enrolling in AL 380 in the spring and/or who hope to become teaching assistants in the ESL Service Courses. To document this experience, you should keep an aiding journal in which you record impressions and experiences about the class you are observing. The following procedure will be used: over the course of the aiding experience, each participant will compose 5 personal entries, and send these entries via e-mail to the instructor and one peer (a different peer for each entry to insure a variety of response). Both the instructor and the peer receiving the journal are responsible for responding within 3 days to the entry. All peer responses should be copied to the instructor. At the end of the term, each students' dialogue journal entries and peer responses will be evaluated.

Applied Linguistics 380
(Supervised Teaching: English as a Second Language)

The Dialogue Journal: You are expected to keep a journal or log of your practicum experience. This will be comprised of your own impressions of the classes you observe, those activities and lessons you plan and teach, comments on materials used, your conferences with the master teacher and with us, your feedback and interactions with other participating students, and any other information you see as useful for your own reflection. Note that the log should include records of both successful and unsuccessful teaching experiences, as both are important in developing your competence and personal style as an ESL teacher.

To keep in better contact with you and your experience, we'll correspond via dialogue journal using e-mail. We'll be using the following procedure: Over the course of the quarter, you will write 5 or 6 entries in the journal. You should send each journal to the course supervisor, and copy the course teaching assistant on the correspondence. Also, we ask that you send each entry to a peer—a different one for each entry. This peer, along with the course supervisor, will be responsible for responding to your entry. All peer responses should be copied to the course supervisor and the teaching assistant. At the end of the term, we'll evaluate the entire log as part of your practicum experience.

APPENDIX B:
SAMPLE PARTICIPANT/INSTRUCTOR/PEER
DIALOGUE JOURNAL EXCHANGE

The participant is an aide in ESL 33C, High-Intermediate English as a Second Language. The peer who responds is aiding in the course one level below, Intermediate English as a Second Language.

Participant Journal Entry

I thought the reading material for this session of 33C was quite interesting. The story was about a young Cantonese girl dealing with ethnic issues in interacting with her American classmates at school and recognizing her culture and identity. She apparently had some eye-opening incidents, such as when she discovered the difference between the lunch she would bring to school and the kind everyone else had. Her riceballs looked very strange to her American schoolmates who had sandwiches. Other topics that were brought up in this story were racial slurs and her family's cultural values. I know that I could definitely relate to a story like this, having grown up in Maryland with nearly all European American kids in my class. I remember discovering these differences that set me apart from the other kids, like my seaweed rolls and my strict parents.

Well, going back to 33C, the students' reaction to this story was much less than I expected. I thought this story would arouse more discussion about either Chinese culture or their own immigrant experiences. I would have hypothesized that the Chinese students in this class would participate even more because of their personal experiences and greater contextual knowledge. But this wasn't the case. Perhaps because they all immigrated here not too long ago, while in their later teens or so, their own immigrant experience was quite different from this little girl's. There probably is a great difference between a child's perspective and a young adult's upon arriving at and acclimating to a new place. Perhaps they thought the story or approach to these heavy issues of race/ethnicity/immigration was dealt with too lightly, portrayed in a child's story. Or perhaps they were just tired!

I enjoyed watching the informal oral presentations, which were given by one representative from each table. They were to describe or create a story for a picture they were given. Each group was particularly attentive to their representative and supportive of him/her. The activity seemed to bring them together in cooperation. It was a nice change of scenery too to have classmates up front. It also seemed good to get the students doing oral presentations, however minor they might be. Something that might've added to the oral presentation experience is the teacher asking the student some questions and/or opening it up for other students to ask questions, serious or nonserious, just to get dialogue going and conversation flowing.

There always seems to be one practical skills activity in each class session. This time, in groups, they came up with steps in doing well on essay exams. The guidelines that they came up with were very general, such as brainstorm and outline, but they probably will remember some of these basic things the next time they have to write an in-class essay. The class got pretty involved in discussing this.

Ok. Til next time.

Instructor Response

Thanks for the interesting account of your own and students' reactions to the reading in 33C.

This is actually a very typical experience in content-based instruction—one picks a theme and/or reading that one thinks will elicit responses and be of interest to students and then it appears that they have much less interest than anticipated.

You give some very likely reasons for students' reactions—either they felt the topic was treated too lightly, it didn't relate closely enough to their own experience, that experience is too far in the distant past, or they were tired. Maybe even a combination of the above???

It's interesting, on the other hand, that you reacted so strongly to the story (I really like it too and had a hand in choosing it, so of course I'm somewhat biased toward it).

What kind of pictures were the students given at their tables? Did these relate in any way to the story? In 33B, the students read a piece from *Farewell to Manzanar.* In that unit, there is a speaking activity where they look at some of the Ansel Adams photos of life in Manzanar and relate what they see to the text they are reading. It's an activity one of our past TAs created. I really like the activity as it gets students discussing the story more. As I read your journal account, I couldn't help thinking that maybe having pictures that related to the story would stimulate discussion. (Kind of like the magazine pictures of "dead end" and "non dead end" jobs I distributed the other day in my demo of the jigsaw got you all talking about jobs and then segued into the pair interviews about your own experiences with dead end jobs.) I'm a strong believer in using pictures as a discussion stimulus in the classroom, in case you hadn't already figured that out.

I agree that even if the guidelines that students came up with are general, they will tend to remember them better since they themselves generated them.

Have a great weekend. See you on Monday.

Peer Response

I enjoyed reading your journal entry. In terms of the exercise dealing with the story of the young Cantonese girl, like you said, it's hard to know why the students didn't respond well—whether it was because these serious issues were portrayed through a children's story, or perhaps because the students felt it was too personal to discuss in class. It would have been interesting to ask a few of them afterward what their thoughts were.

I observe in XL33B, and the teacher recently did an exercise similar to the photo/story activity that you mentioned. This exercise also worked very well in our class. Each table was given a picture of a family. The students were supposed to talk about the people in their picture, describe what they thought their family situations were, and any information they thought was pertinent (e.g., whether the families seemed happy, where they lived, how they were related, etc.) One student then had to report their ideas to the rest of the class. The students had a good time with the exercise. It also gave them a chance to practice their public speaking skills. This activity was used to prepare them for the next theme used in the course, which is "family." In one on-going exercise, they'll be watching a video of a UCLA professor teaching a course on "The History of the American Family," so this was a good way to stimulate some of the vocabulary they'll need for this next stage. Later in the course they also have to give an oral presentation that is graded, so this was good preparation for that task.

I think you mentioned that your class brainstormed ideas about how to do well on essay exams. Our class also relies on practical-skills training. After learning about paragraph and essay formats, the students have done "in-class timed writings," in which they are given 45 minutes to write on various topics. This exercise allows them to practice skills used in essay examinations.

Lastly, our class also utilizes an approach where there's a lot of peer interaction, group work, and learning from fellow students. In many cases, they evaluate each others' writing samples. I agree this seems to be a very effective learning strategy.

Well, thanks for sharing your thoughts and experiences with me.

4

ESL Students in the Mainstream

Observations From Content Area Faculty

Judith W. Rosenthal

Kean University

I first met Niurlys when she was a student in my introductory biology course. She was about nineteen years old, and the year before, had immigrated from Colombia with her parents. Although she completed her senior year in a bilingual program at a local, New Jersey high school, Niurlys hardly knew any English. She was attending Kean University because here she could participate in an intensive English as a Second Language (ESL) Program and concurrently begin working toward her degree by taking a limited number of content-area courses taught using Spanish as the language of instruction. So that is how we met, during Niurlys' freshman year, in my "Spanish speaking" section of "Principles of Biology."

Niurlys was a good student and earned a final grade of "B." She mastered the content, worked well in the laboratory, attended regularly, participated in class discussions, and satisfactorily fulfilled all assignments. Like many other students I have taught from Colombia, Niurlys' previous education was excellent, especially in science, mathematics, and calculus.

For the next year or two, I occasionally would see Niurlys in the hallways of Kean, and she would stop by my office to chat. She completed her ESL coursework and was preparing to be a high school Spanish teacher. Sometimes, I would help her by proofreading assignments she had written in English or coach her in oral presentation skills. As far as I knew, all was going well. Then, one day, Niurlys appeared in my office, sobbing. Apparently, a history professor, put off by her accent, had advised her to "get out of my class until you can speak English".

I remember this incident very clearly. What I cannot recall is whether or not Niurlys withdrew from that history course or if she and the instructor ever sat down and worked out their 'differences.' Nevertheless, I do know that Niurlys remained enrolled at Kean, completing her degree requirements. She is now a teacher. I saw Niurlys at a conference several years ago, and we ate lunch together. In English (still with an accent) she reported to me that life was good and that she was now working on a Master's degree.

As we talked I couldn't help but wonder, what would have happened if Niurlys had taken that history teacher's words to heart, not just dropping his course but perhaps being so discouraged that she withdrew from college? How would that have improved her English? Instead of a successful professional who was continuing her education, we would have had another statistic to add to the dismal educational record of Hispanics in the United States.

—*Judith W. Rosenthal, Professor, Biological Sciences, Kean University*

THE GROWING NUMBER OF NONNATIVE ENGLISH SPEAKING STUDENTS: INTERNATIONAL, IMMIGRANTS, AND REFUGEES

Although no one knows exact numbers, several lines of evidence indicate a dramatic increase in undergraduates of limited English proficiency. This population includes international students ("foreign" students attending college in the United States on temporary student visas) as well as first and second generation immigrants and refugees (permanent residents and U.S. citizens). This growing population of students of limited English proficiency is the result of:

- increasing ethnic and linguistic diversity in the K–12 school population (McDonnell & Hill, 1993; Stewart, 1993; *The Challenge of Change*, 1992; Vernez & Abrahamse, 1996);
- a million or so immigrants and refugees entering the United States each year from countries where a language other than English is spoken (Fix & Passel, 1994);
- growth in the percentage (from 1.52% in 1976 to 2.19% in 1995) of the total undergraduate population represented by international students (*The Chronicle of Higher Education Almanac*, Aug. 29, 1997, p.18);
- increased enrollment in English as a Second Language (ESL) on college campuses (Bers, 1994; Cochran, 1992; Cohen & Ignash, 1992; Gray, Rolph, & Melamid, 1996; Ignash, 1992; Ignash, 1992, 1993);
- results of surveys carried out at various colleges and universities showing that relatively large percentages of students are born outside

the United States and speak a language other than English at home (Cochran, 1992; Rosenthal, 1996, pp. 35–37; Russikoff, 1994).

Not only is no one keeping tabs of the enrollment of nonnative English speakers but also, at most institutions, it is not possible to differentiate between international, immigrant, and refugee students (Gray et al., 1996). Although all of these students are affected to some degree by a lack of proficiency in English, they tend to differ in other respects (Cheng, 1993; Cochran, 1992; Gray et al., 1996; Kinsella, 1997; Sigsbee, Speck, & Maylath, 1997; Stewart, 1993; Vernez & Abrahamse, 1996).

For example, international (or "foreign") students in general are better educated and have fewer financial problems than immigrants and refugees. They have completed their secondary education in their homeland and are well read and literate in their native language. Prior to their arrival in the United States, they have studied English as a foreign language. As a condition for admission to many American colleges and universities, they have scored satisfactorily on an English proficiency test such as TOEFL (Test of English as a Foreign Language). Certain aspects of the English language still may present some difficulties, but English is no longer a major academic obstacle. After completing their studies in the U.S., most international students will return to their homelands to live and work.

Immigrants and refugees are more likely to remain in the United States on a permanent basis and in time may become U.S. citizens. The economic and educational opportunities available in the U.S. usually outweigh the hardships they may encounter as newcomers.

Some immigrants and refugees have completed high school or studied at a university in their native country. However, their academic credentials may not be recognized in the U.S., and their lack of proficiency in English is a handicap. Others, because of political and economic problems in their native countries, have had little formal education. They arrive here with no knowledge of English, low literacy levels in their native language, and with strained financial resources.

The children of immigrants and refugees may begin their schooling in their homeland in their native language and finish their education, in English, here in the United States. Caught between two worlds and two cultures, some end up not knowing either their first (native) or second (English) language particularly well.

Whether international, immigrant, or refugee, the nonnative English speakers attending our colleges and universities are a diverse group. I do not know how important it is to be able to distinguish between them, but I am certain that most nonnative English speakers benefit (as well as many of their underprepared native English-speaking peers) from a style of teaching that takes into consideration their linguistic needs.

MAINTAINING REALISTIC EXPECTATIONS
ABOUT ESL STUDENTS

Although it would make our work as college instructors considerably easier if there were a test of English language proficiency that would predict academic success, no such test exists (Graham, 1987). The types of language skills needed to discuss and analyze a philosophy text, to understand the discipline-specific jargon used in economics, and to comprehend the difference between arithmetic problems that state "divide six by twelve" and "divide six into twelve" are extraordinarily vast. Moreover, other factors—such as previous educational opportunities, motivation, intelligence, and time management skills—contribute to a college student's academic achievement.

Studies have shown that nonnative English speakers, even after successful completion of an ESL program, often feel insecure about their ability to compete in the mainstream classroom (Christison & Krahnke, 1986; Ostler, 1980; Smoke, 1988; Valentine & Repath-Martos, 1997). Similarly, content-area faculty may be frustrated by the language skills of the ESL students enrolled in their courses (Ballard & Clanchy, 1991; Ferris & Tagg, 1996; Hamp-Lyons, 1991; Johns, 1991a; Leki, 1992; Russikoff, 1994; Santos, 1988; Silva, 1997; Vann, Meyer, & Lorenz, 1984; Vann, Lorenz, & Meyer, 1991).

Learning English as a second language is not an easy task, and the vocabulary and skills required to complete an academic program of study are much more extensive than those that make everyday conversation possible (Cummins, 1980). In fact, learning a second language for academic purposes requires a considerable amount of time, generally 5 to 7 years (Collier, 1987; Collier & Thomas, 1989; Cummins, 1981). This certainly is longer than the amount of time a student spends in an ESL program or completing an Associate's or Baccalaureate degree.

Learning a second language also involves making numerous errors (Ellis, 1994; Krashen, 1981, 1987; Leki, 1992; Lightbown & Spada, 1993). Some errors are a result of interference from the first or native language. Others, however, are a part of the developmental process. Just as toddlers and small children make all sorts of errors when learning their native language, so do adults when learning a second language. However, whereas we are tolerant of the errors made by youngsters (and often consider their speech to be "cute"), errors made by adult L2 learners are judged more harshly. Adults are accused of not studying hard enough, not trying hard enough, etc.

If we are going to maintain realistic expectations about the performance of ESL students, we also need to remember that they are not just learning English. By means of English, they are studying a wide variety of subjects—from art and business to literature and zoology. For most, English is a means to an end, not the end in itself. By utilizing those aspects of English in which they are most skilled, ESL students can succeed in college without native-like English proficiency.

ESL STUDENTS IN THE MAINSTREAM: A SUMMARY OF THE LITERATURE

Several studies have been reported in the literature in which questionnaires and/or structured interviews were administered to college students who either had completed their ESL requirements or were taking advanced ESL coursework (Christison & Krahnke, 1986; Ostler, 1980; Sheorey, Mokhtari, & Livingston, 1995; Smoke, 1988; Valentine & Repath-Martos, 1997). The results of these investigations are remarkably similar. The students claim that their ESL studies improve their proficiency in English and, to some extent, help prepare them for further mainstream, academic coursework. Nonetheless, the students do not feel sufficiently prepared when it comes to understanding academic texts, taking notes during lectures, and writing research papers. They express concerns about their test-taking skills, the speed with which they can read in English, their ability to speak (particularly when asking questions in class or meeting with a professor), and their listening comprehension, grammar, and vocabulary. As reported in these studies, the importance of each language skill not only varies with class standing (undergraduate vs. graduate) but also with the academic discipline.

Mainstream faculty members express similar concerns about the academic preparedness and language proficiency of ESL students. Investigations of this type either attempt to identify the skills needed by ESL students to succeed in the mainstream classroom (Horowitz, 1986; Johns, 1981; Powers, 1986), or focus on the importance of one aspect of language such as oral communication skills (Ferris & Tagg, 1996) or written discourse (Santos, 1988; Vann, Meyer, & Lorenz, 1984, Vann, Lorenz, & Meyer, 1991). The results indicate that what is perceived as a problem area or as a necessary skill for the ESL student reflects the particular academic discipline, the pedagogical approach used by the instructor, and certain characteristics of the faculty members themselves (such as gender, age, and whether they are native or nonnative speakers of English). For example, Santos (1988) and Vann, Meyer, and Lorenz (1984) found that professors in the physical sciences were much less tolerant of language errors in the compositions of ESL students than were their peers in the humanities and social sciences. Ferris and Tagg (1996) found that the importance of oral proficiency for ESL students very much depends on the academic discipline, the size of the class, and the instructor's preferred "delivery type" (lecture, discussion, seminar). Thus, a business class with limited enrollment may require class participation and working in small groups whereas large science and engineering lectures rarely require any oral participation.

Apparently, what is especially difficult for ESL students is making the transition from advanced ESL coursework to mainstream, subject-matter courses taught exclusively in English. As one of my colleagues put it,

> I have had many ESL students in my 'Cell Biology' course who have told me that they do well in content-area courses taught in their native language and that they also have completed their ESL requirements. Nonetheless, they do poorly in my class which is taught in English. The abrupt transition from one language to another seems to be very difficult for them.

Some ESL students, by dint of hard work, can successfully make this transition; for others it is a struggle. Content-based ESL instruction such as that described in this volume makes this transition less abrupt, increasing the likelihood that students will be adequately prepared for the challenges they will face in mainstream classrooms.

"DON'T JUDGE A BOOK BY ITS COVER"

Limited English proficiency and obvious "foreignness" can prevent faculty members from seeing the strengths that ESL students bring to the classroom. Some have had much better academic preparation in their homelands than many of the students graduating from high schools in the United States. Their knowledge of history, politics, geography, science, and mathematics may far exceed that of a typical American student. They bring to the classroom new perspectives and alternative points of view. Many nonnative speakers are highly motivated to succeed and may be much more willing to work hard to achieve their goals.

Yes, they may make errors when speaking or writing in English. Yes, it may be difficult for them to express their ideas. Nonetheless, their limited English proficiency does not mean that they lack intelligence or that they cannot learn. (Of course, there will be some nonnative English speakers whose prior academic preparation is so inadequate, whose study skills are so weak, and/or whose motivation is so low that combined with lack of English proficiency, academic failure is not a surprising outcome. We have native English speakers who suffer from some of the same problems.) However, with ESL students we need to be particularly careful not to judge a book by its cover.

> Norma seemed out of place in a woodworking studio. She reminded me of Xavier Cugat's fourth wife, Charo, the 'Coochie Coochie' girl. She had manicured nails, carefully applied make-up, 'big hair', and always wore 3-inch high heels to class. She spoke heavily accented English at hyperspeed and was in the midst of some mid-life career change. Norma was intense, melodramatic. In fact, I could only tolerate the briefest interactions with her. I tired easily in the face of

her unbridled power and rapid-fire speech. However, when it came to woodworking, Norma was a novice.

For one of her assignments in this beginning Furniture Making class, Norma proposed an extensive project, which involved designing and making a headboard for a double bed. The plans she drew up were excellent, and off she went to the lumberyard, with her manicured nails and high heels, to purchase the necessary wood and materials, hauling them in her car back to the woodworking studio. What typically happens in this course is that the semester comes to an end before the students can complete the pieces they are working on, and this was true for Norma.

However, what really surprised me was that over the next two semesters, on her own time, and for no additional academic credit, Norma returned to the woodworking studio to finish the headboard, carving into it the New York City skyline and the George Washington Bridge. It was magnificent. Furthermore, she designed the headboard so that it would come apart to fit into her car. Thus, she was able to take it home, reassemble it, and mount it on the wall by her bed.

Today, Norma is a practicing interior designer, and I am much more cautious about judging students' potential based on initial impressions. I can thank Norma for an important lesson learned!

—*Stuart Topper, Associate Professor, Fine Arts Department, Kean University*

For far too long, ESL instruction has been perceived by many faculty members and administrators as a form of academic remediation. Students may not receive academic credit for successful completion of ESL coursework, and ESL classes frequently are staffed by part-time, adjunct faculty.

However, as the number of students who are nonnative English speakers grows, ESL instruction becomes increasingly important. As researchers learn more about the process of L2 acquisition, it becomes more and more evident that ESL students learn English both in the ESL and in the mainstream classroom. In other words, all faculty, whatever the academic discipline, are contributing to the development of English language proficiency by non-native speakers.

Unfortunately, professors who would like to help ESL students often don't know where to begin or what to do. They may be experts in their academic disciplines but know little or nothing about the linguistic needs of the ESL students enrolled in their courses. Workshops and college-wide programs to train content-area instructors to more effectively teach ESL students are rare. Thus, in the rest of this chapter, I try to provide the kind of background information and suggestions that individual faculty members—whatever their academic specialty—should find useful when teaching ESL students in their mainstream courses.

FREQUENTLY USED LANGUAGE DEPENDENT SKILLS IN THE MAINSTREAM CLASSROOM

In this chapter, I focus on seven broad categories of language-dependent skills, skills that are used in college classrooms regardless of the academic discipline. They include listening comprehension, following instructions, reading, speaking, test taking, vocabulary development, and writing. Because the relative importance of a particular skill depends on the instructor's pedagogical practices as well as the academic discipline, the sequence in which this information is presented does not imply any particular hierarchy or ranking.

I attempt to explain some aspects of these skills that are particularly troublesome to nonnative speakers of English. Through examples, I hope to illustrate how "typical" classroom activities and "everyday" teaching practices may not produce the results that instructors desire with students of limited English proficiency.

As you read through this material, please keep in mind that I am not singling out particular activities and practices as examples of "bad" teaching. Rather, I am trying to raise awareness of the types of things we all do or say in the classroom that fail to take into consideration the linguistic needs of some ESL students. At times, I make suggestions about useful techniques. However, it is up to you to decide if this information is relevant to your classroom practices and whether or not it might help you to reduce linguistic barriers and enhance learning for nonnative speakers of English in your courses.

Listening Comprehension

Understanding spoken English is essential in every academic subject. As they talk, professors transmit content-area information, teach the jargon and discourse style appropriate to the discipline, and provide instructions for successful completion of the course. Students also depend on listening skills when attending guest lectures, watching videos and films, and while listening to their classmates during discussions and oral classroom presentations. No amount of time spent in the ESL classroom can fully prepare a student for the wide range of listening experiences, the differences in individual speech patterns, accents, and dialects, and the idioms, slang, and jokes used by instructors and classmates in a typical classroom.

Academic listening and lecture comprehension are complex skills for both native and nonnative speakers of English (Ferris & Tagg, 1996; Flowerdew, 1994; Powers, 1986). How much students understand depends on the knowledge and skills that they bring to the classroom as well as on characteristics of the lecture delivery, its content, and organization (Mason, 1994). Unlike a book that can be read and reread, a lecture or class discussion happens once.

Unless a student tape records the class, there is no way to go back over what was said by the instructor or what transpired during a discussion. The only record that remains when class ends are the student's notes or any handouts which were distributed.

Some ESL students attempt to write down every word that the professor says because they cannot determine the main points being made nor just how important and relevant is each piece of information. When their classmates laugh at a joke the professor tells, they don't join in because they have no idea what the joke means. And when someone uses an idiom—such as "couch potato" or "it's raining cats and dogs"—ESL students can't imagine what is being discussed. A literal translation just doesn't make sense. Even when students tape record their classes, they admit that they often do not have the time to listen to these tapes.

In order to enhance the listening comprehension of ESL students, instructors can do some of the following:

- Make a conscious effort to speak at a reasonable rate (even when excited about the topic under discussion)
- Write key terminology on the chalkboard, spelling out new words and explaining their meaning
- Use visual aids (slides, models, etc.) to enhance oral presentations
- Distribute copies of lecture notes or outlines
- During lectures and discussions, periodically sum up what has been covered so far in class
- When soliciting questions from students, provide ample time for nonnative English speakers to participate
- When appropriate, take time to briefly explain the jokes and idioms that are met by blank stares on the faces of nonnative English speakers.

Instructors can pick and choose among suggestions such as these to find what works best in their classes. However, what they may note is that many students who are native speakers of English will derive as much benefit from such changes as do the nonnative speakers of English.

Following Instructions

Students are frequently asked to follow instructions. We say or write, "Do this." "Read that." "Write this." "Explain that." "Answer this." "Calculate that." Of course, all of "this and that" is for the students' own good, to help them learn something, to complete an assignment, or meet the requirements of a course. However, instructions that seem simple to any native English speaker can be fraught with difficulty for the recently mainstreamed ESL student. Consider the following examples:

- A professor says in passing, "Read pages 213–245 of chapter 16 of the textbook." The student who is a native English speaker quickly jots down the page numbers of the assignment. However, an ESL student who still has trouble understanding numbers spoken in English may completely miss or misunderstand the assignment.
- A laboratory instructor directs the attention of students to where they can find various pieces of equipment that will be needed to perform an experiment. Although the instructor is well intentioned, these instructions may not be too helpful to ESL students who are not familiar with the English names. Although students may look in the direction where the instructor is pointing, they may have no idea on which object to focus their eyes.

In these examples, the professor and the laboratory instructor have not done anything wrong. Yet, from the point of view of limited English proficient students, some simple modifications would be helpful. The professor could write the page numbers of the assignment on the chalkboard so that students who did not understand the spoken numbers could still copy down the correct assignment. The laboratory instructor could make sure that large labels or name tags are affixed to each piece of equipment. Then when directing the students' attention to each, the instructor could read the name and point to the label as well as the object. ESL students would have more clues to help them identify and remember the names of the instruments. As these examples illustrate, small efforts on the part of mainstream faculty members, gestures that require little time or energy, may significantly increase the likelihood that students can and will follow instructions.

Reading

Reading is at the core of almost every college course. Usually, there is a required textbook, and depending on the subject area, additional reading assignments. Not surprisingly, Powers (1986) found that of the four language skills (reading, writing, listening, and speaking), reading is considered by faculty to be most important for a student's academic success.

Whether or not a student finds a reading assignment difficult depends on a number of factors including the nature of the subject matter, the style in which the material is written, the background knowledge that the student brings to the reading assignment, and his or her general reading ability. To derive meaning from a text requires more than decoding the words, and novice and experienced readers approach assigned tasks differently (Britton, Woodward, & Binkley, 1993; Brown, Armbruster, & Baker, 1986; Swaffar, 1988; Thompson, 1987; Westby & Rodriguez Rouse, 1993).

For ESL students, there is another variable to consider, that is, how well they read in their second language. If they get bogged down in the mechanics of reading and lack sufficient vocabulary, they may benefit little from the reading assignment (Swaffar, 1988; Westby & Rodriguez Rouse, 1993). Not surprisingly, Dornic (1980) found that reading in one's nondominant language is slower and more mentally fatiguing even for "balanced" bilinguals, who are equally competent and fluent in both languages.

According to Sheorey et al. (1995), nonnative speakers (when compared to their native English speaking peers) report spending more than double the time (11.3 v. 4.7 hours per week) doing academic reading; they also perceive significantly more problems with vocabulary and comprehension. As pointed out by the authors of this study, it is not possible to tell if the additional amount of time spent by nonnative speakers doing academic reading indicates difficulties with reading comprehension, increased motivation to do well, or greater dependency on the text because of poor note-taking abilities during class. However, Dornic's study (1980), as well as self-reports by ESL students (Ostler, 1980; Smoke, 1988; Valentine & Repath-Martos, 1997), suggests the former, that comprehension difficulties mean more time spent reading.

An extensive sight vocabulary (words that the reader recognizes automatically) facilitates reading comprehension, but just how big must it be, especially for students doing academic reading in their second language? Laufer (1997) concluded that for nonnative speakers of English (who already know how to read in their native language), beginner level reading in English requires a minimum of 3,000 word families, or approximately 5,000 lexical items. This is considerably smaller than the receptive vocabulary of 14,000 to 17,000 base words known by university undergraduates who are native English speakers (as reported in Hazenberg & Hulstijn, 1996).

Developing an extensive vocabulary is essential for the academic success of ESL students. Therefore, we return to this topic later in this chapter. Meanwhile, I would like to make some final comments about reading and textbook selection.

It is worth keeping in mind that the features that make a text attractive to an instructor or to a selection committee do not necessarily make the book more readable by or comprehensible to students of limited English proficiency (Rosenthal, 1996). Thus, when planning their reading assignments, instructors might want to keep in mind the presence of ESL students in the classroom. This could mean consulting with an ESL specialist when selecting a text, eliminating all nonessential pages and reading assignments, and/or providing a list of vocabulary words and their definitions that will make the assignment more readily comprehensible. For ESL students, assignments such as "Read chapter 15 of the textbook," or, "Summarize the article by so-and-so," may be too vague. Professors may need to assign study questions to guide students in their reading or ask students to identify and write out the main points of what they are reading.

Speaking

Because they rely heavily on the receptive skills of listening and reading, ESL students can succeed in college even if they have difficulty speaking English. Quite simply, they can avoid classes that involve oral participation and select a major that requires as little speaking as possible. Thus, it is not surprising that according to a recent report (*The Chronicle of Higher Education*, Dec. 12, 1997, p. A43), the top fields of study for foreign students enrolled in U.S. institutions are business (21%), engineering (16%), physical and life sciences (8%), and mathematics and computer science (8%). (Of course, data of this type does not reveal whether nonnative speakers of English select these majors because they often require little use of spoken English in the classroom or because these are the academic areas of greatest interest to the students.)

There are a variety of reasons why ESL students may shy away from speaking in public in English. They may be embarrassed about having an accent. They may have difficulty finding the correct words to express their thoughts. They may get discouraged because listeners are impatient, unwilling to give them enough time to formulate their ideas and to put them into words. Fear of speaking may keep students from asking and answering questions in class or from seeking out the professor during office hours.

In the anecdote at the beginning of this chapter, a history professor tells Niurlys to "get out of my class until you speak English." Angry and frustrated by the limited oral proficiency of this ESL student, the faculty member unexpectedly lashed out. Similarly, the reluctance of ESL students to speak up and to participate in class discussions may be perceived by the instructor as lack of preparation or disinterest. Clearly, the inability of ESL students to communicate orally in English can be troublesome and easily subject to misinterpretation.

Although lecturing remains the primary mode of instruction in large survey courses and in some disciplines (such as the sciences), classroom pedagogy is changing. Professors are increasingly turning to a more interactive style of teaching that includes class discussions, small group work, and individual and group presentations (Astin & Astin, 1992; Ferris & Tagg, 1996). Try as they might, ESL students may not be able to avoid oral participation in the classroom. The issue then becomes how to help such students overcome their fear of speaking and how to encourage their participation.

College-age ESL students are adult L2 learners; inevitably, they will end up speaking English with an accent (Harley, 1986; Singleton, 1989). Pronunciation practice and accent reduction courses may bring some improvement, but eliminating an accent may not be possible (nor is it necessarily a top priority for the ESL college student).

As classroom instructors, we need to listen more carefully. Occasionally, we may have to ask students to repeat themselves, but this can be accomplished much more graciously than by frowning and saying, "What?" It is important to let students know just how much we do understand and to encourage them to continue the dialogue. Just because we are having trouble understanding what they are saying does not mean that their comments are trivial. It may be necessary to ask them to write down (and/or e-mail) their questions or comments or to ask other bilingual students in the class to serve as "translators." Working in small groups may ease their way into joining whole class discussions. In a supportive classroom atmosphere, ESL students can be coaxed into participating, little by little overcoming their fears of speaking up in English.

Test Taking

Assessing what a student knows and has learned is an integral part of the educational process. In some courses, students write papers, make oral presentations, and prepare portfolios. However, written tests still remain standard practice across much of the curriculum. Essay questions, short answers, multiple-choice, true–false, fill in the blank, matching, and problem solving are some of the ways that instructors attempt to evaluate the progress that students are making.

Among native English speakers, there may be complaints about tricky language, particularly on multiple-choice tests. A few students may have difficulty interpreting the language of a test question or understanding a word used here or there. However, in general, the effects of the language of the test are relatively "constant."

In contrast, for students of limited English proficiency, language becomes another variable in the test-taking process. The student's performance and evaluation may reflect much more than how much subject matter he or she knows (Ballard & Clanchy, 1991; Hamp-Lyons, 1991; Johns, 1991a, 1991b; Leki, 1992; Santos, 1988; Vann, Meyer, & Lorenz, 1984; Vann, Lorenz, & Meyer, 1991). For example, how quickly and how well students can read and interpret test questions may be just as important as how accurately they respond. This is particularly true for multiple-choice tests (Ballard & Clanchy, 1991).

In the case of essay exams and written compositions, the students' ability to organize and to express their thoughts, as well as how much they know, are not the only variables that influence the assessment of their written work. The reader or person doing the evaluation brings his or her own perspective and standards to the judging process.

For example, several studies investigated faculty tolerance of errors in the writing of ESL students (Janopoulos, 1992; Santos, 1988; Vann, Meyer, & Lorenz, 1984; Vann, Lorenz, & Meyer, 1991). The relative acceptability of incorrect word choices and of spelling, grammar, and punctuation errors have been examined alone, and in relationship to the age, gender, native language, and academic discipline of the faculty member who is assessing the writing. Although some interesting correlations were noted, what is more important are the pedagogical implications of these findings. Just how irritating are such errors? How much do they interfere with the reader's comprehension? How much do they affect the grades that students receive? Can faculty members distinguish between content and English language usage? Are they willing and able to do so, and is it appropriate to be separating language from content? Furthermore, should the writing of native and nonnative English speakers be judged by the same or different standards?

The students' attitudes, values, and rhetorical style also have an impact on a reader's assessment of their written work (Ballard & Clanchy, 1991; Johns, 1991a; Leki, 1992; Scarcella, 1984; Silva, 1997). Raised and schooled in other cultures, ESL students may use a style of writing and express views and beliefs that are quite different from what is expected from typical American students. As a result, the person reading the essay or composition finds that the introduction is too long, that the writing contains unnecessary digressions, and that the writer fails to reach any conclusions. The opinions expressed by the student may make the reader quite uncomfortable. However, for ESL students, what they have written and how they have written it is appropriate to their upbringing and cultural heritage.

Exams and assessment procedures—whatever the type—are rarely as fair and objective as we believe or would like them to be. This is especially true for ESL students. Some of these students have never seen, let alone taken, a multiple-choice test until they arrive in the United States. In their homeland, they were accustomed to writing essay exams. Unfortunately, the type of essay they were taught to write is now deemed inappropriate according to the evaluation criteria used in the United States. Articulate in their native languages, ESL students may have difficulty finding the right words in English to express their ideas. This is particularly true when they are working in a testing situation with time constraints.

Doing well in a test taken in English means that the student not only knows the subject but also is developing the necessary command of the English language. However, not doing well can be the result of inadequate subject matter knowledge and/or lack of English proficiency. Determining the source of difficulty may present a challenge to both the student and the instructor.

Vocabulary

Insufficient vocabulary—to express oneself orally or in writing or to understand reading matter or what others are saying —is a problem for ESL students even at the advanced level (Leki, 1992; Sheorey et al., 1995; Swaffar, 1988). Sometimes the meaning of a word can be figured out from the context in which it is used; sometimes it can't. Some words are deceptive, appearing familiar when they really aren't (such as what happens with literal interpretations of *shorthand* and *headlong*). Stopping to look up every unfamiliar word in a dictionary is not always feasible nor does it guarantee that the student will remember the meaning of a word the next time it is encountered.

Vocabulary is also discipline specific. A student may need to know *metabolism* and *niche* for a biology course and *detente* and *imperialistic* for a history class. Word meaning also depends on the context in which the word is used. Thus, *square* may refer to a shape or to a mathematical operation. No amount of time in the ESL classroom will completely prepare students for the new terminology that presents itself in each content-area course and academic discipline.

Developing an adequate vocabulary is an ongoing problem for ESL students (Coady & Huckin, 1997). Instructors who want to assist ESL students with vocabulary development can do some of the following: Take time to write out new terminology on the chalkboard. Refer students to the glossaries found in the back of many textbooks. Provide synonyms to new and complex terms. Explain the meaning of idioms (such as "ballpark figure" and "beat around the bush"). Assemble and distribute lists of words and their definitions that might help with particularly difficult or long reading assignments. In many cases, it is not just the ESL students in the course who will benefit, but also some of the native English speakers.

Writing

The writing skills of ESL students have been scrutinized from every perspective: analysis of typical sentence-level errors (Leki, 1992; Santos, 1988), faculty responses to such errors (Santos, 1988; Vann, Meyer, & Lorenz, 1984; Vann, Lorenz, & Meyer, 1991), the pros and cons of error correction (Leki, 1992; Zamel, 1985), the ability to write in the style called for by a particular academic discipline and/or audience (Belcher & Braine, 1995; Johns, 1991b), differences in the "composing process" used by first- and second-language writers (Leki, 1992), the influence of students' native language and culture on their writing in English (Ballard & Clanchy, 1991; Johns, 1991a, 1991b; Leki, 1992; Scarcella, 1984; Severino, Guerra, & Butler, 1997), the types of writing tasks expected in different academic disciplines (Horowitz, 1986), and on and on.

There is an immense body of literature about the writing of ESL students. Because this subject is too broad and too complex to cover in this chapter, I mention just two of the problems faced by ESL students when writing for their content-area courses.

One of the challenges is that the standards used to assess written work vary with each academic discipline. For example, Bridgeman and Carlson (1983), as reported in Johns (1991b), found that the criteria used to evaluate essays were ranked differently by faculty members in English and Science/Engineering. In fact "paper organization" and "quality of content" were ranked, respectively, 1st and 7th for English faculty and 5th and 1st for engineering and science faculty. As a result, ESL students may be surprised to find that the kind of essay that works well in one academic discipline is a disaster in another. They may need explicit instruction in the type of writing appropriate to a given subject area.

Another challenge faced by ESL students when writing for their mainstream courses is the diversity of assignments. Horowitz (1986) identified seven categories of writing tasks that college students are assigned: summary of/reaction to a reading, such as a book or journal article; annotated bibliography; report on a specified participatory experience; connection of theory and data; case study; synthesis of multiple sources, such as the library research paper; and the research project based on a survey or experiment carried out by the students. Horowitz recommends that ESL instruction include simulations of university writing tasks, thus providing the kinds of writing skills that students will need in subsequent courses.

Content-area instructors should not expect ESL students to write like their native English-speaking peers. As numerous studies have shown, they won't and don't. Instructors only waste valuable time and energy by getting out the red pen and correcting every error that appears in a report or composition. Although well intentioned, such detailed corrections rarely help ESL students to produce error-free writing.

So what is an instructor to do when evaluating the written work of nonnative speakers in mainstream courses? ESL specialists recommend focusing on content and organization while limiting corrections to the one or two types of errors that are most distracting and irritating (Krashen, 1987; Leki, 1992), such as problems with subject–verb agreement or correct word order. Furthermore, if students are going to learn from their mistakes, they must be given the opportunity to revise what they have written. Nevertheless, as Leki (1992) reminds us, it is unlikely that ESL students will become flawless writers of English and that "their numerous minor errors may be thought of as a kind of foreign accent, only in writing instead of in speech" (p. 129).

CONCLUSIONS

In this chapter, I focused on the receptive language skills of listening and reading as well as the productive skills of writing and speaking. I tried to relate them to "typical" classroom experiences of ESL students across the academic disciplines. However, I do not want to leave behind the impression that the "language barrier" is the only significant factor influencing the performance of ESL students in mainstream classes. These students are also adjusting and adapting to the American academic system and to the American way of life. Nonverbal communication (or what we commonly call *body language*) and differences in learning styles also play important roles in their academic success. However, in this single chapter it was not possible to address these additional topics.

I began this chapter by talking about Niurlys. She in many ways is representative of the growing population of nonnative English-speaking students enrolling in colleges and universities across the United States. She may never speak or write English as well as her native English speaking peers; however, she can communicate effectively in her newly acquired second language. She is a college graduate and is gainfully employed. What remains most remarkable about Niurlys and all the ESL students I have had the privilege to teach is that they will graduate from college not only with an academic degree but also with bilingual proficiency. How many native English speakers can make this claim?

REFERENCES

Astin, A. W., & Astin, H. S. (1992). *Undergraduate science education: The impact of different college environments on the educational pipeline in the sciences.* Los Angeles: Higher Education Research Institute.

Ballard, B., & Clanchy, J. (1991). Assessment by misconception: Cultural influences and intellectual traditions. In L Hamp-Lyons (Ed.), *Assessing second language writing in academic contexts* (pp.19–35). Norwood, NJ: Ablex.

Belcher, D., & Braine, G. (Eds.) (1995). *Academic writing in a second language: Essays on research and pedagogy.* Norwood, NJ: Ablex.

Bers, T. (1994). English proficiency, course patterns, and academic achievements of limited-English-proficient community college students. *Research in Higher Education, 35,* 209–234.

Bridgeman, B., & Carlson, S. B. (1993). *Survey of academic writing tasks required of graduate and undergraduate foreign students.* (Research Report No. 83-18). Princeton, NJ: Educational Testing Service.

Britton, B. K., Woodward, A., & Binkley, M. (Eds.). (1993). *Learning from textbooks.* Hillsdale, NJ: Lawrence Erlbaum Associates.

Brown, A. L., Armbruster, B. B., & Baker, L. (1986). The role of metacognition in reading and studying. In J. Orasanu (Ed.), *Reading comprehension: From research to practice* (pp. 49–75). Hillsdale, NJ: Lawrence Erlbaum Associates.

Cheng, L.-R. L. (1993). Faculty challenges in the education of foreign-born students. In L. W. Clark (Ed.), *Faculty and student challenges in facing cultural and linguistic diversity* (pp. 173–183). Springfield, IL: Charles C. Thomas.

Christison, M. A., & Krahnke, K. J. (1986). Student perceptions of academic language study. *TESOL Quarterly, 20,* 61–79.

Coady, J., & Huckin, T. (Eds.). (1997). *Second language vocabulary acquisition.* Cambridge: Cambridge University Press.

Cochran, E. P., (Ed.). (1992). *Into the academic mainstream: Guidelines for teaching language minority students.* New York: Instructional Resource Center, City University of New York.

Cohen, A. M., & Ignash, J. M. (1992). Trends in the liberal arts curriculum. *Community College Review, 20,* 50–56.

Collier, V. P. (1987). Age and rate of acquisition of second language for academic purposes. *TESOL Quarterly, 21*, 617–641.

Collier, V. P., & Thomas, W. P. (1989). How quickly can immigrants become proficient in school English? *The Journal of Educational Issues of Language Minority Students, 5*, 26–38.

Cummins, J. (1980). The cross-lingual dimensions of language proficiency: Implications for bilingual education and the optimal age issue. *TESOL Quarterly, 14*, 175-187.

Cummins, J. (1981). Age on arrival and immigrant second language learning in Canada: A reassessment. *Applied Linguistics, 2*, 132–149.

Dornic, S. (1980). Information processing and language dominance. *International Review of Applied Psychology, 29*, 119–140.

Ellis, R. (1994). *The study of second language acquisition.* Oxford: Oxford University Press.

Ferris, D., & Tagg, T. (1996). Academic oral communication needs of EAP learners: What subject-matter instructors actually require. *TESOL Quarterly, 30*, 31–55.

Fix, M., & Passel, J. S. (1994). *Immigration and immigrants: Setting the record straight.* Washington, DC: The Urban Institute.

Flowerdew, J. (1994). *Academic listening: Research perspectives.* Cambridge: Cambridge University Press.

Graham, J. G. (1987). English language proficiency and the prediction of academic success. *TESOL Quarterly, 21*, 505–521.

Gray, M. J., Rolph, E., & Melamid, E. (1996). *Immigration and higher education: Institutional responses to changing demographics.* Santa Monica, CA: Rand.

Hamp-Lyons, L. (Ed.). (1991). *Assessing second language writing in academic contexts.* Norwood, NJ: Ablex.

Harley, B. (1986). *Age in second language acquisition.* San Diego, CA: College-Hill Press.

Hazenberg, S., & Hulstijn, J. H. (1996). Defining a minimal receptive second-language vocabulary for non-native university students: An empirical investigation. *Applied Linguistics, 17*, 145–163.

Horowitz, D. M. (1986). What professors actually require: Academic tasks for the ESL classroom. *TESOL Quarterly, 20*, 445–462.

Ignash, J. M. (1992, December). ESL population and program patterns in community colleges. *ERIC Digest (EDO-JC-92-05).*

Ignash, J. M. (1992, December/1993, January). Study shows ESL is fastest growing area of study in US community colleges. *TESOL Matters, 2*, 17.

Janopoulos, M. (1992). University faculty tolerance of NS and NNS writing errors: A comparison. *Journal of Second Language Writing, 1*, 109–121.

Johns, A. M. (1981). Necessary English: A faculty survey. *TESOL Quarterly, 15*, 51–57.

Johns, A. (1991a). Faculty assessment of ESL student literacy skills: Implications for writing assessment. In L. Hamp-Lyons (Ed.), *Assessing second language writing in academic contexts* (pp. 167–179). Norwood, NJ: Ablex.

Johns, A. M. (1991b). Interpreting an English competency examination. *Written Communication, 8*, 379–401.

Kinsella, K. (1997). Creating an enabling learning environment for non-native speakers of English. In A. I. Morey & M. K. Kitano (Eds.), *Multicultural course transformation in higher education* (pp. 104–125). Needham Heights, MA: Allyn & Bacon.

Krashen, S. D. (1981). *Second language acquisition and second language learning.* Oxford, UK: Pergamon Institute of English.

Krashen, S. D. (1987). *Principles and practice in second language acquisition.* Englewood Cliffs, NJ: Prentice-Hall International.

Laufer, B. (1997). The lexical plight in second language reading. In J. Coady & T. Huckin (Eds.), *Second language vocabulary acquisition* (pp. 20–34). Cambridge: Cambridge University Press.

Leki, I. (1992). *Understanding ESL writers.* Portsmouth, NH: Boynton/Cook.

Lightbown, P. M., & Spada, N. (1993). *How languages are learned.* Oxford: Oxford University Press.

Mason, A. (1994). By dint of: Student and lecturer perceptions of lecture comprehension strategies in first-term graduate study. In J. Flowerdew (Ed.), *Academic listening: Research perspectives* (pp. 199–218). Cambridge: Cambridge University Press.

McDonnell, L. M., & Hill, P. T. (1993). *Newcomers in American schools: Meeting the educational needs of immigrant youth.* Santa Monica, CA: Rand.

Ostler, S. E. (1980). A survey of academic needs for Advanced ESL. *TESOL Quarterly, 14,* 489–502.

Powers, D. E. (1986). Academic demands related to listening skills. *Language Testing, 3,* 1–38.

Rosenthal, J. W. (1996). *Teaching science to language minority students: Theory and practice.* Clevedon, England: Multilingual Matters.

Russikoff, K. (1994, March). *Hidden expectations: faculty perceptions of SLA and writing competence.* Paper presented at the Twenty-eighth annual convention of Teachers of English to Speakers of Other Languages, Baltimore, MD.

Santos, T. (1988). Professors' reactions to the academic writing of nonnative-speaking students. *TESOL Quarterly, 22,* 69–90.

Scarcella, R. C. (1984). How writers orient their readers in expository essays: A comparative study of native and non-native English writers. *TESOL Quarterly, 18,* 671–688.

Severino, C., Guerra, J. C., & Butler, J. E. (Eds.) (1997). *Writing in multicultural settings.* New York: Modern Language Association.

Sheorey, R., Mokhtari, K., & G. Livingston (1995). A comparison of native and nonnative English-speaking students as college readers. *The Canadian Modern Language Review/La Revue canadienne des langues vivantes, 51,* 661–677.

Sigsbee, D. L., Speck, B. W., & Maylath, B. (Eds.). (1997). *Approaches to teaching non-native English speakers across the curriculum.* San Francisco, CA: Jossey-Bass.

Silva, T. (1997). Differences in ESL and native-English-speaker writing: The research and its implications. In C. Severino, J. C. Guerra, & J. E. Butler (Eds.), *Writing in multicultural settings* (pp. 209–219). New York: Modern Language Association.

Singleton, D. (1989). *Language acquisition: The age factor.* Clevedon, England: Multilingual Matters.

Smoke, T. (1988). Using feedback from ESL students to enhance their success in college. In S. Benesch (Ed.), *Ending remediation: Linking ESL and content in higher education* (pp. 7–19). Washington, DC: TESOL.

Stewart, D. W. (1993). *Immigration and education: The crisis and the opportunities.* New York: Lexington Books.

Swaffar, J. K. (1988). Readers, texts, and second languages: The interactive process. *The Modern Language Journal, 72,* 123–149.

The challenge of change: What the 1990 census tells us about children (1992). Washington, DC: A report prepared by the Population Reference Bureau for the Center for the Study of Social Policy.

The Chronicle of Higher Education Almanac (August 29, 1997), 18.

The Chronicle of Higher Education (Dec. 12, 1997), A43.

Thompson, I. (1987). Memory in language learning. In A. Wenden & J. Rubin (Eds.), *Learner strategies in language learning* (pp. 43–56). Englewood Cliffs, NJ: Prentice-Hall International.

Valentine, J. F., & Repath-Martos, L. M. (1997). How relevant is relevant? In M. A. Snow & D. M. Brinton (Eds.), *The content-based classroom*: Perspectives on integration of language and content (pp. 233–247). White Plains, NY: Longman.

Vann, R. J., Meyer, D. M., & Lorenz, F. O. (1984). Error gravity: A study of faculty opinion of ESL errors. *TESOL Quarterly, 18*, 427–440.

Vann, R. J., Lorenz, F. O., & Meyer, D. M. (1991). Error gravity: Faculty response to errors in the written discourse of nonnative speakers of English. In L. Hamp-Lyons (Ed.), *Assessing second language writing in academic contexts* (pp.181–195). Norwood, NJ: Ablex.

Vernez, G., & Abrahamse, A. (1996). *How immigrants fare in U.S. education*. Santa Monica, CA: Rand.

Westby, C. E., & Rodriguez Rouse, G. (1993). Facilitating text comprehension in college students: The professor's role. In L. W. Clark (Ed.), *Faculty and student challenges in facing cultural and linguistic diversity* (pp.189–225). Springfield, IL: Charles C. Thomas.

Zamel, V. (1985). Responding to student writing. *TESOL Quarterly, 19*, 79–97.

II

Building English Language Skills Through Content-Based Instruction

⌐

Grammar in Content-Based Instruction

Peter Master

San Jose State University

Content-based instruction (CBI) refers to "the concurrent study of language and subject matter, with the form and sequence of language presentation dictated by content material" (Brinton, Snow, & Wesche, 1989: vii). To this end, CBI uses authentic (i.e., material not originally produced for language teaching purposes) tasks and materials while emphasizing accommodation to language learners' needs through increased redundancy and exemplification and the use of advance organizers, frequent comprehension checks, and frequent, straightforward assignments and assessment procedures. Eskey (1997) defines CBI as follows:

> The content-based syllabus is best viewed as a still newer attempt to extend and develop our conception of what a syllabus for a second-language course should comprise, *including a concern with language form and language function*, as well as a crucial third dimension—the factual and conceptual content of such courses. (p. 14, italics mine)

CBI is the integration of content learning with language aims (Brinton et al., 1989), and for most language instructors, one of the aims of language instruction is to provide learners with a grasp of the grammatical systems that operate in that language. One of the conditions that Brinton et al. (1989) claim CBI to fulfill is "a focus on use as well as on usage" (p. viii), as does Eskey's concern with language form and language function.

93

THE ROLE OF GRAMMAR IN THE CBI CONTEXT

The current notion shared by many in the field of TESOL is that grammar does not exist independently of vocabulary and discourse, but that a focus on form is indeed effective (Lightbown & Spada, 1990; Pienemann, 1989; Spada & Lightbown, 1993; White, Spada, Lightbow, & Ranta, 1991) and necessary. Faris (1997), for example, found that "summary comments *on grammar* appeared to lead to the most substantive revision [of student compositions, while] positive comments almost never led to any changes at all" (p. 330, italics mine). She concluded that "simultaneous attention to content and form … does not short-circuit students' ability to revise their ideas but may in fact improve their end products, because they receive more accuracy-oriented feedback through the writing process" (p. 333). Celce-Murcia, Dörnyei, & Thurrell (1997) noted that the indirect approach of the late 1970s and 1980s, whereby competence was thought to arise from conversational interaction, is giving way to a renewed interest in the direct approach, which "recalls the traditional methods of teaching grammar, whereby new linguistic information is passed on and practiced explicitly …" (p. 141).

This renewed interest in form-focused instruction has come about after more than a decade of doubt as to the efficacy of grammatical instruction in the English for Speakers of Other Languages (ESOL) classroom. The doubt was exemplified in the work of Krashen (1992), who stated, "My interpretation of the research is that grammar learning does have an effect, but this effect is peripheral and fragile" (p. 409). His comprehensible input instructional model, which appeared to instantiate the features of CBI in accommodating to language learners' needs, came under criticism because, although it led to considerable fluency, it was insufficient to develop adequate output accuracy (Higgs & Clifford, 1982; Schmidt, 1983). Schmidt (1991) later argued that efficient learning required paying attention to the learning objective and then practicing that objective until it became automatic. Widdowson (1990) refuted the indirect approach more directly in his view that language pedagogy is "a way of short-circuiting the slow process of natural discovery" (p. 162). Thus, a principled attention to form within the areas of content being studied is considered necessary, especially if the aim is to acquire cognitive academic language proficiency.

CBI is an ideal means of assuring the integration of these aspects of language. By dealing with grammar within the context of understanding content, many of the original criticisms of the grammatical syllabus are satisfied: students no longer deal with decontextualized sentences or spend years learning isolated rules that inhibit their spoken fluency.

THE TREATMENT OF GRAMMAR
IN COLLEGE-LEVEL CBI TEXTS

College-level CBI texts[1] exhibit numerous ingenious ways of linking grammar to content. Dale and Cuevas (1987, pp. 14–15) utilized comparative structures, prepositions, the passive voice, and logical connectors in solving mathematical problems.

- Comparative structures: *less/greater than, n times as much as, as . . . as, -er . . . than* (from Knight & Hargis, 1977).
  Examples: All numbers *greater than* 4 . . .
  Hilda earns *six times as much as* I do.
  Wendy is *as old as* Miguel.
  Miguel is *three years older than* Frank.

- Prepositions: *by, into* (from Crandall, Dale, Rhodes, & Spanos, 1985).
  Examples: Eight divided *by* four . . .
  Eight *into* four . . .
  Two multiplied *by* itself two times . . .
  X exceeds two *by* seven.

- Passive voice: (from Crandall, Dale, Rhodes, & Spanos, 1985).
  Examples: Ten *is divided* by two.
  X *is defined* to be equal to zero.
  When 15 *is added* to a number, the result is 21.

- Logical connectors: *if . . . then, if and only if, because, that is, for example, such that, but, consequently, either . . . or*
  Examples: For every real number there is a unique real
  number *-a, such that a* $+ (-a) = 0$ and $(-a) + a = 0$.
  If a is a positive number, *then -a* is a negative number.
  The opposite of *-a* is *a; that is,* $-(-a) = a$.

Brinton et al. (1989, pp. 109, 156, 157) made use of restrictive and nonrestrictive relative clauses to describe the work of B. F. Skinner, comparison and contrast to describe the differences between the executive and legislative

---

[1]Texts concerned with "context-based grammar" (e.g., Fingado, Freeman, Jerome, & Summers, 1991) are not considered because they represent efforts to provide contextualized reasons for using a specific grammar point rather than using context as the point of departure. Fingado et al., for example, exploit the use of gerunds and infinitives in discussing the generation gap, acceptable professions for young people, parental expectations, and tastes in popular music. However, the grammar appears to drive the selection of content (albeit quite cleverly) rather than the content determining the grammatical focus.

branches, and conditional subordinate clauses to describe stimulus–response relationships.

- Restrictive and nonrestrictive relative clauses
  Examples: Events, objects, and activities *over which you have control* can act as reinforcers.
  The Skinner Box, *which is used to study animal behavior*, was developed by B. F. Skinner.

- Comparison and contrast (e.g., *however, in spite of the fact that, unlike, similarly, while, in contrast, even though*)
  Example: The executive branch makes treaties *while* the legislative branch can only ratify them.

- Conditional subordinate clauses
  Example: *If animals in a Skinner box touch a lever*, they receive food.

Hubbard, Cohen de Fernandez, & Nagore (1992, p. 59) used relative clauses to identify or describe famous people.
- Relative clauses
  Example: Leonardo da Vinci was the man *who painted the Mona Lisa*.

Harrington (1993, p. 92) used nonfinite clauses to show sequences of historical events.
- Nonfinite clauses
  Example: *Having studied Emerson*, Thoreau went to live at Walden Pond.

Pakenham (1994, pp. 5, 20) described the grammar of cause and effect in relation to advances in health care.
- The grammar of cause (C) and effect (E) (e.g., *C causes* E, *C results in* E, *C creates* E, C gives rise to E, *C leads to* E).
  Example: According to scientists, a great deal of pollution *is caused by* power plants that produce electricity by burning coal.

Weidauer (1994, p. 53) focused on verb tense consistency in a passage about the pedagogy of poverty.
- Verb tense consistency
  Example: Why *did* I react that way? Surely many six-year-olds in my class *would not have reacted* as I had. I think partly it *was* that I *was* very insecure about my relationship with my

teacher, and partly that I *hadn't yet learned* to feel comfortable about my school.

Silverman (1997, p. 24, 27) used comparisons to describe artifacts.
- Comparisons (e.g., *like, -er, more, less, fewer*).
  Example: South Coast vessels have flatt*er* bottoms and are decorated with *more* colors.

Tapper & Storch (1997, pp. 294–295) used relative clauses and verb tense and voice in reconstructing a text about Australian society (Jamrozik, 1994, pp. 37–38).
- Noun clauses
  Example: Hennessy does, however, accept *that aboriginal tribal law should have a special place in the judicial system*, unlike the cultures and laws of other groups.

- Verb tense and voice
  Example: Chief Justice Martin's decision *was made* in response to a submission from Walker's barrister, John Tippett, that his client, or a member of his client's family, *would receive* tribal punishment for killing a man.

Gadjusek (1997, p. 226) used subordinate clauses to separate core facts from description in describing the life of Martin Luther King.
- Subordinate clauses
  Examples: In 1929, Martin Luther King was born in Atlanta, Georgia, *which was a segregated southern city with a large, middle-class African American population*. [focus on life of MLK]
  In 1929, Atlanta, Georgia, *where Martin Luther King was born*, was a segregated, southern city with a large, middle-class African American population. [focus on history of Atlanta]

The grammatical explanation in these texts ranges from none at all to fairly extensive treatments (especially in more recent publications). However, in general the focus on grammar is quite limited, which leads one to wonder whether the antigrammar stance of the 1980s is still operative for many CBI authors and publishers, making them reluctant to deal with grammar in any overt fashion. This apparent reluctance can manifest itself in two ways: a limited range of grammatical items focused on, and a dearth of grammatical metatext in an effort to "simplify" grammatical explanations.

LIMITED RANGE OF GRAMMATICAL ITEMS

The grammatical items that best lend themselves to exploitation in CBI contexts are those that are linked to rhetorical structure. Thus, comparison and contrast (e.g., -er, more, less, fewer, in contrast, even though, differ from), logical connectors (e.g., in addition, however, therefore), the various forms of subordination (noun, adverb, and adjective [relative] clauses; gerunds and infinitives; nonfinite clauses), and verb tenses are the most common areas of grammar mentioned in CBI texts, although CBI texts eschew the teaching of grammar altogether.

Teacher Texts.   Texts designed for practicing teachers and teachers in training often suggest the linkage of grammatical explanation to a specific task related to the content. In Crandall (1987), of the three content areas discussed (mathematics, science, and social studies), only mathematics explicitly mentions the grammar of comparatives, prepositions, passive voice, and logical connectors. The UCLA Freshman Summer Program (Brinton et al., 1989) covered relative clauses, comparison and contrast, and conditional subordinate clauses.[2] However, the description of the sheltered Introduction to Psychology class at the University of Ottawa indicates that the teacher "helps the students with specific language problems, but there is *no explicit teaching of grammar*" (p. 47, italics mine), although "a lesson on comparison and contrast might use ESL materials to present the vocabulary for expressing such relations (e.g., "analogous," "is like", "difference")" (p. 52).[3] Holten (1997) described the use of fronted adjective clauses in poetry. In Brinton and Master (1997), the three lessons (out of 77) that deal with grammar in CBI concern comparisons (Silverman, 1997), relative clauses and verb tenses (Tapper & Storch, 1997), and subordinate clauses (Gadjusek, 1997).

Student Texts.   In texts designed for lower proficiency levels, Christison and Bassano (1992) provided excellent science content but no grammar focus at all. Bailey (1990) provided an excellent content reader with verb tenses reduced throughout to the simple present, representing a different way of limiting the range of grammatical items. Although a laudable effort to exploit the narrative present tense, this technique leads to sentences such as "Until they sail away and discover America, Europeans live in a small world" (p. 1) and "South Vietnam loses the war. The United States has to pull out, but at least it's over" (p. 185), neglecting the fact that the narrative present is usually situated

---

[2]The syllabus for the course includes article usage, passive constructions, gerunds and infinitives, and tense usage (p. 228), but these are not mentioned in the text.

[3]Wesche appears to differentiate CBI from ESL with the implication that grammar is really only the concern of ESL, not CBI.

in the past before it is used. At more advanced proficiency levels, Pakenham (1994) provided limited coverage of the grammar of determiner cohesion, cause and effect, definitions, and comparison and contrast.

In contrast, Weidauer (1994), the low-advanced level of the *Tapestry* series,[4] covered a wider array of grammatical items, including verb tense and agreement, adverb clause reduction, pronominal reference, noun compounds, passive voice, articles, cause and effect, correlative conjunctions, and parallelism. Furthermore, two recent college-level CBI textbooks included a very wide range of grammatical coverage. Jensen, Repath-Martos, Frodesen, and Holten (1997) provided an impressive breadth of coverage, including adjective sequencing, fronting adverb phrases, adverbs, passive voice, embedded questions, participial phrases, subordination, subject–verb agreement, relative clauses, articles with proper nouns, cause and effect, modals, and clarification connectors. Part 2 of the same series, (Frodesen, Holten, Jensen, & Repath-Martos, 1997), covered conditionals, *of* -phrases, adjective clauses, passive voice, complex sentence subjects, participial phrases with *by*, *it* -constructions, past modals, subordination, articles, complements with *to* and *-ing*, parallelism, indirect speech, determiner cohesion, and verb tense consistency.

With the exception of the last texts mentioned, most CBI student texts are characterized by a narrowed treatment of the grammatical aspects that are covered. Furthermore, one rarely finds mention in CBI texts of the auxiliary and negation systems, the object system (i.e., direct, indirect, objects of prepositions), the pronoun system (including existential *there* and *it*), the determiner system, the adjective system (i.e., sequence of adjectives, attributive vs. predicate adjectives), or the particle system (i.e., phrasal verbs, separable vs. nonseparable, particles with prepositional verbs). This is no doubt because they would require more overt grammatical explanation than most CBI authors and publishers are willing to provide.

LIMITED METATEXT

In many cases where grammatical explanations are included, there is a reluctance to use grammatical terms to adequately explain the point. For example, Hubbard et al. (1992) included with each unit a section entitled "Language Focus," but it reveals an effort to downplay grammatical explanation with potentially serious results. In one example, the language focus is *who, which,* and *that.* The grammatical explanation provided (p. 59) is the following:

Who follows people: Leif Ericson was the man who discovered America.

---

[4]The Tapestry series also includes a separate reference book for students called *The Tapestry Grammar* and "a Grammar Strand composed of grammar 'work-out' books at each of the levels in the Tapestry Program" (p. X).

That follows people: Leif Ericson was the man that discovered America.

or

things: Earth is a planet that goes around the sun.

First of all, the word *that* has many functions. It can be a relative pronoun (as in this case), a complementizer, a pronoun, or a determiner. Thus, the suggestion that *that* always "follows" is incorrect. Even as a relative pronoun, it is not true that *that* always follows people because this relative pronoun generally occurs only when there is a certain distance between the speaker and the person described, most often in definitions. A better solution would have been to show the common linkage of people + *who* and things + *that*, with a footnote describing the exceptional use of people + *that*, but that does not solve the problem of the various functions of *that*, which would have been removed if the term relative (or adjective) clause had been somewhere mentioned. This is not a disparagement of the text as much as an indication of the problems that may arise from efforts to avoid dealing with grammar in the CBI context.

Harrington (1993), one of the first CBI books on American history and one that contains excellent content, included an explicit section entitled "Structures" in each unit with the following rationale: "The underlying principle has been to engage students interactively with both historical *and* grammatical content by providing the opportunity for creative response to structural models" (p. xiii, italics in original). Harrington included an impressive variety of grammatical items but provides minimal (in most cases no) grammatical explanation. The consequence for the student is that the exercises may easily lead to confusion or even to false generalizations. For example, in the structure exercise in Unit I, the directions state, "Following the model, change the sentences below. Rewrite the sentences" (p. 15). The following model is provided: *Gaining international prestige was not easy —> To gain international prestige was not easy.* The generalization that may be deduced from this exercise is that gerunds are always transformed into infinitives. In Unit II, an exercise requires the matching of *Jackson's family came to America in search of a better life* with *They must have had problems in Europe* (p. 30), with no explanation of why singular *family* requires the plural pronoun *they*. In Unit III, the directions state, "In the paragraph below, fill in the blanks with the correct compound words. Choose from the following list: *whatever, whenever, however, whoever*" (p. 45). The problem is that the compound words (a confusing term in itself) comprise a mix of adverbial and noun clause markers that are only superficially similar (*whatever* and *whoever* are noun clause markers; *whenever* and *however* are adverbial clause markers). This is followed by a matching exercise in which only noun clauses appear. The generalization that may be deduced is that all words that end in *-ever* are noun clause markers. My purpose in pointing out these problems is again not to denigrate the text, which contains many fine readings and exercises, but to show how an emphasis on content and a concomitant deemphasis on grammar may not foster the understanding that is intended.

PROBLEMS WITH INCOMPLETE COVERAGE OF THE SYSTEM

Widdowson (1990) argued that incidental acquisition of form was "a long and rather inefficient business" (p. 145). Dyson (1996), having cited Long's (1991) statement that "a syllabus with a focus on *form* ... overtly draws students' attention to linguistic elements as they arise incidentally in lessons whose overriding focus is on meaning, or communication" (p. 46, italics in original), also questioned the implications of a form-focus occurring only "incidentally" (p. 61). Although she did not explain what her concerns might be, it is clear that she meant to suggest that such a focus should be something more than incidental.

Hutchinson and Waters (1989) provided a similar warning in the ESP context: "If the learner sees it [language] as just a haphazard set of arbitrary and capricious obstacles, learning will be difficult, if not impossible" (p. 51). Furthermore, they praised the structural syllabus in that it "provides the learner with a systematic description of the generative core of the language—the finite range of structures that make it possible to generate an infinite number of novel utterances. For this reason the structural syllabus continues to be widely used in spite of criticism from advocates of functional, notional or use-based descriptions [such as CBI] of English" (p. 26). The weakness of the structural syllabus, they noted, is that it does not provide the learner with an understanding of the communicative uses of language. However, "[a]ll communication has a structural level, a functional level, and a discoursal level. They are not mutually exclusive, but complementary ... " (p. 37).

Furthermore, ESOL students have always demanded a focus on form in the classroom. In a study of student perceptions of the CBI curriculum in the ESL Service Courses at UCLA, Valentine and Repath-Martos (1997) found that grammar and vocabulary were the skills most often mentioned as having been given too little emphasis. Observation determined that, although grammar and vocabulary were covered covertly,

> Only one student [out of 78] seems to have fully grasped that through the writing process in this CBI model, grammar and vocabulary instruction take place indirectly. For many students, however, it was difficult to get beyond expectations of a traditional language skills curriculum with an overt grammar component and weekly vocabulary lists. In an effort to deal with these expectations, we feel that it is fundamental for the students to have a clear understanding of the CBI model, and that the instructor must overtly state the rationale for each

classroom activity. It may also be necessary and useful to include more explicit grammar and vocabulary instruction, perhaps through incorporation of a grammar reference book within the content-based instructional context. (p. 245)

What might a focus on form that is more than incidental look like? This question raises the issue of whether the chance coverage of grammar is indeed sufficient to provide mastery or at least, to paraphrase a member of the audience in a grammar colloquium at TESOL 1997, the self-confidence that native speakers have in knowing the whole system. In other words, in allowing content to dictate what elements of grammar are covered in class, are we not debilitating our students in those areas that are not likely to be focused on? [5]

SOLUTIONS

Two problems concerning focus on form have been identified in CBI textbooks and classrooms: a limited range of items covered and limited explanation of those that are covered. A few recent publications have begun to address these problems by including a much wider range of grammatical items and by including more precise explanations, which inevitably require more grammatical metatext. It is clear, though, that a textbook cannot do everything. It is ultimately the CBI instructor who must make sure that grammar is sufficiently covered, both in terms of range and explanation.

One way to use the content as the starting point for a focus on grammar is to focus on the specific usage encountered in a text but then to expand on that area of grammar in a systematic way (see, for example, Master, 1996) for a presentation of the major systems in English grammar). For instance, the appearance of a nonrestrictive relative clause in a text might occasion (especially if there are student queries about the structure) a discussion of the relative clause system and its three major elements: the relative pronouns, the nonrestrictive and restrictive forms, and the ways in which relative clauses may be reduced. This can be linked back to the content by discussing in the particular instance that triggered the grammatical focus what the effect would be of using a different relative pronoun, of changing the clause to a restrictive one, or of applying different kinds of reduction.

The following example illustrates my point. Harrington (1993) provided these sentences in a section on Booker T. Washington: "[H]e never forgot the day when news of emancipation reached his family. 'My mother, *who was standing by my side*, leaned over and kissed her children, while tears of joy ran down

---

[5]A similar point showing need for greater grammatical coverage in CBI was made by Brinton & Holten (1997). Their conclusion was that there was a need to reassess the CBI paradigm and rethink certain aspects of classroom practice.

her cheeks'" (p. 184). Having learned the three major elements of the relative clause system, students would be in a position to discuss the ramifications of altering the grammar of the underlined relative clause.

Relative Pronoun (structural).   Since the clause is restrictive, the only possible relative pronouns are the WH-forms *who, whom, which,* and *whose* + NOUN (i.e., *that* is excluded). Of these, *which* is not possible since the subject (*mother*), is human; *whom* is not possible because the clause is a subject-form, not a predicate- (or object-) form relative clause; and *whose* is not possible because no possession of the subject's is indicated and no noun follows the relative pronoun. Thus, *who* is the only choice possible in this clause; any other choice would have been grammatically incorrect.

Restrictive vs. Nonrestrictive (functional).   If the clause were changed to the parallel restrictive form, it would become *My mother who was standing by my side leaned over and kissed her children* ... This form, however, is an unlikely one since it indicates that the speaker has one mother who is standing by his side and implies that there is another mother elsewhere (since a restrictive relative clause is only used when one noun must be differentiated from another). The nonrestrictive form is thus the only likely choice in this case, though it is not grammatically incorrect and might be appropriate if one had two (e.g., one metaphorical) mothers.

Reduction (discoursal).   Subject-form reduction allows the deletion of the relative pronoun + *be* when *be* is followed by a VERBing form, a VERBed form, or a preposition. Thus, in this case it would be perfectly correct to reduce the clause in the original sentence, leading to *My mother, standing by my side, leaned over and kissed her children* ... If both the reduced and the nonreduced forms are grammatically correct, why did the author choose to use the nonreduced form in this case? The reduced clause moves the predicate of the clause (*standing by my side*) closer to the subject, thereby suggesting that there is some causal linkage between the two. Such a linkage can be interpreted in a number of ways (e.g., the speaker cannot stand—either physically or morally—without the aid of his mother, the kiss from the mother was meant to express the joint feeling of the speaker and his mother). However, the author chose to squelch any such associations by using the full form of the clause, which simply sets the scene of the utterance, that is, she happened to be by his side when he heard the news of the emancipation, not in another room or outside in the garden. Furthermore, this is the first time that the mother is mentioned in the text.

Such a lengthy process would no doubt be shunned by many CBI practitioners and would certainly only be appropriate at a fairly advanced level. I provide it merely to demonstrate what it may mean to include coverage of a grammatical item with all of its ramifications. The trouble is, as Holten (1997) admits, that CBI instructors "often deemphasize grammar in favor of what seem to be more pressing issues" (p. 384). Most aspects of grammar are not nearly so complicated, however, and a full explanation need not be offered all at the same time.

The term CBI (content-based instruction) was originally coined as "content-based language instruction." In too many cases, like some of those just described, the emphasis seems to be far more on content than on language, and the expectation that L2 learners, especially at the college level, will somehow miraculously develop both receptive and productive language skills by being exposed to content sounds very much like Krashen's comprehensible input hypothesis, which has already been shown to be insufficient for language acquisition.

CONCLUSION

Because a language makes use of a large number of grammatical systems in any given text,[6] it is only knowledge of the entire system that effectively enables a nonnative speaker to read and write at the college level. On the other hand, an effective balance between language and content can provide the student with control of the linguistic system of English while simultaneously providing novel and interesting content. What I suggest is that the content still come first, helping the learner appreciate the fact that any particular usage is not an isolated event; then the grammatical system in which that usage is embedded can be fully explained and practiced. Finally, the original content is examined in light of the grammatical system, which thus becomes an exemplar and proof of the relevance of that system. When this process is repeated for a range of grammatical systems, grammatical knowledge may be acquired that the learner can generalize to productive endeavors, such as writing essays and term papers. The practice of dealing only with grammar that arises incidentally from content may aid receptive decoding skills (although even these may require a more systematic treatment of grammar; see Deyes, 1987), but it is not true content-based language instruction.

---

[6]This sentence, for example, makes use of the following grammatical systems:
1. adverbial clauses [fronted]/subordination (*since* ...)
2. verb tenses (*makes, is, will enable*)
3. particles (*makes use of, knowledge of*)
4. articles (e.g., *a language, Ø grammatical systems, the entire system*)
5. prepositions (*of, in, at*)
6. determiners (*articles, any*)
7. noun clause/subordination (*that* ...)
8. *it*-focus/cleft constructions (*it is only knowledge ... that* ...)
9. infinitive complements/subordination (*to read and write*)
10. coordination (*read and write*)
11. noun compounds (*college level*)

REFERENCES

Bailey, J. (1990). *From the beginning: A first reader in American history.* Studio City, CA: JAG Publications.

Brinton, D. M., & Holten C. (1997, February 14). *Does the emperor have no clothes? A re-examination of content-based instruction.* Plenary address delivered at the 1997 Los Angeles ESL Conference, University of Southern California.

Brinton, D. M., & Master, P. (1997). *New ways in content-based instruction.* Alexandria, VA: TESOL.

Brinton, D. M., Snow, M. A., & Wesche, M. (1989). *Content-based language instruction.* Boston: Heinle & Heinle.

Celce-Murcia, M., Dörnyei, Z., & Thurrell, S. (1997). Direct approaches in L2 instruction: A turning point in communicative language teaching? *TESOL Quarterly, 31*(1), 141–152.

Crandall, J. (1987). *ESL through content-area instruction: Mathematics, science, social studies.* Englewood Cliffs, NJ: Prentice Hall Regents.

Crandall, J. A., Dale, T. C., Rhodes, N., & Spanos, G. (1985). *The language of mathematics: The English barrier.* Paper presented at the Delaware Symposium on Language Studies VII. University of Delaware, Newark, DE (cited in Dale & Cuevas, 1987).

Christison, M. A., & Bassano, S. (1992). *Earth and phsyical science: Content and learning strategies.* Reading, MA: Addison Wesley.

Dale, T. C., & Cuevas, G. J. (1987). Integrating language and mathematics learning. In J. Crandall, (Ed.), *ESL through content-area instruction: Mathematics, science, social studies* (pp. 9–54). Englewood Cliffs, NJ: Prentice Hall Regents.

Deyes, T. (1987). Towards a minimum discourse grammar for ESP reading courses. *Reading in a Foreign Language, 3*(2), 417–428.

Dyson, B. (1996). The debate on form-focused instruction: A teacher's perspective. *ARAL, 19*(2), 59–78.

Eskey, D. (1997). Syllabus design in content-based instruction. In M. A. Snow & D. Brinton (Eds.), *The content-based classroom: Perspectives on integrating language and content* (pp. 132–141). White Plains, NY: Longman.

Faris, D. (1997). The influence of teacher commentary on student revision. *TESOL Quarterly, 31*(2), 315–339.

Fingado, G., Freeman, L. J., Jerome, M. C., & Summers, C. V. (1991). *The English connection: A content-based grammar* (2nd ed.) New York: Newbury House.

Frodesen, J., Holten, C., Jensen, L., & Repath-Martos, L. (1997). *Insights 1: A content-based approach to academic preparation.* White Plains, NY: Longman.

Gadjusek, L. (1997). Building a life. In D. M. Brinton & P. Master (Eds.), *New ways in content-based instruction* (pp. 220–226). Alexandria, VA: TESOL.

Harrington, K. L. (1993). *America past and present: The challenge of new frontiers (Vol. II).* Boston: Heinle & Heinle.

Higgs, T. V., & Clifford, R. (1982). The push toward communcation. In T. V. Higgs (Ed.), *Curriculum, competence, and the foreign language teacher* (pp. 57–79). Lincolnwood, IL: National Textbook Company.

Holten, C. (1997). Literature: A quintessential content. In Snow, M. A. & Brinton, D. M. (Eds.), *The content-based classroom: Perspectives on integrating language and context* (pp. 377–387). White Plains, NY: Longman.

Hubbard, P. S., Cohen de Fernandez, E., & Nagore, G. (1992*). Prism: An intermediate English course*. Orlando, FL: Harcourt Brace Jovanovich.

Hutchinson, T., & Waters, A. (1989). *English for Specific Purposes*. Cambridge: Cambridge University Press.

Jamrozik, W. (1994). White law, black law. *The Independent Monthly*, May, 1994 (cited in Tapper & Storch, 1997).

Jensen, L., Repath-Martos, L., Frodesen, J., & Holten, C. (1997). *Insights 2: A content-based approach to academic preparation*. White Plains, NY: Longman.

Knight, L., & Hargis, C. (1977). Math language ability: Its relationship to reading in math. *Language Arts, 54,* 423–428 (cited in Dale & Cuevas, 1987).

Krashen, S. (1992). Teaching issues: Formal grammar instruction. *TESOL Quarterly, 26*(2), 409–411.

Lightbown, P. M., & Spada, N. (1990). Focus on form and corrective feedback in communicative language teaching: Effects on second language learning. *Studies in Second Language Acquisition, 12,* 429–448.

Long, M. (1991). Focus on form: A design feature in language teaching methodology. In De Bot, K., Coste, D., Kramsch, C., and Ginsberg, R. (Eds.), *Foreign Language Research in Cross-Cultural Perspective*. Amsterdam: John Benjamins.

Master, P. (1996). *Systems in English grammar: An introduction for language teachers*. Englewood Cliffs, NJ: Prentice Hall Regents.

Pakenham, K. J. (1994). *Making connections: An interactive approach to academic reading*. New York: St. Martin's Press.

Pienemann, M. (1989). Is language teachable? Psycholinguistic experiments and hypotheses. *Applied Linguistics, 10*(1), 52–79.

Schmidt, R. (1983). Interaction, acculturation, and acquisition of communicative competence. In N. Wolfson, & E. Judd (Eds.), *Sociolinguistics and second language acquisition* (pp. 137–74). Rowley, MA: Newbury House.

Schmidt, R. (1991). *Input, interaction, attention and awareness: The case for consciousness raising in second language learning* (Anais do X Encontro Nacional de Professores Universitáros de Lingua Inglesa I). Rio de Janeiro, Brazil: Pontificia Universidade Católica.

Silverman, M. (1997). Identifying and comparing ancient artifacts. In D. M. Brinton & P. Master (Eds), *New ways in content-based instruction* (pp. 24–27). Alexandria, VA: TESOL.

Spada, N., & Lightbown, P. M. (1993). Instruction and the development of questions in L2 classrooms. *Studies in Second Language Acquisition, 15,* 205–221.

Tapper, J., & Storch, N. (1997). Paragraphing and linking: A reconstruction activity. In D. M. Brinton & P. Master (Eds). *New ways in content-based instruction* (pp. 293–296). Alexandria, VA: TESOL

Valentine, J. F., & Repath-Martos, L. M. (1997). How relevant is relevance? In M. A. Snow & D. M. Brinton (Eds.), *The content-based classroom: Perspectives on integrating language and content* (pp. 233–247). White Plains, NY: Longman.

Weidauer, M. H. (1994). *Modern impressions: Writing in our times*. Boston: Heinle & Heinle.

White, L., Spada, N., Lightbown, P. M., & Ranta, L. (1991). Input enhancement and L2 question formation. *Applied Linguistics, 12,* 416–432.

Widdowson, H. (1990). *Aspects of language teaching*. Oxford: Oxford University Press.

C

The Short Story as a Bridge to Content in the Lower Level ESL Course

Loretta F. Kasper
Kingsborough Community College/CUNY

Because he scored only 350 on the Test of English as a Foreign Language (TOEFL), Kamel was placed into a lower level ESL course. He is a conscientious student with ambitions of one day earning a Master's degree in Business Administration. Although Kamel speaks English fairly well, his writing skills are very weak. He has trouble expressing ideas grammatically, so it is often difficult to understand his written work.

Kamel will need to make dramatic improvement in his written expression if he is to pass the college writing skills assessment test, a test that will require him to present a coherent and grammatical written argument. Until he passes this test, Kamel will not be able to take the mainstream courses he needs for his major. Worse, if he is unable to pass this test within 2 years, he will have to leave college.

Whereas many lower level ESL programs are totally skills-based, college students like Kamel need ESL programs that are also aimed at the need to achieve fluency in and to master the vocabulary of academic discourse. A skills-based program of instruction may give Kamel grammatical exercises to help him practice verb tenses or subject–verb agreement. He may read one- to two-page passages and answer comprehension questions on those passages. He may attend a language laboratory where he listens to tapes and practices the sounds of English.

Although each of these activities may offer Kamel some improvement in his basic English *skills*, they do not give him the opportunity to develop the skills that are most critical to college level work. To succeed in college, Kamel must also develop the ability to use English to acquire interdisciplinary information, to analyze and associate that information with previously learned information, and finally to articulate his knowledge through various modes of written expression.

Is there a method of instruction that can develop both basic English language skills *and* the ability to use English to acquire interdisciplinary information? The answer lies in content-based college ESL instruction. As Crandall (1995) puts it, in content-based courses, "The focus is not just on learning the language, but in using [the language] as a medium to learn something else" (p. 3). Although studies have shown that content-based courses help college ESL students improve basic language skills—reading, writing, listening, and speaking—by requiring them to use English to learn interdisciplinary information, these studies have generally targeted high intermediate to advanced level ESL populations (Black & Kiehnhoff, 1992; Brinton, Snow, & Wesche, 1989; Kasper, 1995, 1997a; Raphan & Moser, 1993/94).

Higher level students have been targeted for two reasons. First, students at higher levels of English language proficiency are ready to make the transition from the ESL program to the college mainstream. In fact, passing college assessment examinations in reading and writing is often a requirement for exiting these higher level ESL courses and moving on to full matriculation in the college mainstream. Second, the level of linguistic sophistication found in content-based texts is often quite advanced, so that these texts have generally been deemed too difficult to be used with lower level ESL students. Yet, lower level students like Kamel are the very students who need to develop English language proficiency more rapidly than ever before because colleges and universities are beginning to place strict limitations on the number of semesters a student may remain in developmental courses.

Failure to meet institutional standards for English language proficiency within these set time limits may have serious consequences on ESL students' academic, professional, and personal lives. Therefore, ESL educators need to find ways to make CBI materials more accessible to lower level students, so that these students may also enjoy their proven benefits.

USING SHORT STORIES AS A BRIDGE TO CONTENT

Short stories can provide an excellent foundation for introducing content-based topics, and subsequently academic texts themselves, into lower level ESL courses. Short stories are especially useful as a starting point because they are authentic literary texts written for a native-speaking audience. Using short stories in a lower level ESL course exposes students to the real-life English that they can expect to read and to hear in their mainstream college courses, and in the process builds vocabulary, enhances fluency in reading, and engages students actively in learning (Song, 1995). I have successfully used a number of short stories as foundations for content-based units with students having entry level TOEFL scores as low as 350. The key to the success of this instructional model is teaching the short story, and related content-based topics, through a variety of highly integrated multimedia content-based activities.

The multimedia approach helps lower level ESL students develop all four basic language skills—listening, speaking, reading, and writing—as it introduces them to content matter through both print and audiovisual instructional materials. This chapter illustrates how to use this multimedia approach and the short story, *Flowers for Algernon* by Daniel Keyes (1964), as the foundation for a lower level content-based unit in psychology.

This classroom-tested, multimedia approach incorporates a variety of learning activities that are meaning-driven, student-centered, and unintimidating (Kasper, 1997b). The activities used encourage lower level ESL students to take an active role in learning, to engage in self-monitoring, to make guesses in their search for meaning, and to communicate in the second language. The result is increased levels of English language literacy with overall enhancement of the four basic language skills.

TYPES OF ACTIVITIES

The multimedia activities include prereading exercises such as advance organizers and analogies, reading and writing activities, and audiovisual activities. The advance organizers and analogies help to activate students' preexisting knowledge on the topic of the short story, thus bridging the gap between the knowledge the ESL student already has and the knowledge he or she needs to comprehend the text. The reading and writing activities help lower level ESL students to acquire information in a meaningful context and then to expand on that information through various forms of writing. The audiovisual materials (i.e., cassette tapes and videos) help consolidate learning by making the subject matter more concrete to the lower level ESL student, thereby facilitating comprehension.

MATERIALS AND PROCEDURE

Prerecorded audio and videotapes are used throughout the course to develop listening skills. Reading, writing, and speaking skills are then developed through a variety of other multimedia activities. In this approach, production activities in speaking and writing grow naturally out of comprehension activities in listening and reading.

Completing all of the activities as described in this chapter requires approximately 3 to 4 weeks of class time for a course meeting 6 hours per week. This time-line includes time to complete and discuss each of the reading and writing exercises and time to listen to or view and discuss each of the audiovisual materials.

The short story, *Flowers for Algernon*, is about a developmentally disabled man who is chosen for an experimental operation that results in his becoming a genius. The main character, Charlie Gordon, keeps a journal of his progress throughout the story. Like Charlie, the ESL students will also keep a journal in which they describe their thoughts and feelings, as well as their progress in English, as they read, listen, speak, and write throughout this lesson. Thus, by describing analogous experiences, lower level ESL students are encouraged to become more deeply involved not only with the characters in the story, but also with the English language itself.

Prereading Activities

Each prereading activity is designed to tap into students' personal experience with and knowledge of psychology, in general, and the developmentally disabled, in particular. Before the story is read, students are provided with an advance organizer, a prereading worksheet, that can be done as a writing or a conversation exercise. This worksheet asks the students to describe a special person that they know who has the characteristics of warmth, understanding, an open nature, and little formal education. They are asked to discuss the simple, touching things this person has done.

The second prereading exercise presents the students with a list of psychological references and terms that provides them not only with some of the new words they will encounter in this story, but also with some new ideas and concepts grounded in the discipline, psychology. Students are required to use these references and terms in subsequent reading, writing, and vocabulary exercises.

A writing exercise asks students to edit the first entry of Charlie Gordon's journal as presented in the short story. Lower level ESL students now have a chance to correct someone else's writing and to test their own knowledge of spelling, punctuation, vocabulary, and grammar. This exercise helps these lower level students to develop insights into finding and correcting errors in their own writing by prompting them to take an active role in learning and to monitor their own work. Finally, this correction exercise provides students with a general introduction to the short story itself.

Reading and Writing Activities

In the second stage of the lesson, students are assigned to read the short story for homework. After students have read the story at home, they complete several different comprehension exercises in class. First, students are given a short, multiple-choice reading comprehension exercise that provides a quick indication of how well they understood the story and the characters. A copy of this exercise is provided in Appendix A.

Next, they are given a writing assignment that asks them to connect Charlie's experiences with their own. Several times in the story, Charlie must take a number of tests that cause him great anxiety. The writing assignment asks students to relate their own experiences with test taking and to compare them with Charlie Gordon's. This writing exercise encourages these lower level ESL students to tap into the emotions they feel when they have to take an important test in college. Thereby, the exercise helps students to identify and to "bond" with Charlie's character.

The next series of exercises focuses on vocabulary development. A vocabulary building exercise requires students to complete sentences by choosing words taken from the story. Students then work together in small groups to complete a crossword puzzle using the words from the vocabulary building exercise (see Appendix A). Students remain in these small groups for the final vocabulary exercise, which consists of a letter written by Charlie Gordon to Dr. Strauss. Students are provided with prefixes, suffixes, and roots that, when correctly combined, make up the words in the letter (see Appendix 1). Students do this exercise without the aid of the story. After they have completed the sentences in this exercise, students use the syllables provided to form and define additional new words used in the story but not in the exercise. Lower level ESL students find these vocabulary building exercises, especially the crossword puzzle, to be a great deal of fun. They enjoy having the opportunity to practice vocabulary in the context of the story and to share their knowledge with classmates.

Finally, students do a character analysis of Charlie Gordon, focusing on how he changes throughout the story. They list the individual factors that led to each of the changes in Charlie's character. This character analysis also asks students to describe what they have learned about the developmentally disabled from this story. They then use this information to write an essay on the topic, "How did Charlie fit into society before and after his operation?"

Consolidating Activities

The consolidating activities incorporate visual media, such as films, to extend the ideas and concepts presented in the short story. These films are especially important for lower level ESL students because they present graphic, visual illustrations of key critical thinking concepts, thus helping to consolidate and reinforce learning by making the subject matter more concrete. Moreover, the films challenge students to match images elicited from the printed texts with visual representations on the screen, further engaging them in critical thinking tasks (Kasper & Singer, 1997).

As a follow-up to the reading of *Flowers for Algernon*, students view the movie, *Bill* (Wiley & Jameson, 1981), a true story about a developmentally disabled man who spent 47 years in a mental institution. They also watch an episode of the ABC television series, *Life Goes On* (Stewart & Page, 1990), which describes the attitudes toward and the handling of developmentally disabled children in two different families.

The short story, *Flowers for Algernon*, and the films, *Bill* and *Life Goes On*, present three different attitudes toward the developmentally disabled. In the final writing assignment for the short story, students compare and contrast how people feel about and deal with the developmentally disabled characters in each of these three stories.

Thus, the integration of carefully designed multimedia activities helps lower level ESL students acquire background information on a topic within the discipline, psychology. Students then elaborate on this background information as they complete related oral and written activities. This multimedia integration is important to the development of English language proficiency because research has shown that overall linguistic skill acquisition is facilitated when instructional activities involve as many of the senses as possible (Collie & Slater, 1987; Taylor, 1987).

As described, the instructional activities used in this multimedia approach encourage lower-level ESL students to take an active role in learning, to engage in self-monitoring, and to make guesses in their search for meaning. In the process, lower level ESL students learn to construct meaning from information stored in memory, to extract relevant information from the larger text context, and to filter out redundant or irrelevant information. Each of these has been identified as critical to developing English language literacy (Gajdusek & van Dommelan, 1993).

In addition to helping these lower level ESL students develop literacy in the English language, these multimedia activities help keep ESL students motivated (Kasper, 1994a, 1994b), and this motivational factor is extremely important in improving overall linguistic performance (Westphal Irwin, 1986).

THE NEXT STEP

Reading *Flowers for Algernon* and engaging in the activities described in this chapter provides lower-level ESL students with a concrete foundation in a number of topics in psychology. Students can then draw on that foundation as they move on to reading more academically based texts. For example, the lesson on *Flowers for Algernon* gives students a list of psychological references and terms, and this information facilitates their comprehension of a subsequent academic text, *The History of Psychology,* contained in the textbook, *Teaching English through the Disciplines: Psychology* (Kasper, 1997c), which describes the development of psychology as an academic discipline and the theories of several famous psychologists. The language in this text, although not overly complex, does represent academic English requiring a higher level of linguistic sophistication than is traditionally expected of lower level students (see Appendix B for a sample of the text). However, the short story and the corresponding multimedia activities have established a strong foundation that prepares lower level ESL students to take the next step up the "linguistic ladder" and enables them to deal successfully with new, and more advanced, material.

While presenting them with content information, the academic text, *The History of Psychology* also continues to develop students' English language skills through vocabulary and comprehension exercises. The comprehension exercises require students to write a sentence or two to answer questions on the reading. In addition, students' writing and critical thinking skills are developed through an essay prompt that requires them to link the information in the academic text with the previously read short story. The essay prompt asks students to choose one of Charlie's behaviors and then explain that behavior referring to one of the psychological theories described in the academic text. Thus students might discuss Charlie's determination to beat Algernon in the maze race, referring to the psychological theory, functionalism, as they explain how beating the mouse would help Charlie develop confidence in his intelligence and make it easier for him to fit into society.

To further increase accessibility of the academic material, additional multimedia activities are incorporated into the lesson. The video, *The Stimulating World of Psychology* (1996), helps reinforce vocabulary and content information as it offers an entertaining and easy-to-understand visual presentation of the psychological concepts discussed in the academic text.

ADDITIONAL SHORT STORY LINKS TO CONTENT

Flowers for Algernon is an extremely effective bridge to content information in psychology. Other short stories may also be used in lower level ESL courses as links to additional content areas (see Appendix C). Like *Flowers for Algernon,* these stories should be taught through a multimedia approach incorporating print and audiovisual activities designed to develop English language skills and, at the same time, to teach content area information. Another story that I have classroom tested and found to work well as a link to content in a lower level ESL course is *There Will Come Soft Rains.*

There Will Come Soft Rains by Ray Bradbury (1991) is a wonderful link to a content-based unit on computer technology. Computer technology is a field of growing interest to college students, and many lower level ESL students may wish to enroll or may already be enrolled in computer courses. Bradbury's short story describes a world where computers are the only survivors of a nuclear war. This essay is an effective bridge to academic texts describing the evolution of computer technology and modern computer applications. Essays like

The History of the Computer and *Artificial Intelligence Research*, both contained in the textbook, *Interdisciplinary English* (Kasper, 1998a), respectively trace the development of the computer from the abacus to Pentium machines and describe computer applications that can perform tasks as humans do, much like the machines described in Bradbury's story.

Once again audiovisual materials help to make these materials more accessible to the lower level ESL student. Students can listen to an audiotape of Bradbury reading his own story. This tape can be interspersed with the reading of the story to provide listening practice and to encourage students to make predictions as they read. The texts relating to computer technology are supplemented by the National Geographic video, *Miniature Miracle: The Computer Chip* (1992). This film enables students to witness the miracles of the technological revolution as it traces the development of the computer from its early history to more recent applications in fields like robotics and medicine.

STUDENT FEEDBACK IN MULTIMEDIA CONTENT-BASED COURSES

The instructional approach described in this chapter, incorporating content-based materials into the lower level ESL class, yields very positive results in terms of both student feedback and student performance. ESL students say that the wide variety of activities is enjoyable, interesting, and highly motivating. Students report that as they acquire relevant vocabulary and identify important issues surrounding the topics presented, they are able to read, speak, and write about those topics more easily. The content-based topics presented in this type of course encourage lively class discussion and foster critical thinking in English. Lower level students learn that they have a lot to say. They develop confidence in their ability to say it, and this motivates them to write about what they think and what they know. Overall, feedback from lower level ESL students indicates a belief that multimedia CBI, as described in this chapter, not only improves their English language skills but also teaches them about important issues in society and education.

ASSESSMENT IN THE LOWER LEVEL CONTENT-BASED COURSE

Lower level students taught using the multimedia CBI approach described in this chapter outperform lower level students in noncontent, skills-based courses on reading and writing assessment measures at both the departmental and the college level. Reading assessment measures, at both levels, present the students with a battery of questions that require a written answer of several sentences. Students may be asked to describe intertextual connections, to draw inferences, and/or to summarize information presented in related texts.

Writing assessment measures, again at both the department and the college level, require that students compose a clear and cogent expository essay in which they discuss an educational or societal issue of interest. At my college, the average pass rate on departmental measures of assessment has traditionally been only 65% for students in skills-based lower level ESL courses. In contrast, this pass rate has soared to 95% since the implementation of content-based lower level courses. In addition, students who have been in content-based lower level courses are able to pass college skills assessment tests after fewer semesters (Kasper, 1998b).

Because they have been exposed in the CBI context to the kinds of questions contained on institutional assessments, students feel more comfortable and more confident at test time. Moreover, the materials used in the content-based course have introduced students not only to the question types, but also to the language contained therein. As they read and respond to these materials during the course of the semester, lower level students gradually become more familiar with the language of academic texts. This, in turn, helps improve their performance on final measures of assessment.

CONCLUSION

Using a short story as a bridge to content in a lower level ESL course helps students develop both the linguistic and the academic skills they need to succeed in college. These courses give students a variety of opportunities to use the English language to express their thoughts and feelings as well as to expand on newly acquired knowledge. Each of the activities incorporated into the multimedia approach helps students develop confidence in their ability to use English to acquire academic information. Because they have practiced the vocabulary and the structures that they need to comprehend and to express ideas, lower level students are motivated not only to read content-based texts in English, but also to articulate their reactions to this content in written and spoken English.

This step-by-step approach, incorporating both print and audiovisual materials with gradually increasing levels of linguistic sophistication, enables even lower level ESL students to enjoy the benefits of CBI. Thus, these lower level ESL students can be given the opportunity to progress more rapidly in their English language development. This, in turn, enables them to meet institutional standards of English language proficiency more quickly, so that they can succeed in fulfilling their academic goals.

REFERENCES

Black, M. C., & Kiehnhoff, D. M. (1992). Content-based classes as a bridge from the EFL to the university classroom. *TESOL Journal, 1*, 27–28.

116 CHAPTER 6

Bradbury, R. (1991). "There will come soft rains" in *Tales of fantasy*. (Audiotape). Listening Library.

Brinton, D. M., Snow, M. A., & Wesche, M. B. (1989). *Content-based second language instruction*. Boston: Heinle & Heinle.

Collie, J., & Slater, S. (1987). *Literature in the language classroom*. Cambridge: Cambridge University Press.

Crandall, J. (1995). Content-based ESL: An introduction. In J. Crandall (Ed.), *ESL through content-area instruction* (pp. 1–8). McHenry, IL: The Center for Applied Linguistics/Delta Systems.

Gajdusek, L., & van Dommelan, D. (1993). Literature and critical thinking in the composition classroom. In J. G. Carson & I. Leki (Eds.), *Reading in the Composition Classroom* (pp. 197–217). Boston: Heinle.

Kasper, L. F. (1994a). Developing and teaching a content-based reading course for ESL students. *Teaching English in the Two-Year College, 22*, 23–26.

Kasper, L. F. (1994b). Improved reading performance for ESL students through academic course pairing. *Journal of Reading, 37*, 376–384.

Kasper, L. F. (1995). Discipline-oriented ESL reading instruction. *Teaching English in the Two-Year College, 22*, 45–53.

Kasper, L. F. (1997a). The impact of content-based instructional programs on the academic progress of ESL students. *English for Specific Purposes 16*(4), 309–320.

Kasper, L. F. (1997b). Teaching the short story, "Flowers for Algernon," to college-level ESL students. *The Internet TESL Journal, 3*(8). [Online]. Available: http://www.aitech.ac.jp/~iteslj/Lessons/Kasper-Algernon/index.html

Kasper, L. F. (1997c). The history of psychology. In L. F. Kasper (Ed.), *Teaching English through the disciplines: Psychology* (2nd ed., pp. 3–9). New York: Whittier.

Kasper, L. F. (1998a). *Interdisciplinary English*. (2nd ed.). New York: McGraw-Hill.

Kasper, L. F. (1998b). Meeting ESL students' academic needs through discipline-based instructional programs. In T. Smoke (Ed.), *Adult ESL: Politics, pedagogy and participation in classroom and community programs* (pp. 147–157). Mahwah, NJ: Lawrence Erlbaum Associates.

Kasper, L. F., & Singer, R. (1997). Reading, language acquisition, and film strategies. *Post Script, 16*, 5–17.

Keyes, D. (1964). Flowers for Algernon. In D. A. Sohn (Ed.), *Ten top stories* (pp. 5–36). New York: Bantam.

Miniature Miracle: The Computer Chip. (1992). (Film). National Geographic Video.

Raphan, D., & Moser, J. (1993/94). Linking language and content: ESL and art history. *TESOL Journal, 3*, 17–21.

Song, B. (1995). Incorporating writing into the lower-level ESL reading classroom. *Journal of College Reading, 2*, 57–60.

Stuart, M. (Producer), & Page A. (Director). (1981). *Bill*. (Film). Star Classics, Inc.

Taylor, B. (1987). Teaching ESL: Incorporating a communicative, student-centered component. In M. H. Long & J. C. Richard (Eds), *Methodology in TESOL: A book of readings* (pp. 45–60). New York: Newbury.

The Stimulating World of Psychology. (1996). (Film). Cerebellum Corporation.

Westphal Irwin, J. (1986). *Teaching reading comprehension processes*. Englewood Cliffs, NJ: Prentice Hall.

Wylly, Sr., P. (Producer), & Jameson, J. (Director); (1990). *Life goes on*. Hollywood: Warner Brothers, Inc.

APPENDIX A:
EXERCISES USED TO TEACH "FLOWERS FOR ALGERNON"[1]

Reading Comprehension

Directions: Choose the letter of the best response to each of the following statements.

1. Why is Charlie Gordon picked for the operation?
   a. because Charlie trusts and respects Prof. Nemur
   b. because Charlie is motivated to learn
   c. because Charlie will not tell anyone else about the experiment
2. Why does Charlie want the operation?
   a. because he thinks that if he were smart, people would not make fun of him
   b. because he thinks that if he were smart, Alice Kinnian would like him
   c. because he thinks that if he were smart, he would have more friends
3. Immediately after the operation, Charlie is disappointed because
   a. he cannot visit his family
   b. he does not feel any smarter
   c. Alice does not come to visit him
4. One reason Algernon wins the maze races is that
   a. Charlie lets him win
   b. Algernon is smarter because of the operation
   c. Dr. Nemur makes Charlie nervous when he watches Charlie take the tests
5. Nemur wants to keep the operation a secret because he
   a. is afraid that it won't work and people will laugh at him
   b. knows that what he is doing is unethical
   c. wants to protect Charlie from reporters.
6. Why does Dr. Nemur bring Charlie a television?
   a. to keep him from worrying about his problems
   b. to teach him and help him remember more
   c. to change the way his brain works
7. Charlie goes to therapy sessions because he
   a. worries that he is crazy
   b. thinks therapy will make him smarter
   c. begins to dream and remember
8. Charlie's determination is revealed by his

---

[1](from Kasper, 1997b)

a. desire to read and write
b. determination to win the maze race
c. promotion at his bakery job
9. Charlie's "friends" at the bakery show they are really no friends at all by
   a. getting him in trouble with his boss
   b. telling him that the operation didn't work
   c. getting Charlie drunk as a joke
10. After Charlie beats Algernon at the maze race,
    a. Dr. Strauss believes that the operation was a success
    b. Charlie becomes friends with Algernon
    c. Alice Kinnian falls in love with Charlie

Vocabulary Exercise

Combine the following syllables to create words found in Charlie's letter to Dr. Strauss on June 4.

al ap co con da di dix dromes du ef fect for gence glan la in lar li mu na ob or pen pid port ra re scure struc syn ta tel though tin tion ture ue

1. Under separate cover I am sending you a copy of my _____ entitled:
2. "The Algernon-Gordon_____: A Study of _____ and Function of
3. Increased_____," which may be published if you see fit.
4. I have included in my report all of my formulas, as well as _____
5. analyses of the_____ in the_____.
6. The more sensational aspects of my rapid climb cannot _____ the facts.
7. Reviewing the data on Algernon: _____ he is still in his physical youth, he has regressed mentally.
8. Motor activity impaired; general reduction of _____ functioning;
9. accelerated loss of _____ ; and strong indications of _____
10. As I show in my report, these and other physical and mental deterioration _____ can be predicted with statistically significant results by the application of my new _____.
11. As long as I am able to write, I will _____ to put down my thoughts and ideas in these progress reports.
12. However, by all indications, my own mental deterioration will be quite _____.

Crossword Puzzle

Down
2. Empty; Without Feeling
3. Only Friends
6. Stranded; All Alone
9. A Nice Way of Saying
   Something Difficult
10. Lively and Full of Energy

Across
1. Self-contradictory
4. Turn away
5. Period between events
7. Insult
8. Evil and immoral
11. Too Fancy
12. Trigger
13. Tame and Obedient

Choose your answers from among the following vocabulary items:
stimulus   affront   paradoxical   docile   vacuous   baroque   marooned   avert   animated   platonic   interim   depraved   euphemism

Crossword Puzzle Answers

```
V          P
PARADOXICAL
  C        AVERT
  U        T
  O        O
  U        N
  S        INTERIM
           C        AFFRONT
           R
           O
           O
           N
           E
           DEPRAVED
              U  N
              P  I
              H  M
      BAROQUE  A
              M  STIMULUS
              I  E
              S  DOCILE
              M
```

APPENDIX B:
SAMPLE FROM THE TEXT,
"THE HISTORY OF PSYCHOLOGY"[2]

Sample of Text:

Functionalism: The Uses of the Mind. *The functionalist school was concerned with the functions of mental processes and structures. It developed as a result of Darwin's theory of evolution in England and the US, as people began asking about the adaptive significance of psychological processes. This means they wanted to know how our behavior helps us to deal with changes in our environment; how we adapt our behavior so that we may survive changing situations.*

John Dewey (1859–1952) initiated functionalism at the University of Chicago in 1894. Dewey argued that psychological processes were continuous, ongoing events; he talked about "the stream of consciousness." Dewey emphasized studying behavior in its natural context to determine its functions.

Functionalism emphasized applied activities such as mental tests and education, and helped introduce the study of lower organisms into psychology" (p. 6).

Sample of Comprehension Questions:

What scientist influenced the Functionalist school?
How would the Functionalists explain mental illnesses such as schizophrenia, where a person withdraws from reality? (pp. 14–15).

APPENDIX C:
OTHER SUGGESTED SHORT WORKS
MATCHED WITH CONTENT AREA[3]

The following is a list of short works I have used successfully with lower level ESL students. There are many good collections of short works available. The sources for short works listed in this appendix are: *21 Great Stories* edited by Abraham Lass and Norma Tasman (Mentor, 1969); *Ways of Reading* edited by David Bartholomae and Anthony Petrosky (St. Martin's, 1993); and *The Retold Classics Series* (Perfection Form, 1987). The Perfection Form Company of Logan, Iowa also provides the *Tale Blazer* series, which enables the instructor to select individual short stories of interest and have these bound together into one collection. In this way, instructors can custom design a collection of the short stories most appropriate for use in their classes. Each story comes complete with vocabulary, reading comprehension, and writing questions.

---

[2](from Kasper, 1997c)
[3]Works other than short stories are identified by parentheses.

Audiotapes and films are also available for some of these works as indicated. The interested instructor should keep in mind that because these works were written or translated for native speakers of English, lessons should be designed to include both extensive vocabulary development and detailed comprehension questions.

Content Area	Short Work
Sociology	"War" by Luigi Pirandello
	"The Lottery" by Shirley Jackson (film available)
Linguistics/Language Acquisition	"What Stumped the Bluejays" by Mark Twain
	"Aria"/"The Achievement of Desire" from *Hunger of Memory* by Richard Rodriguez
	The Miracle Worker (a play) by William Gibson (film available)
Environmental Science	"Wine on the Desert" by Max Brand
	"Leningen vs. the Ants" by Carl Stephenson
	"To Build a Fire" by Jack London (film available)
History	"An Occurrence at Owl Creek Bridge" by Ambrose Bierce (film available)
	"The Devil and Daniel Webster" by Stephen Vincent Benet
	"Incidents in the Life of a Slave Girl" by Harriet Jacobs
Business	"The Law" by Robert M. Coates
	"Cosby Knows Best" by Mark Crispin Miller
	Death of a Salesman (a play) by Arthur Miller (audiotape and film available)
Child Psychology	"Eve in Darkness" by Kaatje Hurlbut
Diet and Nutrition	*The Best Little Girl in the World* (a novel) by Steven Levenkron (film available)
	The Moon is Broken (a novel) by Eleanor Craig
	"Dr. Heidegger's Experiment" by Nathaniel Hawthorne
Culture	"The Mark of the Beast" by Rudyard Kipling
Computer Science	"There Will Come Soft Rains" by Ray Bradbury (audiotape available)

7

Film Imagery

A Visual Resource for Clarifying Content and Developing Academic Writing Skill

Loretta F. Kasper
Kingsborough Community College/CUNY

A high intermediate level ESL class has been studying language acquisition as part of a content-based unit on linguistics. They have learned about the critical period theory and about the nature–nurture debate as presented in the language acquisition theories of Chomsky and Skinner. They have also read about Genie, a young girl who was shut away by her father and deprived of language for 11½ years of her life. The students have been asked to write about Genie's case, explaining it in terms of the critical period theory and the nature–nurture debate. This writing assignment requires not only that they understand concepts in the field of linguistics, but also that they be able to analyze and evaluate Genie's language use within the framework of those linguistic concepts. To do this, students must have a clear and vivid image of how Genie used language and of what her life and language development were like after she was found. Unfortunately, although the ESL students in this class have all been moved by this incredible story, they have not really been able to imagine how Genie must have looked and sounded when she was finally found at the age of 13, nor what her life and her language development were like afterwards.

A chorus of "Oohs" and "Aahs" ring out from the classroom as the video monitor comes to life with images of a young girl stumbling across a yard. She is thin and very frail. When she speaks, her language is incomprehensible, yet

122

it is evident that she is struggling to communicate, to reach out and connect with other people. As they watch the film, *Secret of the Wild Child* (1994), these ESL students suddenly and immediately become a part of what they have previously only read about. "She looks so pretty," one young woman says "When I read the text, I didn't imagine her this way." Another student joins in, "It is so sad, yet so amazing that she survived such great punishment. It was hard to really understand what her life and her language were like before we saw the movie. Now, I think, it will be easier to write about her."

INTRODUCTION

To be successful in college, ESL students must develop strong academic skills. They must be able to comprehend, analyze, and interpret information presented in English. Furthermore, they must be able to use English to articulate conceptual relationships within and among various disciplines of study. This chapter takes the position that a content-based perspective that uses both print and visual texts can effectively develop ESL students' linguistic skills and broaden their academic base of knowledge (Bloome & Bailey, 1992; Costanzo, 1985; Kasper & Singer, 1997).

Although print materials are the most common instructional resource in language classes, there is a strong interdisciplinary rationale for using visual imagery to develop linguistic skills and the schematic knowledge base. Research in psychology maintains that not only is visual processing at the foundation of our language development (Piaget & Inhelder, 1971), but also that the mind stores and manipulates linguistic information pictorially (Paivio, 1979; Salomon, 1981). In 1970, Gordon Bower pointed to the value of imagery in language acquisition, demonstrating that the use of imagery strengthens the association between already existing knowledge and new incoming information, and in 1978, Gruneberg found that creating imaginal associations to linguistic items improves learning and that the more vivid and interactive (i.e., relating to more than one factor, such as sound, vision) the images are, the more effective. More recently, in the field of linguistics, Weiner (1995) extolled the value of imagery in building the reading and writing skills of developmental students. Weiner suggested that developmental students can broaden their schematic knowledge base and draw inferences about incoming information by using their visual, imaginative skills.

This research suggests that imagery, such as that provided by film, might offer a useful visual resource for helping ESL students develop the linguistic skills and broaden the base of knowledge they need to succeed in academic reading and writing tasks. This chapter discusses how film imagery may be used to clarify information presented in content-based texts by filling gaps in comprehension that may result from missing or inappropriate information in the schematic knowledge base. The chapter also describes, through classroom-tested examples drawn from several subject areas, how the structure and content of film can be used as a model for various rhetorical modes of discourse and so help ESL students build skill in the written exposition and analysis of content-based issues.

USING FILM TO CLARIFY CONTENT INFORMATION

A CBI model views language and learning as interdependent, and lasting learning, intellectual growth, and language as inextricably connected. Content-based print texts expose ESL students to academic language and can provide valuable raw material for the in-depth written analysis and discussion of salient interdisciplinary issues. However, for students to derive linguistic and academic benefits from content-based texts, they must be able to construct meaning from those texts. In their attempts to construct meaning from print texts, students call on their previous experience and information in the schematic knowledge base. Unfortunately, gaps in comprehension may result if the concepts presented and the linguistic structures used are abstract and do not fit with the student's existing schematic knowledge base. These gaps in comprehension can cause L2 learners to lose their way as they attempt to use preexisting schemata to construct meaning from the printed word (Bransford & Johnson, 1972).

In contrast, the visual learning experience created through the use of film can help ESL students deal successfully with sophisticated textual material. Film imagery strengthens the association between already learned information and new incoming information by providing ESL students with both relevant schema background and authentic natural language (Pincas, 1996). Through careful film selection, purposeful lesson planning, and the integration of a variety of meaning-based activities, ESL students can build both linguistic skill and content knowledge (Stoller, 1988). Whether viewing the complete film or excerpted sequences, ESL students benefit from a graphic, visual illustration of key critical thinking concepts as they are challenged to match outer visual representations of content-based concepts with the inner mental representations of these concepts developed through their readings of print texts (Kasper & Singer, 1997). Further, as MacDonald and MacDonald (1991) noted, film naturally calls on a variety of language skills as students must decode dialogue, read criticism, discuss perceptions, and write commentary.

Thus, film becomes a means to opening the window of comprehension, empowering ESL students in their efforts to analyze and explore content-based issues in a critically probing way. ESL students' reactions to film imagery, which are the product of their individual experiential and cultural backgrounds (Corrigan, 1994), can be directed to and examined within the context of various areas of academic discourse, such as psychology, environmental science, law, and others, to broaden the verbal and written perspective (Kasper & Singer, 1997). Thus, film imagery incorporated into CBI provides

ESL students with a multimedia context for language learning that stimulates the imagination, reinforces both language and content, and helps to maintain motivation, thereby producing better readers and writers (Collie & Slater, 1987; Kasper, 1995).

The following example from a content-based lesson dealing with language acquisition illustrates how film imagery may be used to clarify content information. *The Miracle Worker* (Gibson, 1956) is a play that lends itself well to a discussion of the process of language acquisition and of the many factors that impact that process. The dining room scene in Act 2 of this play portrays a powerful physically and emotionally charged interchange between Annie Sullivan and a young Helen Keller that ultimately paves the way for Helen's language acquisition. In the print version of the play, the entire scene is conveyed through italicized screen directions. Although ESL students may read and understand much of the individual vocabulary contained therein, the intricate emotional and linguistic nuances that pass between Annie and Helen during this powerful encounter are expressed through fairly complex language structures, and so may not be obvious to the nonnative speaker of English. As a result, the full significance of this scene will be lost.

However, the film (*The Miracle Worker*, 1962) conveys these intricate nuances visually. As students listen to the language and watch the action, they receive both verbal and visual cues to the information presented. The resulting cognitive representation of the text is multimodal, consisting of the collaborative effects of both types of cues (Chun & Plass, 1997), and so it is stronger than that created by simply reading the play. Hence, students exposed to film imagery are better able to comprehend the power and the violence of the scene as well as better able to appreciate this scene as a turning point in the lives of the characters. Grasping the full significance of the scene, ESL students are then better prepared to deal with it on a cognitive and a critical thinking level, drawing on previous knowledge and experience to formulate and express an opinion.

Thus, through exposure to content-based print and film, ESL students can broaden their schematic knowledge base, in the process shaping and refining their perceptions of experience. This results in enhanced ability to both interpret texts and define relationships between concepts (Langer & Applebee, 1987). Film supports ESL students' attempts to construct meaning from print texts by offering visual elements that can be examined in detail through classroom discussions and individual responses. In this way, film can also be used to facilitate the development of skill in written academic discourse.

USING FILM TO DEVELOP ACADEMIC WRITING SKILLS

By clarifying content and synthesizing learning, the visual experience provided by film leads to higher levels of text comprehension. The greater students' comprehension, the better able they are to engage in the written analysis and exposition of complex interdisciplinary concepts. Because film links disciplinary perspectives, stimulates the imagination, and motivates reaction and analysis (Aiex, 1988), it may be used to both provide an effective stimulus and serve as a visual model for various forms of academic writing, such as comparison–contrast, cause–effect, and argumentation.

Comparison–Contrast

Learning how to define equivalencies between experiences and learning how to perceive differences involving similar phenomena is critical to understanding content and to developing proficiency in written academic discourse (Dyson, 1994). For students to be able to make use of newly acquired information, they must recognize how and why that information is related to or is different from information in their existing knowledge base. In fact, the ability to compare and contrast information and concepts is a prerequisite for other written forms of academic discourse, including cause–effect analysis and argumentation. Moreover, college ESL students will be asked to demonstrate knowledge through comparison–contrast writing not only in English courses, but also in many of their mainstream courses. For example, in a behavioral science course, students may be asked to describe the similarities and differences between the various schools of psychology, or in a chemistry course, to compare and contrast the properties of various chemical elements, or in a business course, to compare and contrast various marketing strategies. Therefore, to increase their chances for success in college courses, ESL students need to become proficient in the written analysis of comparison–contrast.

The process of language acquisition is a content-based topic that is rich with possibilities for comparative analysis. Students may read about contrasting theories of language acquisition, including the critical period theory and the nature–nurture debate embodied in the work of Chomsky and Skinner. They may also read about the famous case of Genie, the young girl who was deprived of exposure to language from the age of 18 months to 13 years. Genie's rare and complex case raises issues spanning a number of different content areas as the events surrounding this case point to the intricacies of language acquisition and psychosocial development.

As described in the anecdote that began this chapter, if presented solely through print texts, these events may be somewhat difficult for ESL students to grasp and therefore to write about. It is here that the power of film, both to facilitate comprehension and to serve as a model for comparison–contrast writing, is strikingly evident. As Barsam (1985) explained, film, particularly film documentary, is effective in teaching comparison–contrast because the cinematic language contained in this film genre often reflects exposition in this rhetorical mode. Furthermore, the structure of film documentary bears a close relationship with this rhetorical mode in that it states a problem, explores various solutions, and may express a preference for one solution over another.

The film documentary *Secret of the Wild Child* (1994), produced by Linda Garmon, offers many possibilities for written analysis involving comparison–contrast as it depicts in graphic detail Genie's life after her discovery, introduces the many doctors and teachers who worked with this young girl, and describes the linguistic theories surrounding her case. After viewing this film, students might be asked to compare Genie's language development with that of normal children, defining and explaining the critical period theory and discussing Genie's language development within the framework of that theory. They might also be asked to explain Genie's language development in terms of the contrasting theories put forth by Chomsky and Skinner. Finally, students might compare and contrast Genie's relationship with each of the doctors and teachers who worked with her after she was found.

Garmon's film also compares and contrasts the Genie case with that of another child who, like Genie, was deprived of language. This child, Victor, the so-called "Wild Boy of Aveyron," lived in France during the 1800's. As students watch the film and see the descriptive images it presents, the similarities and the differences between the lives and the language development of these two children gradually become clearer to them. Students might then be asked to write an essay in which they compare the Genie case with the 19th century case of Victor as described by the narrator of the film documentary. Directing their attention to the various comparison–contrast relationships expressed, *Secret of the Wild Child* helps students to build schemata for, and so develop skill in, this rhetorical mode.

In the following essay excerpt, reprinted with permission, a high intermediate level ESL student addresses the question of how we acquire language, contrasting the theories of Chomsky and Skinner and then applying those theories to a discussion of Genie and Victor:

> The question of how people acquire language has been analyzed by some scientists and experts. Among them were the linguist Chomsky and the psychologist Skinner, who developed two different theories of language acquisition. The main idea of Chomsky's theory is that all children had an innate knowledge of the grammar of their native language. They speak without thinking of the word order. According to Chomsky's theory the human being has a hidden mechanism to start using the native language. ... In contrast, Skinner's theory is that nothing can come by itself. Nothing can substitute parent's love and attention, normal communication, and strong process of study. People reach different levels of language acquisition because they grow up in different environments.
>
> Examples like Genie and Victor represent that language should be studied in the human environment with certain relation from parents, adults, and teach-

ers. ... These cases show that methods like punishment, abuse, harassment could cause very serious problems in acquiring language, possibly even brain damage. Vice versa, when children are surrounded with love and care, they accept language with positive emotions and big interest. The brain cannot advance without a normal environment ... both of these things are necessary for acquiring language.

Cause–Effect Analysis

Although comparison–contrast is a basic form of academic writing, many assignments in college courses require that students be able to articulate similarities and differences among events and that they also be able to define causal relationships among those same events. Thus, the written analysis of cause and effect may be considered a more advanced skill.

Global warming, or the greenhouse effect, is a content-based issue that lends itself well to teaching ESL students the written analysis of cause and effect because this issue has both immediate and possible future impacts on our weather, and resulting effects on issues in content areas such as business and nutrition. The greenhouse effect is a somewhat abstract topic, one that requires some understanding of complex chemical interactions. Film provides visual imagery that helps to clarify and concretize these abstract scientific concepts and thereby facilitates comprehension as it serves as a model for the written analysis of cause and effect.

After reading a text that defines the greenhouse effect, explains the cause–effect relationship between greenhouse gases and global warming, and details the environmental, chemical, and political implications of ozone depletion and global warming, students watch the film documentary *Crisis in the Atmosphere* (1989), produced by Lionel Friedberg. This film describes the problem and the process of global warming, focusing the camera on actual (although sometimes simulated) situations. Thus, the documentary creates a feeling of "being there" as it chronicles, step by step through spoken narration, the events leading to global warming. In this way, the film documentary bears a close relationship to the format of a cause–effect essay.

Crisis in the Atmosphere (1989) also provides students with many facts to support a written analysis of cause and effect. The film takes students inside a glacier to study "fossil" air, teaches them about chlorofluorocarbons (CFCs), and examines the environmental effects of Chernobyl, the Exxon Valdez spill, and the burning of the Amazon rain forests. One of the key sequences in the film documentary is a visual depiction of the chemical process through which ozone is destroyed by CFCs. Here, film imagery takes a difficult scientific concept and brings it to a level of visual understanding by depicting step by step, through clear and vivid pictures, the chemical destruction of ozone. This helps to clarify content information and so better enables students to articulate their knowledge of the effect of chemical pollutants on our atmosphere in an intelligent way.

Another key sequence in the film documentary shows the air in Los Angeles viewed over the course of a day through time-lapse photography. This sequence presents a powerful visual image that reinforces the effect of greenhouse gases on our air by putting this scientific phenomenon into the context of everyday life. Thus once again, the film works very effectively to clarify information presented in the print text, as well as the cause–effect relationship of greenhouse gases to environmental pollution as it stimulates students' interest in and responses to the problem.

The vivid images presented in the film documentary give students a concrete stimulus for a written analysis of cause and effect that requires them to explore predictions about the future condition of the earth's environment and to draw inferences concerning complex cause/effect relationships. For example, students might be asked to imagine that it is the year 2050, and although governments and their citizens were warned about the dangers of the greenhouse effect as early as the 1970's, they did not take the necessary steps to prevent it from worsening. Taking into account continued global warming and ozone depletion, students are asked to write about life in the year 2050 under these conditions. Through the powerful visual images it presents, the film provides a visual model for this written analysis of cause and effect, and students may call on this visual model to help them develop skill in this form of academic writing.

In their written projections for the earth's future, students are encouraged to combine facts and imagination. The following excerpt, reprinted with permission, clearly illustrates the power of film imagery as presented through one student's view of life in 2050:

> When I was born in 1950, the Earth was clean and beautiful. But people did not take care of it. They began to build a lot of factories, many cars and other things that polluted the air. ... When I was 15, the scientists discovered that there was a big hole in the ozone layer—the Earth's natural protector against UV radiation. ... Because of the ozone hole a lot of people started getting sick and died. ... Because of pollution and the ozone hole, there was a 'greenhouse effect,' the temperatures rose very fast, and now there are very hot climates everywhere. The equator area in 2030 became a desert without any signs of life. In 2045, all the Earth's glaciers melted away and water flooded a lot of lands. ... Now in 2050 everyday life is hard because of lack of food, polluted air, and strong hurricanes. People struggle with each other for every piece of land, for food and water to drink. ... Sometimes I remember the past times, and I reflect upon why we did not take the necessary steps to protect our world. ... I think that [people] forgot that the Earth is a wonderful gift that needs to be treated with respect and love.

Argumentation

Both comparison–contrast and cause–effect represent key modes of written academic discourse. As ESL students build skill in the written analysis of comparative and causal relationships, they also become familiar with the essential components of an effective written argument. This is important because ESL students are often required to produce written arguments on institutional skills assessments, which may be used by colleges to indicate students' readiness for mainstream courses. Therefore, proficiency in argumentative discourse is a skill ESL students must have if they are to succeed in college.

Expressing and supporting an opinion is a skill valued in American English writing; however, this is not the case in all cultures (Raimes, 1996). For this reason, ESL students may find written argumentation, in which they state a strong thesis and take a firm stand on an issue, difficult. Watching films in which conflicts are depicted and arguments put forth can help students to visually perceive both the stance taken by the characters and how the characters convey and defend that stance to the audience. This helps students develop the schematic knowledge they need to compose an effective written argument.

Human evolution is a content-based topic that has sparked controversy, particularly in the early part of the 20th century. Darwin's theory and the religious and political controversy stirred up by this theory resulted in the Scopes Monkey Trial of the 1920s. Students may read texts describing Darwin's theory and the Scopes Monkey Trial; however, understanding the complex moral, educational, legal, and social issues surrounding the trial and its outcome requires a clear understanding of the American judicial system and the social and religious climate of America in the 1920s.

The film *Inherit the Wind* (1960), directed by Stanley Kramer, offers a visual and a creative representation of the many complex moral, educational, legal, and social issues brought up by the Scopes Monkey Trial. Therefore, the film may be used to clarify concepts initially introduced through print text. This film also provides an effective means for stimulating critical thinking and for teaching ESL students how to construct an effective argument through the antithetical positions it presents to the viewer: custom versus progress, religion versus science, intolerance versus tolerance, old versus new (Kasper & Singer, 1999). By watching and analyzing the opposing arguments presented by the attorneys in the film, students learn how to develop an effective argument, from the emotional to the intellectual; they learn what Raimes (1996) has called the essential elements of a persuasive argument—a strong thesis stating the issues and/or questions to be answered, supporting evidence, and a call to action.

With *Inherit the Wind*, the method and effectiveness of the legal arguments are the fundamental pedagogical concerns; one need not agree with a particular character's point of view, as long as that point of view can be evaluated and eventually written about. As they watch the film, students may be asked to list the important points made by each lawyer in his courtroom argument for or against Darwin's theory of evolution. After the film, students can present their views on each legal position in a written summary that identifies and evaluates the arguments they found most persuasive and explains why they consider these arguments to be effective.

Their interactions with text and film teach ESL students about the intricacies of the American judicial system. They consider the difference between "rights" and "legality" as they discuss whether Bertram Cates should have had the right to teach Darwin's theory even though there was a state ordinance prohibiting it. Students can open a discussion, taking and defending their positions on the following questions: Should an unjust law be respected at the cost of individual human freedom? Should it be broken? Which is more important in a free society—individual freedom or the law?

As students listen to and discuss the conflicting emotional and legal views presented in *Inherit the Wind*, with the purpose of defining the most convincing argument and writing about it, they are encouraged to suspend their own preconceptions and to develop an open mind. Used in this way, the film becomes both an effective stimulus for critical thought, helping students to organize and shape their ideas toward an issue (Trillin, 1985), and an apparatus for producing meaning (Tremonte, 1995). The model of argumentation depicted in the film visually illustrates for students the active process of inquiry and communication necessary for developing and presenting an effective written argument (Susser, 1994). In this way, using a film like *Inherit the Wind* as a rhetorical teaching device can help to focus ESL students' attention on the process of writing, and on the critical analysis and interpretation required by that process.

The method of argumentation presented in the film also provides students with a springboard for taking a firm written stand on other issues. For example, students may be asked to choose an issue about which they have a strong personal opinion and to write a persuasive essay in which they argue their position on this issue. They must be sure to include a rebuttal of the opposing viewpoint in the essay. Multiple drafts and revisions of these essays should be used to facilitate genuine growth for students as they learn to approach writing as a process in which one develops, articulates, and refines ideas.

The following excerpt, reprinted with permission, comes from an essay on racial prejudice written by an intermediate level ESL student. It clearly demonstrates this student's ability to take a firm written stand and argue a point of view:

> In our history from earliest years to our time, some people don't like other people; some of them even hate others who are different from them. ... Time has passed from old times and now we are living in a cruel and difficult world. At this moment, one would think all nations have to be together and live without hating each other, but some people up to today still hate others who are different from them. Many times they hide this hate deep, deep in their souls.

When I think about it, I become very angry. I want to meet these people and argue with them up to when they will finally understand that all people are like anybody else. When I was in school, I had a friend who was kind and good, but people would always be cruel to her. They would say mean things to her because she was different from them. I wanted to tear them, but my friend calmed me down and always said, 'You have to respect all people.' But how could I respect them when they hated her for nothing, just because she was different from them? ...

All people in the whole world have to be together, they have to live without hating or killing. If for example, the whole world blows up and just two persons survive, these two people will help each other to survive, and they won't see which nationality they are because they will need to be together like ground and grass. They will need each other even if they are different from each other. But now people don't understand that. I will never understand how there can be so much hatred and cruelty in our world.

STUDENT FEEDBACK AND PERFORMANCE

This chapter put forth the premise that film imagery improves comprehension of content-based information, and it provided examples to illustrate how film may be used to develop and strengthen the critical thinking skills necessary for written exposition and analysis of key issues. The effectiveness of film as a visual resource for clarifying content and developing academic writing skill is supported both by students' feedback and by their progress as writers. When asked to complete questionnaires requesting their feedback on the use of film, ESL students' responses are overwhelmingly positive. Students say that the films make the work clearer and help them to understand the texts better. They say that if a concept is unclear when they first read about it, seeing the film enables them to visualize it. In addition, students say that the films add interesting variety to the course. The students say that the films "let them study the material in a different way." They say that after they see the films, "it is easier to write about the topic because the film gives extra material to talk about in their essays." Finally, when asked if they believe that the films help them to write better, students say that the films, "show them how to put an essay together" and "how to talk about similarities and differences, and also causes and effects." Students' feedback also indicates that they believe that the films help them learn "how to collect evidence, form an opinion, and make an argument for or against an issue."

In terms of their progress as writers, on a qualitative level, students' writings become more critical and insightful as they use images and information from the films as support in their writing. By providing several perspectives from which students may articulate and analyze conceptual relationships and issues, film leads them to explore topics at a deeper level. Moreover, on a quantitative level, pass rates on final reading and writing assessments increase (from 72% to 95%). These improved pass rates enable students to progress more quickly to higher levels of English language and content area study.

A FINAL ANALYSIS

Whether popular or documentary, film can be used as a visual apparatus to aid ESL students in constructing meaning from content-based texts and in developing academic writing skills. There are many popular films and film documentaries that may be used as visual resources and rhetorical teaching devices in content-based lessons. *Jurassic Park, Trading Places,* and *Dead Poet's Society* are popular films that are easily integrated into lessons dealing with topics in science, business, and psychology–sociology. *The Miniature Miracle, The Stimulating World of Psychology,* and *The Geometry of Life* are film documentaries that are appropriate visual resources for lessons dealing with topics in computer science, psychology, and biology.

Presenting content-based information through both print and film gives ESL students multiple tools with which to construct meaning from interdisciplinary texts and to articulate that meaning through expository, analytical written pieces spanning a variety of rhetorical modes. Used as a visual adjunct to print texts, film provides a clear and comprehensive examination of interdisciplinary issues, themes, and ideas, and helps to develop and strengthen critical thinking skills, such as analysis, interpretation, inference, and synthesis of knowledge. These are skills that ESL students will need if they are to meet the linguistic and academic challenges of college coursework.

REFERENCES

Aiex, N. K. (1988). Using film, video, and TV in the classroom. *ERIC Digest No. 11, (ED300848).* Washington, DC: ERIC.

Barsam, R. (1985). Nonfiction film and/as composition. In J. Spielberger, (Ed.), *Images and words: Using film to teach writing* (pp. 19–26). New York: The City University.

Bloome, D., & Bailey, F. M. (1992). Studying language and literacy through events, particularities, and intertextuality. In R. Beach, J. L. Green, M. L. Kamil, & T. Shanahan (Eds.), *Multidisciplinary perspectives on literacy research* (pp. 181–210).Urbana, IL: NCTE.

Bower, G. (1970). Analysis of a mnemonic device. *American Psychologist, 58,* 498–510.

Bransford, J. D., & Johnson, M. K. (1972). Contextual prerequisites for understanding: Some investigations of comprehension and recall. *Journal of Verbal Learning and Verbal Behavior, 61,* 717–726.

Chun, D. M., & Plass, J. L. (1997). Research on text comprehension in multimedia environments. *Language Learning and Technology, 1*(1), 60–81.

Collie, J., & Slater, S. (1987). *Literature in the language classroom.* Cambridge: Cambridge University Press.

Corrigan, T. (1994). *A short guide to writing about film* (2nd ed.). New York: HarperCollins.

Costanzo, W. V. (1985). Visual thinking in the writing class. In J. Spielberger (Ed.), *Images and words: Using film to teach writing* (pp. 69–78). New York: The City University.

Crisis in the atmosphere. (1989). (Film). Producer, Lionel Friedberg. QED Communications, Inc. and The National Academy of Sciences.

Dead poet's society. (1989). (Film). Director, Peter Weir. Touchstone Home Video.

Dyson, A. H. (1994). Viewpoints: The word and the world—Reconceptualizing written language development or, do rainbows mean a lot to little girls? In R. B. Ruddell, M. R. Ruddell, & H. Singer (Eds.). *Theoretical models and processes of reading* (4th ed.). (pp. 297–322). Newark, DE: IRA.

Gibson, W. (1956). *The miracle worker.* New York: Bantam.

Gruneberg, M. M. (1978). The practical application of memory aids. In M. M. Gruneberg & P. Morris. (Eds.), *Aspects of Memory* (Vol. 1.). London: Methuen.

Inherit the wind. (1960). (Film). Director, Stanley Kramer. MGM/UA.

Jurassic park. (1993). (Film). Director, Steven Spielberg. Universal Studios.

Kasper, L. F. (1995). Using multimedia integration in a thematic-based ESL reading course. *Journal of College Reading, 2,* 19–29.

Kasper, L. F., & Singer, R. (1997). Reading, language acquisition, and film strategies. *Post Script, 15,* 5–17.

Kasper, L. F., & Singer, R. (1999). Inherit the text: An interdisciplinary perspective on argumentation. In E. Bishop (Ed.), *Cinema-(to)-graphy: Film and writing in the contemporary composition course* (pp. 116–124). Portsmouth, NH: Heinemann.

Langer, J. A., & Applebee, A. N. (1987). *How writing shapes thinking.* Urbana, IL: NCTE.

MacDonald, G., & MacDonald, A. (1991, March). *Variations on a theme: Film and ESL.* Paper presented at the annual meeting of TESOL, New York.

Paivio, A. (1979). *Imagery and verbal processes.* New York: Holt, Rinehart, & Winston.

Piaget, J., & Inhelder, B. (1971). *Mental imagery in the child.* New York: Basic Books.

Pincas, A. (1996). Memory and foreign language learning. *Modern English Teacher, 5,* 9–17.

Raimes, A. (1996). *Keys for writers: A brief handbook.* Boston: Houghton Mifflin.

Secret of the wild child. (1994). (Film). Producer, Linda Garmon. WGBH Educational Foundation.

Salomon, G. (1981). *Interaction of media, cognition, and learning.* San Francisco: Jossey-Bass.

Stoller, F. (1988). Films and videotapes in the ESL/EFL classroom. *ERIC Digest (ED299835).* Washington, DC: ERIC.

Susser, B. (1994). Process approaches in ESL/EFL writing instruction. *Journal of Second Language Writing, 3,* 31–47.

The geometry of life. (1988). (Film). Vestron Video.

The miniature miracle. (1989). (Film). National Geographic Video.

The miracle worker. (1962). (Film). Director, Arthur Penn. United Artists.

The stimulating world of psychology. (1996). (Film). Cerebellum Corporation.

Trading places. (1983). (Film). Director, John Landis. Paramount Pictures.

Tremonte, C. M. (1995). Film, classical rhetoric, and visual literacy. *Journal of Teaching Writing, 14,* 3–19.

Trillin, A. (1985). Film and the teaching of writing. In J. Spielberger (Ed.), *Images and words: Using film to teach writing.* (pp. 13–18). New York: The City University.

Weiner, H. S. (1995). Inference: Perspectives on literacy for college reading students. *Journal of College Reading, 2,* 3–18.

9

Speaking Science

Developing ESL Materials for University Students in Academic Disciplines

Sharon A. Myers
Texas Tech University

There are a relatively large number of content-based materials available to develop reading and writing skills; however, those available to develop listening and speaking skills are few in number. Listening skills are critical to academic success, and speaking skills govern interactions in classrooms and laboratories. Thus, students need materials that target these areas and allow them to develop English language proficiency in listening and speaking. Commercially produced materials unfortunately do not fulfill this need because they are limited in the number of academic fields they represent, as well as the level and kinds of field-specific knowledge they assume students possess. Of the more than 457,000 international students enrolled in United States higher education institutions in the academic year 1996–1997, almost 40% came to study physical and life sciences, mathematics, computer science, social sciences, and engineering; another 21% came to study management and business (*Open Doors*, 1996, 1997). These students need resources that prepare them to understand and use the language of diverse technical fields. For this reason, teacher-prepared materials are needed to fill the gap, so that students can get precisely what they need.

This chapter illustrates how to develop field-specific materials for language learning that address students' listening and speaking needs. It describes the production and use of discipline-specific audio recordings, that I created originally for my international teaching assistants (ITAs) in the sciences, and offers suggestions for how to use other published materials to develop ESL students' listening and speaking skills. Although the chapter deals primarily with materials produced for students in the sciences, interested readers should note that the general procedures described may be applied to developing materials based on the content of virtually any mainstream discipline.

RATIONALE

Although content-based materials that specifically target listening and speaking skills are not widely available, there are a number of reasons why these materials would be highly effective in enabling ESL students to become more proficient listeners and speakers of English. The first reason is increased student motivation. Gardner and MacIntyre (1991) pointed out that student motivation may be influenced by instrumental factors (i.e., interest in the material and professional advantages to be gained) and/or by integrative factors (i.e., interest in the language and culture of English speakers). These researchers further noted that instrumental motivation alone can be a powerful force in learning, suggesting that the best results are achieved when faculty take advantage of student motivation by providing instruction that focuses on the language forms and functions that students perceive as most useful in achieving their educational and professional goals. Indeed, the history of content-based L2 teaching, including the English for Specific Purposes (ESP) movement that emerged out of increasing demand for technical English classes in the early 1970s, defines relevant and interesting course content as a key to effective instruction (Hutchinson & Waters, 1987).

Another reason for using content-based materials derives from the field of cognitive psychology, specifically Ausubel's notion (1968) that learning is meaningful when we can relate it to what we already know, and thus easily integrate new knowledge into the existing cognitive structure. The value of this concept has since been elaborated through studies of the effect of background knowledge on language comprehension (e.g., Carrell & Eisterhold, 1983; Johnson, 1982; Markham & Latham, 1987; Rumelhart, 1980) and expressed in contemporary language teaching methods as an emphasis on the importance of contextualizing language instruction (e.g., Asher, 1982; Ellis, 1990; Krashen & Terrell, 1983; Lewis, 1993; Richards & Rodgers, 1986; Savignon, 1983; Wilkins, 1976). College-level ESL students, across their many first languages and ethnicities, share to some extent a core of knowledge, a scaffolding of related ideas built by their previous training. In the presence of content-related L2 materials, this background gives them power to infer and to predict meaning, and therefore provides a cognitive map with which to navigate a new language more easily.

MEETING STUDENTS' NEEDS
THROUGH FIELD-SPECIFIC AUDIOTAPES

Many of my ESL university students are incoming graduate students who are expected to work as international teaching assistants (ITAs) in their respective departments at Texas Tech University. International students are admitted to my university with scores of 550 or more on the Test of English as a Second Language (TOEFL), but the TOEFL does not predict speaking proficiency nor assure a specialized vocabulary. In fact, many students who score at 550 or above on the TOEFL may rarely have communicated with a native English speaker. Recruited by their departments primarily for their scientific skills, these students often find that the position of ITA makes heavy, sometimes unrealistic demands on their L2 skills.

Their role as ITAs requires that these students be skilled users of both basic interpersonal and cognitive academic language (Cummins, 1981). Thus, they must be able to understand and convey information in their specific fields, which necessitates that they acquire not only overall, but also field-specific proficiency in vocabulary, listening, and speaking. I decided to try to meet my ESL students' listening and speaking needs by producing content-based audiotapes to be used in a 3-week summer training and evaluation workshop designed to prepare students for their work as teaching assistants. This 3-week preparatory workshop provides what English training is possible in that short a time, what compensatory skills are possible to help students communicate while they reach a higher level of proficiency (for example, learning how to use the board and audiovisual aids), and whatever cultural information they need to interact successfully in an English-speaking academic environment.

The audiotapes would also be used in a semester-long follow-up course held from August through December for those students who, at the end of the summer workshop, are evaluated as not yet ready for classroom teaching. At the end of this follow-up course, these students are reevaluated and recommendations made to their departments regarding whether they are ready to teach with routine supervision, with close supervision, or are still not ready to teach.

Before they are ready to begin their work as ITAs, all of my students need to work on pronunciation, stress, and intonation, but they also need, with equal urgency, to learn the vocabulary necessary to teach chemistry, physics, computer science, economics, range and wildlife, biology, mathematics, pathology, civil engineering, and all the other fields they represent. To meet students' needs, with the help of a native English-speaking linguistics graduate student interested in teaching ESL/EFL, I began to prepare hour-long audiotapes specific to each of the ITAs' fields. Since then, I have prepared, recorded, and stored more than 100 hours of field-specific audiotapes and their matching scripts in our university language laboratory. These materials are available to all ITAs, ESL students, and foreign instructors who wish to use them, and have become a great resource for teaching, not only ITAs, but other international students who are placed in proficiency classes in oral skills, grammar, and composition.

PRODUCING THE TAPES

Tape Content

Determining tape content was a key consideration because to be most useful to my students, the recordings needed to address linguistic forms and functions as they related to conveying field-specific information. This meant that, for the purposes of the tapes, content and language were inextricably linked, and both were determined by the immediate, identifiable, and specific needs (Johns, 1997) of my students.

I began by going to different academic departments and requesting copies of the materials the ITAs were actually going to use in their teaching. These included syllabi, lab manuals, textbooks, and workbooks. The materials that seem best for recording vary, but I have found that lab manuals are often straightforward and yield useful field-specific vocabulary and rich clusters of important lexical phrases.

Of course I needed to obtain copyright clearance, and I found that publishers are usually willing to give permission to copy their materials through both tape recording and photocopying, as long as the copies are not being sold, are limited in number, and are limited to use in the lab. In the case of university produced material, such as the physics manuals composed and published by our university, I have been able to get permission for students to make their own cassette copies in the lab to take home.

Because teaching assistants usually teach the lowest level courses in their departments, often introductory level courses for freshmen, the discipline-based concepts involved are comprised of very basic, practical selections of language, and so are approachable by people who, like me, are unsophisticated in the fields. In addition, the basic introductory course in any of these fields tends to include the same overall topics each year. So, even if a given department or instructor changes the presentation or sequencing of the content, the basic concepts—and the vocabulary needed to express those concepts—remains. This makes the tapes useful year after year, not only to the ITAs, but also to any of the university's ESL students or foreign scholars studying in the fields for which recordings have been made.

The content of a typical 60-minute tapescript consists of a meaningful, self-contained chunk of language, say a chemistry lab manual's assignment to carry out a series of copper transformations. This self-contained chunk of language, read out loud in its entirety, represents the kind of meaningful, comprehensible input advocated by Krashen (1982, 1985)—input that challenges students "to reach beyond the linguistic and to use previous knowledge and communicative context to glean the meaning of unfamiliar structures" (Kasper, chap. 2, this volume). A paragraph is read first, uninterrupted, so that the student can hear what the text sounds like when it is connected in a chunk longer than a sentence. Then the same chunk is read in what Chafe and Danielewicz (1987) called "intonation units." These are natural intonation contours followed by a pause. These authors described these units as consisting, most of the time, of a clause, but "some contain an entire verb–complement construction while others are no more than a prepositional phrase, or even just a noun phrase, or a syntactic fragment of some other kind" (p. 95). Sometimes the intonation units inhabit whole breaths, but never more than a natural breath. On the tape, after each intonation unit is read, the reader pauses for a comparable length of time, leaving a silent space during which the student can repeat. Table 8.1 illustrates sample tape content.

The next thing that the student hears on the tape is the instruction, "Please listen and do not repeat," and the next chunk is read. The student has a complete copy of the text, which can be read while the tape is listened to. Often these texts also have illustrations that serve as good graphic organizers of the material.

TABLE 8.1

Sample Tape Content for Chemistry

The tape instructs: "Please listen, and do not repeat."

The first chunk is read: "Purpose of the experiment: Carry out a series of chemical transformations, beginning and ending with pure metallic copper. Determine the mass recovery of copper metal at the end of the series."

Tape: "Please repeat."

Tape: "Purpose of the experiment"

Silence

Tape: "Carry out a series of chemical transformations,"

Silence

Tape: "beginning and ending with pure metallic copper."

Silence

Tape: "Determine the mass percent recovery"

Silence

Tape: "of copper metal"

Silence

Tape: "at the end of the series"

Silence

As the first side of the tape visually approaches its end, I find a natural place to interrupt and say, "This is the end of Chemistry tape number 19, 'Copper Transformations,' Side A." I then turn the tape over, and record the other side with the continuation of "Copper Transformations" until the text ends or the tape ends, whichever comes first. Each tape is a self-contained unit; I never begin another lesson or a different text on the same tape.

Recording the Tapes

Recording well takes some effort, and it is important to note that these are not commercial quality materials. In fact, our "recording booths" are simply tiny soundproofed rooms, and our recording medium is a good quality tape recorder. However, teachers should not be intimidated by the lack of commercial quality, for the materials we make always fit our students' needs precisely.

Producing good tapes requires reading clearly with good diction at a natural pace and natural volume. It is important to leave an appropriate time interval for the student's repetition. This requires a sense of timing and rhythm; I often silently bring the palm of my hand down on the opposite arm, repeating the syllable cadence mentally, giving each one a "beat" and, of course, leaving just a little more time (but not too much) to allow for L2 processing.

Although tapes that are recorded slowly, in very short intonation units, are appreciated by the least proficient students, they are frustrating for the more advanced students, who become bored and disengage from the tape if it is too slow. I have found it better to keep the language clear but the rate natural, challenging the less proficient students, who will usually be motivated to keep pace even if they lose some text.

Occasionally I am unsure of the correct pronunciation of unfamiliar terms. This was true of chemistry and pathology much more often than of other fields, and I sometimes had to check on how to read some math symbols and equations or units of measurement across fields. When I was recording the pathology tapes, a professor of pathology helped out by providing a sheaf of autopsy reports with all identifying patient information removed and by going over some of the terms with me. A couple of times I took a tape recorder over to the chemistry department and enlisted the help of a chemist. However, I was able to clarify some field-specific terms simply by using a dictionary or making a quick phone call.

Despite careful efforts to clarify pronunciation, sometimes I did read a term incorrectly. Students delighted in discovering and pointing out these errors to me. When they do, I thank them for catching and making me aware of my error, and I promise to check with the department and then to correct the error. Strevens (1988) had three suggestions concerning the lack of knowledge we may have in relation to our students' fields: to become familiar with the course materials, become familiar with the language of the subject, and allow students to correct us if necessary. As ESL faculty, we should never make any pretense about having knowledge in these fields. The students are happy to forgive our ignorance—after all, we are language teachers and they know it—but they don't forgive arrogance. I have found that it is important to read and make notes on the chosen course materials beforehand, and to take those notes into the recording session. Over time, between making the materials and interacting with the students, an instructor becomes more and more familiar with the field-specific language.

The most problematic dimension in making the tapes is the time required to do so. It usually takes 1 hour and 20 minutes to produce a 1-hour tape, composed of relatively straightforward text, in disciplines such as economics, range and wildlife, or political science. Producing a tape in more technical disciplines like chemistry, pathology, calculus, or physics might take up to half an hour longer, sometimes more if it is necessary to meet with an expert in the field. These time frames include time to preread, make notes, find answers to things unknown, actually record, and mark the tape. I also make copies of the original tapes and place them in the language laboratory so that students can have access to the copies and their respective transcripts for individual work outside of class time. Although the time it takes to create a tape far exceeds the amount of recorded material, the subsequent use of the tapes by teachers and students delivers many valuable instructional hours and solid practice in the content area(s) of interest.

USING THE TAPES

A language laboratory offers the ideal setting for using these tapes. However, when a language laboratory is not available, the tapes can still be used in the classroom for listening comprehension exercises, dictation, group repetition, and individual student study. The language laboratory at my university is set up for three channels, which means that three separate field-specific tapes can be played from the console to individual student booths. This means that it is possible to have a few chemistry students, a few biology students, and several physics students listening to and repeating their respective tapes simultaneously.

Frequently, students in the lab come from more than three fields. In that case, students go to the section of the lab not hooked up to the broadcasting channels. There each student has an individual tape, listens to it on an individual tape recorder, and repeats. Through the console, it is possible to tune in, listen to, and communicate privately with each student. For example, there might be two students in computer science and one in range and wildlife doing this, and although the console is not broadcasting into their booths, it is still possible to monitor what they say and communicate with them.

We never ask students to work with the tapes for more than 20 or 25 minutes because we have found that time period to be the upper limit before most students burn out doing this kind of imitative practice. Training students to improve their attending skills helps. Cohen (1990) suggested that students can "be (made) more aware of how their attention wanders—that is, when they start tuning out. It may well be that tuning out begins to happen the more passively the students handle the input" (pp. 147—148). Therefore, to avoid passivity and to increase attention span, I instruct students to focus on the meaning of what they are saying, and I caution them that their attention may begin to wander. "Pretty soon, your mind may start to go somewhere else," I say, gesturing with my hand away from my head, "That is absolutely natural. It's OK. It may happen again and again. Just grab your mind like this,"—I grab it gesturally—"and pull it back, like a kite. Think about the meaning, if you can. If your mind starts floating off again, just pull it in and put it back on the meaning again."

As students listen to the tapes, the teacher at the console monitors student after student, sometimes listening to only one intonation unit, sometimes to longer utterances, before going on to the next student. This is a great opportunity for completely individualized instruction, and I try to make it a rule to give at least as much time to encouraging students as to correcting them. I move swiftly from student to student keeping them on their toes and listening carefully so that they can repeat as accurately as possible. On these runs around the console, it is possible to make eye contact with a shy student and provide encouragement: "Sounds better today," or "That was good," or "Keep it up," or "Good intonation." It is also possible to break into the flow of other students who are repeating to provide specific instruction: "Again, did you say 'molality' or 'molarity'?" or "You are dropping your endings, let me hear those 'eds' and 't' endings," or "Repeat after me," and give an immediate model. I have found that if students are monitored over and over again in quick succession, they perform at their best and they clearly appreciate individual attention and encouragement. There is no question that using the tapes requires hard work, but motivated students will and do work.

FOLLOW-UP MATERIALS

Whereas teacher-produced tapes most directly address students' specific language and content needs, some published materials, such as student texts, may also be adapted to be used in the language classroom as a follow-up to work done in the lab. Maze, modified cloze, and cloze activities based on a unit in the student text are particularly effective in developing specialized vocabulary (see the Appendix for examples of these activities).

The language of graphical representation of knowledge, especially coordinate graphing, seems to be the lingua franca of technical fields, and assignments that ask students to describe and interpret graphs, tables, and charts teach them necessary field-specific vocabulary. Although familiarity with graphical representation of knowledge is integral to the sciences, college students in all fields will at some point be called on to plot, read, describe, and interpret graphs, and therefore need to learn appropriate vocabulary and language structures.

To familiarize my students with the language of graphs, I give them a handout with graph vocabulary (x-axis, y-axis, horizontal axis, vertical axis), words that describe patterns (increase, decrease, rises, reaches a plateau), and vocabulary for interpretation (As x increases, y decreases; y is inversely proportional to x; The graph indicates that ...). The vocabulary used in relation to these coordinate graphs also includes frequent expressions of quantitative description (twice as many, three times as much, double the [unit of measurement], as high as, as low as) and comparison/contrast (in comparison with, in relation to, with the exception of, unlike).

After I introduce this vocabulary, I ask students to bring a field-specific graph to class where they must present it orally or describe and interpret it in writing. This activity helps to make field-specific English language material more accessible to ESL learners and encourages them to produce and respond to their own original material, enabling them to progress to the autonomous stage of language use (Kasper, chap. 1, this volume). The oral presentations do not need to be long and may include some questions from the audience. Students also read and respond to each other's written descriptions of the graphs. A recent class assignment was very successful and yielded the following graphs: "Velocity Fluctuation in Turbulent Flow along an Automobile Side Window," "Voter Turnout for Presidential Elections Expressed as Percentage of Voting Age Population, 1932–1992," "Demand Curve," "Spectral Distribution of Losses for a Typical Multimode Silica Fiber," and "The Relationship between Stress and Strain in a Tensile Testing Experiment." My ESL students practiced and developed cognitive academic language skills as they explained and discussed the highly sophisticated field-specific concepts depicted in these graphs.

I also give students graphs, tables, or charts and ask them to work together in class to prepare written or oral descriptions and interpretations of these materials. One highly interesting set of such visuals, published yearly by *Open Doors*, provides information about both international students studying in the U.S. and students from the U.S. studying abroad. These visuals depict ratios of male to female students across different nationalities, numbers of students across time, geographic origins and destinations, and popular fields of study. The statistical profiles kept by most colleges and universities (e.g., degrees granted; numbers of students in fields; demographics) provide additional useful and interesting resources. Other profiles available through student career centers, government, and popular sources contain descriptive and statistical information about the geographical areas in which students live, employment opportunities, and jobs and income levels. Finally, the UNESCO Statistical

Yearbook (1997) contains information related to the different countries of the world, including, of course, the countries from which our students come. Particularly interesting is the intranational and international statistical information concerning science, technology, and education.

STUDENT RESPONSE

Student response to the use of the laboratory tapes and follow-up classroom materials has been overwhelmingly positive. In a survey of the ITSs taught using these materials, more than half reported that they felt that the materials had not only improved their pronunciation, grammar, and listening comprehension, but had also increased their confidence to teach or present in their respective fields (Myers, 1995). Students say that they appreciate individualized instruction in pronunciation, stress, and intonation. They often remark that they appreciate knowing how to say the field-specific words that they have frequently only read. From low proficiency students who are just learning to segment language at the word level, to the very advanced students refining their prosody, all like being able to practice and work *out loud* for long stretches of class time rather than sitting in polite silence with relatively few opportunities to practice in the classroom. Their interest in the material is clear from their posture, voice quality, gestures, and alertness.

ASSESSMENT

Assessing success using the materials described in this chapter depends on students' proficiency level. Listening comprehension tests at the beginning levels can confirm or disprove passive recognition of words, phrases, or larger units of language represented in these materials, and at the more advanced levels, production can be evaluated through oral presentations and writing assignments.

I found that use of the audiotapes benefitted all my students, even those who did not pass the initial 3-week training workshop and so needed to take the follow-up course. This latter group experienced a significant gain of, on average, 43 points in their comprehensibility scores on the Speaking Proficiency English Assessment Kit (SPEAK) test (1985); (the institutional version of the ETS Test of Spoken English). This gain was achieved by the end of one semester of study. Moreover, in evaluations of field-specific oral presentations required at the end of the semester, both I and the two outside evaluators, who included members of students' major departments, found these students considerably more intelligible and more fluent than they had been at the end of the initial training workshop.

As always in educational research, there are many variables in addition to instructional materials at work, and students' gains were likely also influenced by instructor enthusiasm and by experiences outside of class during the semester. Nevertheless, the results were very positive. I continue to use these materials, and incoming students still work hard with them, still appreciate them for the same reasons, and still continue to make good improvement in their communicative and academic language skills.

CONCLUSION

All of the materials and assignments described in this chapter are meant to facilitate the learning of field-specific language needed by college-level ESL students. Although I developed the materials to help graduate ITAs acquire the English language proficiency they needed to teach their classes, the tapes are certainly applicable to any and all college level ESL students. ESL students in college come to learn more than English; they come to study and become proficient in a variety of different disciplines. To do this, however, they need to become familiar with the language of these fields. A content-based ESL course offers the ideal setting to introduce students to field-specific language, and at the same time, to give them the practice they need to develop strong listening and speaking skills in English.

As teachers of college level ESL students studying many diverse fields, we need to recreate, insofar as possible, content-based contexts in which students can act out various modes of discourse. We can model various discourse modes; for example, the role of a person trying to enter a debate, or one trying to change a subject. We can then have students practice these discourse modes in small groups or with the class at large. The in-class presentation of audiovisuals provides a context for teaching the language of these functions, and one in which students can rehearse their roles as professionals engaged with other professionals.

For the most part, international students work hard to understand their subjects and they intend to continue working hard. They need to develop the ability to listen, understand, and speak about their areas of study; in short, they need to develop the ability to function autonomously in an English-speaking academic environment (Kasper, chap. 1, this volume). As Hutchinson and Waters (1987) reminded us, these students come to us as a valuable instructional resource. By designing content-based activities that capitalize on and further develop the rich, field-specific knowledge base that ESL students bring to our courses, we can help them shine and give them the power to become full members of the academic community.

REFERENCES

Asher, J. (1982). *Learning another language through actions: The complete teacher's guide*. Los Gatos, CA: Sky Oak Productions.

Ausubel, D. (1968). *Educational psychology: A cognitive view*. New York: Holt, Rinehart, & Winston.

Carrell, P. L., & Eisterhold, J. (1983). Schema theory and ESL reading pedagogy. *TESOL Quarterly, 17*, 553–573.

Chafe, W., & Danielewicz, J. (1987). Properties of spoken and written language. In R. Horowitz & S. J. Samuels (Eds.), *Comprehending oral and written language*, (pp. 83–113). San Diego, CA: Academic Press.

Cohen, A. D. (1990). *Language learning: Insights for learners, teachers, and researchers*. New York: Newbury House.

Cummins, J. (1981). The role of primary language development in promoting educational success for language minority students. In J. Cummins (Ed.), *Schooling and language minority students: A theoretical framework* (pp. 1–50). Los Angeles: Evaluation, Dissemination, and Assessment Center.

Ellis, R. (1990). *Instructed second-language acquisition*. Oxford: Basil Blackwell, Ltd.

Gardner, R. C., & MacIntyre, P. D. (1991). An instrumental motivation in language study: Who says it isn't effective? *Studies in Second Language Acquisition, 13*, 57–72.

Hutchinson, T., & Waters, A. (1987). *English for specific purposes*. Cambridge: Cambridge University Press.

Johns, A. M. (1997). *Text, role, and context: Developing academic literacies*. Cambridge: Cambridge University Press.

Johnson, P. (1982). Effects on reading comprehension of building background knowledge. *TESOL Quarterly, 16*, 503–516.

Krashen, S. (1982). *Principles and practice in second language acquisition*. Oxford: Pergamon.

Krashen, S. (1985). *Input hypothesis: Issues and implications*. New York: Longman.

Krashen, S., & Terrell, T. (1983). *The natural approach: Language acquisition in the classroom*. Englewood Cliffs, NJ: Alemany/Prentice Hall.

Lewis, M. (1993). *The lexical approach: The state of ELT and a way forward*. London: Language Teaching Publications.

Markham, P., & Latham, M. (1987). The influence of religion-specific background knowledge on the listening comprehension of adult second-language students. *Language Learning, 37*, 157–170.

Metz, P. (1997). *Chemistry 1107 Principles of Chemistry I Laboratory Manual*. Palmyra, PA: Chemical Education Resources.

Myers, S. A. (1995). Using written text to teach oral skills: An ITA training class using field-specific materials. *English for Specific Purposes, 14*(3), 231–245.

Open Doors (1996/97). New York: Institute of International Education. [Online]. Available: http://www.ne.org/opendoors/forstud6htm [April 17, 1998]

Richards, J. C., & Rodgers, T. S. (1986). *Approaches and methods in language teaching: A description and analysis*. Cambridge: Cambridge University Press.

Rumelhart, D. (1980). Schemata: The building blocks of cognition. In R. Spiro, B. Bruce, & W. Brewer (Eds.), *Theoretical issues in reading comprehension*. Hillsdale, NJ: Lawrence Erlbaum Associates.

Savignon, S. J. (1983). *Communicative competence: Theory and classroom practice*. Reading, MA: Addison-Wesley.

Speaking Proficiency English Assessment Kit (1985). Princeton, NJ: Educational Testing Service.

UNESCO Statistical Yearbook (1997). [Online]. Web Table of Contents. Available: http://www.unesco.org/generallenglTOC.html [17 April, 1998]

Strevens, P. (1988). The learner and teacher of ESP. In D. Chamberlain & R. J. Baumgardner (Eds.), *ESP in the classroom: Practice and evaluation*, ELT Document 128, (pp. 39–44). Modern English Publications in association with the British Council.

Wilkins, D. A. (1976). *Notional syllabuses*. London: Oxford University Press.

APPENDIX:
SAMPLE MAZE, MODIFIED CLOZE,
AND CLOZE ACTIVITIES[1]

Original text:

In 1789, Antoine Lavoisier proposed the theory that matter is neither created nor destroyed during a chemical transformation. During such processes, chemical bonds in reactants are broken, and new bonds are formed in products, but the number and identity of individual atoms remain unchanged.

Maze activity using this text:

In 1789, Antoine Lavoisier proposed the (theory/theorem/theorist) that matter is neither (fixed/created/reacted) nor (detracted/destroyed/detonated) during a chemical transformation. During such processes, chemical (bond/band/bonds) in reactants are broken, and new (bonds/band/bind) are formed in products, but the number and identity of individual (atoms/atom/random) remain unchanged.

Modified cloze activity, using the same text:

In 1789, Antoine Lavoisier proposed the (t) _____ that matter is neither (c) _____ nor (d) _____ during a chemical transformation. During such processes, chemical (b) _____ are formed in products, but the number and identity of individual (a) _____ remain unchanged.

Cloze activity, using the same text:

In 1789, Antoine Lavoisier proposed the _____ that matter is neither _____ nor _____ during a chemical transformation. During such processes, chemical _____ in reactants are broken, and new _____ are formed in products, but the number and identity of individual _____ remain unchanged.

---

[1](adapted from Metz, 1997, p. 5)

III

Incorporating Technology Into Content-Based Instruction

9

Computers as Content and Context in a Cross-Cultural Language Field Experience

Joy Egbert
Indiana University

*N*ow, I'm in the education building to complete my slideshow. But, I'm afraid that my slideshows are not so great as others' and that I'm a little worried about tomorrow's going to meet children 'cause I'm all thumbs about computer. I don't think I can teach or help them anything. However, I'll have confidence.

While I was taking this class, I realize how much similarity I and American kids have even though we different from nationality and culture. I think there are not many difference between them and Korean kids.

These comments were made as entries in ESL students' e-mail journals as part of an Intensive English Program (IEP) elective course called "Kids and Computers." The comments emphasize two of the roles that technology may play in content-based ESL instruction—the technology can serve as the content of the course, and it can also provide the context in which other content learning, for example, culture, takes place.

Content-based college ESL courses have proven successful in helping students develop language skills as English becomes their means to acquire knowledge. However, although students study within an English-speaking context, few assignments or classes encourage or require them to get out into the environment with native speakers. Incorporating a content-based field experience into the ESL course can provide students with a valuable opportunity for linguistic interaction, within the native speaker community, on both a basic interpersonal and a cognitive academic level. This interaction supports many real world conditions, especially authentic audience, social interaction, and authentic task.

In other words, such classes can be critical to creating what many recent (and some not as recent) L2 acquisition–instruction theories describe as an optimal learning environment (see, for example Egbert, 1993; Spolsky, 1989; Vygotsky, 1978). According to the literature, such an environment includes the following eight conditions (from Egbert, 1993):

1. Learners have opportunities to interact and negotiate meaning.
2. Learners interact in the target language with an authentic audience.
3. Learners are involved in authentic tasks.
4. Learners are exposed to and encouraged to produce varied and creative language.
5. Learners have enough time and feedback.
6. Learners are guided to attend mindfully to the learning process.
7. Learners work in an atmosphere with ideal stress/anxiety level.
8. Learner autonomy is supported.

Content-based instruction (CBI) incorporating community-based field experience as an extension of the classroom language learning environment can help teachers to develop tasks that provide the possibility of meeting these eight conditions and of optimally facilitating students' language acquisition. By tapping primary English language resources with whom students can interact for real purposes, supporting students' active learning, and providing students with choices in approach to the content, these tasks encourage students to learn and use language as a vehicle for further learning, and not as an end in itself. As Hanson-Smith (1999) noted,

> [Researchers] have described fairly completely how students can acquire collocations and related vocabulary items when they are studied not in isolation, but rather with the purpose of mastering an area of learning that the student is already interested in or may have some expertise with in his/her own language, such as business, geography, history, technology, literature, art, etc. [This] is an outgrowth of the belief that students learn best when the content of instruction is a subject matter rather than the language itself. (p. 1)

Making native speakers part of the learning process teaches and supports practice in the pertinent language skills and vocabulary (a critical component of CBI; cf. Richard-Amato & Snow, 1992), makes the study of these skills more authentic, and creates a "highly participatory, dynamic classroom environment in which students are challenged to achieve goals and realize their full potential" (Richard-Amato, 1992, p. 283). By working with native speakers outside of the classroom, purposeful content (the academic goals) and implicit content (pragmatics, social rules, and so on) can become the medium through which authentic, content-based language is learned.

According to Hilles and Lynch (1997, p. 376), "culture ... is a critical topic which should be addressed in content-based instruction" because "a knowledge of culture is essential if we are to truly understand diversity." Engaging ESL students in an intercultural interaction with native speakers of English creates an authentic context for using language to share information and to negotiate meaning. I have found that a cross-cultural language field experience offers highly relevant content for English language instruction, and that the context in which this content instruction takes place may be broadened and strengthened through computer-based activities. Computer technology can serve as the content of the class, and it can also be a tool as part of the context in which the learning of other content (i.e., culture) takes place.

This chapter describes the development of an elective class in the Intensive English Program (IEP) at Indiana University. This class, which was ultimately called, "Kids and Computers," began as an intercultural exchange and broadened to a project in which computers provided both the content of the course and the context for learning culture as an additional content component. The "Kids and Computers" course engaged IEP students in a cross-cultural, computer-based field experience with 2nd and 3rd grade American students. The objectives of this course were to give international students exposure to and practice with native English speakers while giving native-English-speaking students the opportunity to speak with and learn from international students (e.g., exchanging cultural information), and to assist both groups of students in acquiring computer knowledge and skills.

THE FIRST STEP: EXPLORING CULTURE AS CONTENT

Initially, I began by exploring culture as content for ESL instruction. I decided to set up a language arts–social studies miniproject in which my IEP students would go to a local elementary school and conduct 30-minute cultural workshops with the children. I had made some connections with teachers at the elementary school, and they agreed to participate in this mini-project, which paired my college- or profession-bound international students with classes from kindergarten through sixth grade. These IEP students, who came from Korea, Argentina, Italy, Japan, Indonesia, and Venezuela, had been placed in my advanced level (Level 7 out of 7) ESL reading–writing class based on successful completion of previous levels or their score on the in-house placement test.

This type of cross-cultural, cross-age interaction seemed to be a fruitful and effective way not only of bringing the IEP students and the community closer together, but also of meeting many of the conditions for an optimal language learning environment. Not only did the language learners have an authentic audience with whom to interact, they also had control over their topics and methods of presentation, and plenty of time and help to develop their ideas. With "culture" as the content emphasis, the IEP students more easily generated topics to write about, focused more clearly on the vocabulary and language skills necessary to present their ideas, and interacted with the community on a topic of interest or relevance to them. My IEP students wrote process essays on the topic of their workshop—for example, learning regional dances, making ethnic foods, or creating native crafts—and, after working with the children, revised their compositions.

Although my reading–writing course involved other activities, this miniproject was by far its most successful aspect and one that the IEP students across the board noted as their favorite language learning experience in the United States. They said that learning about American culture while interacting with native speakers, rather than simply reading about it in a text, enhanced their understanding of American customs and at the same time gave them much-needed practice with the language. They stressed that basing this interaction on a topic on which they were experts (i.e., aspects of their home culture) made them more comfortable interacting in English. All of the students commented that studying culture as a way to learn reading and writing skills was much more interesting than studying only those skills. The success of this mini-project encouraged me to search for other content-based ways to connect the IEP students with classrooms in the community in language field experience.

STEP TWO: INTEGRATING COMPUTERS AND CULTURE

Although I began by focusing on the value of culture as content, I soon realized that the context of instruction could be broadened and strengthened by the use of computer technology. While visiting the local elementary school during the miniproject just described, I noticed that the school had computer technology but did not seem to have a set agenda for using it. This surprised me because computers have so much to offer as part of CBI. They not only deliver and support the discussion of content, but they also allow students to explore and shape it in ways suited to their learning styles and preferences. I was also aware that the IEP students wanted to learn about computers because computer electives were among the most popular in the IEP. I therefore decided to broaden the focus of my content-based course, addressing culture, technology, and English language issues while bringing IEP students together with native speakers in the community. The result was the "Kids and Computers" elective class.

I was lucky enough to have as a student a computer-using teacher from a local elementary school who was enthusiastic about putting together a computer-enhanced project that would pair her combined 2nd and 3rd grade elementary school class with my IEP students. With a minigrant from the ESL magazine *Hands-On English,* we began planning a project.

Developing the Project

While the elementary school teacher put together a schedule for the project and initiated a World Wide Web home page for it, I put together a syllabus for the elective course and hoped that enough IEP students would sign up to make the project work. The elementary school teacher and I discussed what projects we could do, what software we would need, and how the project would work given the college semester time constraints, her classroom setup, and the technology available to us. It took some revising and rethinking of our initial ideas, but we came up with a workable plan and the "Kids and Computers" elective was created.

The project's primary goal was for IEP and elementary students, to form teams and for these teams to develop computer slide shows describing similarities and differences among group members. For the IEP students it was advertised as a course with computers and American culture (specifically children and the U.S. school system) as content, with part of the course taking place at the elementary school. I expected, based on registration trends at my college, that students mainly interested in learning about computers would join this class. For the elementary children, project objectives included gaining understanding of other cultures, learning about computers, practicing reading and writing, and being creative.

Blending Language, Literacy, and Computers

Our work started from the themes of "similarities" and "differences" in children's texts such as *We Are All Alike, We Are All Different* (Cheltenham Elementary School Kindergartners, 1994), and *Yo! Yes?* (Raschka, 1993), both of which present a variety of links between characters of different cultures. *Yo! Yes?* focuses on the need for all people to have friends and the perceived barrier of cultural differences, and *We Are All Alike, We Are All Different* compares basic physical and abstract similarities and differences among peoples and cultures. These books were chosen because we felt that their succinct, basic introduction to cultural themes would provide a good springboard to content for all of the students involved in the project.

STEP THREE: GETTING READY

The elective course met for 4 hours per week for 7 weeks. The eight advanced level IEP students who signed up for the course were from Korea, Colombia, and Brazil, and, to my surprise, most of them joined the class to learn about culture from the children rather than to specifically learn about computers.

These IEP students spent the first 2 weeks of the 7-week session in a campus lab learning about computers. They established e-mail accounts through which they would send me weekly messages as an electronic journal assignment. They also trained in the use of Broderbund's *Kid Pix* software. *Kid Pix* is a basic presentation package that allows users to draw or construct a series of individual screens or "slides" and make them into a slide show with sound and transitions. We chose this software because it is simple enough to be accessible to both groups of students in the short period of time we had and because the elementary school children were already somewhat familiar with it.

The IEP students created slide shows with scanned images, sound, animation, color, and imported graphics. They called these slide shows "All About Me." The theme, "All About Me," was chosen as a prelude to and demonstration for a subsequent slide show project, "All About Us," that we hoped the IEP and elementary school students would put together based on similarities and differences between their cultures. Figure 9.1 shows some of the slides from the IEP students' shows.

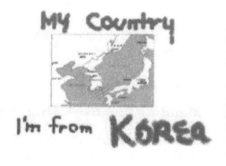

FIG. 9.1. "All About Me" slides (without color or animation).

During this project, the IEP students would be teaching the elementary school students about computers and showing them how to scan, draw, input sound, and make slide shows in *Kid Pix*. The IEP students were excited and a bit nervous about meeting with and dealing with the children for the first time because they were not sure how to act and whether they would be able to understand and communicate with the children. Excerpts from their weekly e-mail messages reveal this excitement and apprehension:

"How are you doing today? I am very excited about the class and the kids whom I will teach. I believe they must be cute and so lovely. I love kids and that is why I decided to take this class. Last night I read the book "Kid Pix", but it's a little confusing because I just read without computer."

"I'm a little nervous about teaching the kids. However, I think I can do it well. My minor is English education, so next year I will go to junior high school to teach students just for one months. I'm supposed to get credit from the teaching but it's not a real kind of teaching. So I'm thinking about the way to teach English to junior-high school students effectively. It's a very hard question. Anyway, I believe that this class would be great experience for me."

"Hi! At that time when I saw this class on the bulletin of this session, I was so excited and actually somewhat surprised at the fact that someone had come up with such an interesting and cool idea. Therefore, I wondered what kind of person the teacher of this class would be like. I like children so much that people around me would say to me, 'You should have become a kindergarten or elementary teacher.' Anyway, I'd like to say that I hope I'll enjoy this class with your help. Good luck."

My interacting with the IEP students via computer during the course (in other words, using the computer as an integrated part of the context) helped us meet the conditions for optimal language learning in several ways. Students received feedback from me whenever they asked for it, in the amounts that they asked for. In addition, this interaction helped to lessen the students' debilitative feelings of anxiety and helped them to focus their stress in productive ways. None of my messages from the early part of the course commented on specific language skills (or the lack of them); instead, students were focused on the content of the course and on using their language to communicate in authentic ways.

Starting in Week 3, the IEP students went to the elementary school twice a week and met on campus the other two class days. The elementary teacher had already made teams of four to five children each, and during their "school" days, the IEP students worked in pairs, one pair to each team of children.

THE PROJECT AND ITS OUTCOMES

Problems and Solutions

A number of problems came up over the course of the project, and working together to find solutions to these problems enabled students to progress culturally, linguistically, and academically. During the first day with the children, my students chatted about themselves and their projects; they had meant to present their "All About Me" demonstration slide shows, but had made a mistake saving things on their computer disks. Although this error threw our plans a bit off schedule, it taught students a valuable lesson about using computers. Thus, it was a good learning experience that would help them avoid similar problems in the future. On the second visit, the IEP students showed their slide shows as models; however, things got off to a slow start because of cultural differences—the children weren't used to the IEP students, and the IEP students weren't used to the "freedom" of American classrooms or dealing with children (e.g., keeping their attention, managing their learning). In addition, logistically there were only five computers in the elementary school classroom—one for each group—so that all of the members of each team were not able to work on the computer at once.

Once we started going to the elementary school, the content of the course changed of necessity. Rather than learning about computers, we discussed American education, children, and related topics. The role of the computer changed, too, from the focus of the class to a tool for communication (e-mail) and a context for building group understanding. To help the IEP students understand the children better, on the days when they were not at the elementary school, these students had problem-solving or working sessions in the computer lab on campus. During one of their first problem-solving sessions, the IEP students received and discussed this handout (Fig. 9.2), based on the acronym "TEACH," and designed to guide them in their interactions with the children.

During these sessions we also discussed problems and questions such as what to do with the children who weren't at the computer, how to deal with time, and so on. The IEP students voiced some of their pleasure and concerns to me both in class and through e-mail, in messages like these:

"I have a great time whenever I go to the school, but I'm worried that I'm not a good teacher. As you know, it's really hard to keep the kids be interested about our project. Today, I tried to find something common between ourselves. You told us that we'd better to find common things not just from our group but also from all kinds of people. I tried to talk to them about that we all have two eyes, a mouth, a nose, and two ears. After that, I thought it's too general, so I changed the topic to something we all like. At the end of the class, I felt that the kids were

---

Kids and Computers

- Try to encourage the kids to use their creativity—encourage them and let them do things their way unless it's inappropriate.
- Everyone needs time to understand—repeat yourself as many times as it takes.
- All of your kids have something to say. Make sure that you pay equal attention to all of them.
- Create a friendly environment. Be fair with computer time!
- Handle with care—don't take the mouse away from students or change anything they do because you personally don't like it. Put your hand on their hand on the mouse to guide them if they need it, and help your group to work well together and agree on things.
- Have fun!!

FIG. 9.2.

getting losing the interests to find common things. I think next time will be better (or harder) to get the interests again because we're gonna teach the drawing tools."

"I asked SY [one of the other IEP students] about teaching after the class. I think she knows a lot better than me. I love kids but I'm not a good teacher so far. However, I'm not disappointed yet. I'm still trying to be a good teacher. Can you give me a piece of good advice for the teaching and controlling the kids? Thank you for reading me.

p.s. Whenever the teacher stands next to our group, I can't say anything to the kids. Because I'm worried that they can think I'm stupid. Isn't it stupid that I think like this?"

"My project is not working so well. I realize that I'm so old that it is so difficult to imagine the world of the children. I'm trying to think about my childhood, and to find out the common thing that I can share with the children. Please, give me some tips."

Benefits

Despite some difficulties, each of the students involved in the project derived significant benefits as they worked together with team members solving problems and building cross-cultural friendships. The IEP students' comments reflect their deep involvement in the project and indicate an increase in their awareness not only of factors related to culture and age, but also of ways to handle problems that came up in the interpersonal exchange.

In addition, the course emphasis on content and the relationship between CBI and optimal learning was reflected in students' comments, more in what they didn't say than what they did; they were intent on using language as a vehicle for communication, teaching, and learning, and were not consumed with worries about discrete grammar points or how this course would help them to pass the Test of English as a Foreign Language (TOEFL). The IEP students, involved in social interaction with their kids about the course content, were engaged in motivating, authentic tasks.

The elementary school children also benefitted because their classroom teacher kept them involved and motivated, prepping them for our arrival, reading and discussing the books on culture noted before, explaining the task, seeing that the students did their homework, and getting in touch with experts when we had computer or other problems.

Producing the Computer Slideshow

To promote cohesiveness, teams were encouraged to create team names. The teams chose names such as "Friends 'til the End," "Boys and Girls," and "Paper Airplanes." Working from ideas in the childrens' texts previously mentioned, the IEP students and their elementary school partners listed their similarities and differences, decided which were worth attention, and divided those into categories for which the children would draw slides. The children were given worksheets to create their slides; they completed some of this work in class, some for homework. The teams then arranged their slides in order on a storyboard and decided to take turns using the team's computer. Students took turns at the computer with one student helper and one of their IEP students to assist. During this time, the second IEP team leader worked on relevant activities with the rest of the team or with the class. At the beginning, these activities involved just casual chatting or discussing the project, but as the project progressed, the IEP and elementary students got involved in such pastimes as creating origami, learning Brazilian dance, perusing photos, postcards, and other artifacts of the IEP students' home cultures, and discussing popular American children's TV shows, toys, and hobbies.

Several times during the project, the IEP students wrote e-mail to the children on their teams, encouraging them, reminding them to do their homework, and saying "Hi." During the final week of the project, the children came to the university for a day-long field trip to use our computer lab and put their slides together into shows. In addition to eating lunch and playing games, the children also participated in a group brainstorming session to evaluate the project.

On our last meeting day at the school, we had a party with food representing the IEP students' countries. During this final class session we also showed each group's slide show to the whole class on a projection screen. These slide shows

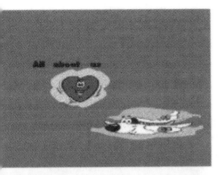

FIG. 9.3. Still Slides From the Group Slide Shows.

were made exciting and interesting through sound, color, and animation. Figure 9.3 shows examples of still depictions of some of these slides.

Students' Feedback on the Project

In their final e-mail messages as part of their electronic journals, the IEP students shared some of their thoughts on the outcome of the project with me. Interestingly, although computers had served as the content for the course, very few of the comments addressed the computer aspects of the course. Rather, most of their comments revealed what the intercultural exchange had taught them about diversity:

> "In this class I learned how is an American elementary school, I learned about the American kids, some things they like and dislike, what are they like when they are in a class. I liked to go there but sometimes it was hard for me to manage the kids, especially some of them."

> "Computer&Kids class. Especially In my team, there was a girl who was not active and not smile. At the first time when we met, she seemed to be very shy and

not so interested. But as class goes on, she began to not only feel enjoyable but also like me so much. What a wonderful experience it is!"

"Through that experience, I could learn about children. I want to be a teacher, so it is really helpful to me. I am also delight because I got through American school system. If I will be a teacher, I will take advantage of that experience. Korea's school system is very hard, but American school system is very freely. I thought that I want to be a pioneer who can change our country's education system."

"... this class is wonderful. I've learn, it's difficult to understand kids and how they think. This time I was trying to think about how kids think for the first time, it is very good experience. I got an idea about what the elementary school system a little. It's gonna be good to compare with our school system in Korea. and I've good relationship with other students, it's wonderful."

"I really enjoyed this class. I learned how to use computer, most of all, I was very happy that I could teach elementary school students. Yesterday, I felt sorry that I couldn't see them any more. But I think it was really good time with kids. I could realize how my English is poor. Because, although I know grammar and vocabulary very well, when speaking, I make a lot of mistakes such as tense, articles, and accordance. But they used accurate grammar and, even though they couldn't understand well, they listened to me. As time went by, kids showed me how they like me and I was so happy."

"Sometimes kids tried to teach slang or some words that kids use. Whenever they did, I wanted to learn that words, but there were many which they could not explain."

CONCLUSIONS AND SUGGESTIONS

By getting out into the community and interacting with native speakers in a real-world context for authentic language use, the IEP students learned not only about kids and computers, but also about many social–pragmatic aspects of communicating in English. Although the project didn't turn out exactly as the elementary school teacher and I had originally envisioned it, it was a great experience for all of us. We had expected that the teams would address culture in more specific ways, but they generally stayed at the level of individual likes and dislikes. We had also hoped that the projects would be more complex, but insufficient time and technology problems affected the final results.

Nevertheless, this project, using computers as content and context in a cross-cultural language field experience, helped to create an optimal language learning environment for the IEP students. Applying a CBI approach and extending the notion of "classroom" environment to include a community of native speakers helped to ensure an ideal atmosphere for many of the students because the task and audience were authentic, and the students not only had control over parts of their learning, but also had the structure and feedback necessary to help them succeed. The IEP students were clearly cognitively engaged and motivated, and the social interaction within their teams, among students themselves in the classroom, and between individual students and myself provided them with authentic contexts in which to use and learn language.

Learning about computers in the process of an intercultural exchange enabled students to learn relevant vocabulary and language skills while developing their computer skills. The integration of e-mail into the context of the course provided a means by which both the IEP students and their elementary school partners could receive encouragement and other crucial forms of feedback and participate in social interactions outside of class.

Although we were able to meet many of the conditions for optimal learning, unfortunately the 7-week session did not allow us to meet the condition of optimal time, for we could have used at least another week or two to allow for adequate follow-up. However, both groups of students gained an awareness of intercultural differences and similarities as they practiced new language and computer skills. The choice of the *Kid Pix* software was a good one in that the program is simple to use but can also support more advanced slide show features. This made it easier to focus on the content of the project instead of on students' computer skills.

There are, however, many ways to improve the project to make it not only a more effective language and culture learning experience for the IEP students, but also a more efficient way to learn content. There are many more great trade books that deal with issues of culture and diversity, and it would have been helpful to do more reading and to connect the reading more closely to the slide show project. We also should have planned for providing the IEP students with more training in how to deal with young children, adding readings and perhaps guest speakers from the School of Education and local schools to the problem-solving portion of the course.

Interested readers should be aware that there are many ways of creating optimal classroom language learning environments for ESL learners of all ages and levels. Visiting other schools and working with content that is authentic to all participants, as in the course described in this chapter, is only one way. Depending on the content of the course, native speakers with relevant knowledge and language can be found in a great many places. For example, students can also make content-based connections with other classes in their own school, they can connect with experts in the community, and they can take advantage of the global community that the Internet provides (for more on the Internet and language learning, see Egbert & Hanson-Smith, 1999). Connections can be made between college ESL classes and retired persons groups, high school language students, or penpals anywhere in the world. The main point to remember is that while the content and context of the cross-cultural language field experience are flexible, the benefits to be derived from this experience are many.

ACKNOWLEDGMENT

This project was made possible by the participation of J. Spilotro and her S.M.I.L.E. 2nd and 3rd grade combined class at Templeton Elementary School in Bloomington, Indiana, support from the Center for English Language Training at Indiana University, and a minigrant from *Hands-on English*. All examples are used with permission.

REFERENCES

Cheltenham Elementary School Kindergartners (1994). *We are all alike, we are all different*. New York: Scholastic.

Egbert, J. (1993). *Learner perceptions of computer-assisted language learning environments: Analytic and systemic analyses*. Unpublished doctoral dissertation. Tucson, AZ: University of Arizona.

Egbert, J., & Hanson-Smith, E. (Eds.). (1999). *CALL environments: Research, practice, and critical issues*. Alexandria, VA: TESOL.

Hanson-Smith, E. (1999). Content-area tasks in CALL environments. In J. Egbert & E. Hanson-Smith (Eds). *CALL environments: Research, practice, and critical issues* (pp. 137–158). Alexandria, VA: TESOL.

Hilles, S., & Lynch, D. (1997). Culture as content. In M. A. Snow & D. M. Brinton (Eds.) *The content-based classroom: Perspectives on integrating language and content* (pp. 371–376). New York: Longman.

Raschka, C. (1993). *Yo! Yes?* New York: Scholastic.

Richard-Amato, P. (1992). Peer teachers: The neglected resource (chap. 18). In P. Richard-Amato & M. Snow (Eds*)., The multicultural classroom: Readings for content-area teachers* (pp. 271–284). White Plains, NY: Longman.

Richard-Amato, P., & Snow, M. (Eds.) (1992). *The multicultural classroom: Readings for content-area teachers*. White Plains, NY: Longman.

Spolsky, B. (1989). *Conditions for second language learning*. Oxford: Oxford University Press.

Vygotsky, L. (1978). *Mind in society: The development of higher psychological processes*. Cambridge, MA: Harvard University Press.

10

The Keyboard to Success

An ESL/Basic Writing Internet Partnership

David A. Tillyer
The City College of New York

Louise S. Wood
Tri-County Technical College

Electronic mailing was the best thing I have encountered in my days of living.

Martha,[1] a developmental English student,[2] wrote this enthusiastic response following her participation in an intercultural electronic mail exchange between our classes, a basic writing[3] class at Tri-County Technical College (Pendleton, South Carolina) and an English as a Second Language (ESL) class at City College of New York.

We came up with the idea of an intercultural exchange because we saw a strong need for an interesting and real situation to spawn spontaneous, purposeful writing. Our students viewed writing as what they were required to produce for a grade, not as a lively, organic means to express their joys, their

---

[1] All students' names are pseudonyms and student writings are unedited to preserve authenticity.

[2] Developmental English courses are designed to prepare students for college-level English. Students are assigned to these courses on the basis of placement scores.

sorrows, and their curiosities. We saw the intercultural exchange as an opportunity to introduce our students to culture as a content area (Hilles & Lynch, 1997) and to encourage them to explore and articulate cultural diversity.

Martha and other students like her have shown us that such a venture can excite and motivate reluctant writers by providing an opportunity for dynamic, authentic communication and a context for intercultural friendship. In this chapter, we draw from our experiences working together for three semesters to explain our reasons for participating in an exchange, describe the process of conducting one, consider problems encountered, and enumerate positive outcomes. In addition, we offer guidelines for a productive intercultural e-mail exchange.

Although ESL and basic writing (BW) students differ in their language needs, both groups are struggling to gain a level of proficiency in English necessary for the rigors of college-level work. As such, many feel insecure, believing that they lack the status of more advanced students. For both ESL and BW students, electronic mail acts as a confidence builder. In fact, when our students gain access to the Internet and become proficient at using e-mail, they have a skill that many of their fellow students lack.

This added confidence is highly beneficial and helps our marginalized populations feel a greater sense of belonging. Just as significant as the added confidence, however, is the motivation to write provided by the e-mail project. We found that both ESL and BW students groups hungered for communication, and both groups found real satisfaction in the exchange. The exchange, however, met differing needs in the two groups, and, as instructors, our reasons for participating differed somewhat. Consequently, we will discuss our rationale from both the basic writing and the ESL perspective.

LOU: THE BASIC WRITING PERSPECTIVE

For the BW student, e-mail correspondence provides a valuable "real world" writing experience that allows for purposeful communication with a responsive partner. As Daly (1985) wrote, "How one writes—indeed, whether one writes—is dependent on more than just skill or competence. The individual must also want to write or, at the very least, must also find some value in the activity" (p. 44). Most BW students who enter my classes, however, do not want to write and are not in the habit of communicating through writing; in fact, most do not perceive writing as a legitimate means of communication. Writing is an activity they reluctantly perform for a teacher as a course requirement, and, as such, it serves no useful purpose that they can see. As Shaughnessy pointed out concerning BW students who have repeatedly experienced failure, writing may be viewed as "a trap, not a way of saying something to someone" (Shaughnessy, 1977, p. 7). Shaughnessy further reports that "they [BW students] have been writing infrequently, and then only in such artificial and strained situations that the communicative purpose of writing has rarely if ever seemed real" (p. 14).

E-mail correspondence, with its easy, conversational tone, provides a reason to write and a way to overcome this reluctance by allowing students to write in a non-threatening situation that seems natural, not "artificial and strained." Although basic writers are by no means a homogeneous group, my developmental students typically do not see themselves as writers and have not been successful in previous attempts, and generally display a negative attitude toward writing. Such a negative attitude can impede learning, whereas activities that foster positive emotions like "confidence and curiosity" aid in learning (Smilkstein, 1993). E-mail correspondence counters negative attitudes and builds confidence because students succeed. Their partners welcome their words and respond to them, and the screen bears no red marks. As genuine communication takes place, students become eager to write. Until I began using e-mail in my BW class, I had never found my students waiting to get into the classroom at 7:45 a.m. when I arrived.

The partnership with ESL students offers additional benefits for basic writers. Because BW students are native speakers, corresponding with partners who are learning English elevates them to the unfamiliar role of "expert," and they delight in explaining idioms and other terms or phrases unfamiliar to their partners. The constructivist school tells us that students engaged in dialogue are better able to build "a personal knowledge base that they understand" (Brooks & Brooks, 1993). Judy, for instance, a particularly conscientious BW student, took her role of teacher quite seriously and brought in several pages of idioms that she and her family had spent hours recalling. She periodically made these available to the New York group and was pleased that the ESL students clamored for more. Interestingly though, at the same time that they enjoyed this new role, my students also felt a kinship with their ESL partners because they both were working to improve their proficiency in English. Robert, a BW student, sensed this complementary need when he wrote to his partner Olga, a Russian immigrant:

> Yes, the English language can be a complicating subject. Take me for instance, I have lived in the United States all of my life, and I have trouble speaking, spelling, and writting. We are nearly all in the same boat.

The intercultural aspect of the exchange adds another dimension to the classroom. Exchanging ideas and establishing relationships with students from other cultures can enrich the class and engender understanding as no textbook can. Susan (a BW student) wrote about her experience, "This helped me by bringing to light how we all label people we don't know or understand. I gained a new friend from a culture I didn't understand, but I do ... now." For many of my rural BW students, knowledge of the world is limited largely to their rural South Carolina communities. Learning about life in their partners' native countries, as well as urban New York City, broadens their outlook and stimulates thinking, and the whole process becomes an energizing force in the basic writing classroom.

DAVID: THE ESL PERSPECTIVE

At CCNY our computers are battered XTs left behind when the Psychology Department moved up to more powerful machines to run their statistics packages. However, despite the hand-me-down technology with a grueling log-on procedure, our students grow really enthusiastic about e-mail. The difficulty is in stopping the writing process when the next class is hovering. The intercultural nature of the exchanges has been an eye-opener for the urban immigrants at CCNY. As denizens of an international city, my students rarely meet "real" Americans, much less talk to them. Even native-born New Yorkers seem to be somewhat apart from the American mainstream. Therefore, an exchange with South Carolina folks who talk about their daily routines, their problems, and their aspirations offers my students a broader perspective on their new country.

Krashen (1987) pointed out that high motivation, robust self-confidence, and low anxiety are the recipe for positive language "acquisition," which he distinguishes from "learning." I have found that using computers for writing to new friends helps to put students in a frame of mind that encourages language acquisition (Dulay & Burt, 1977; Krashen, 1987). There is something uniquely inviting and motivating about a screen that will transport their thoughts to caring partners 600 miles away. Because the ESL and BW students have common needs, they develop a kind of mutual regard for the welfare of their study partners. This regard is plain in the kinds of life stories that they exchange and the kind of advice that they pass back and forth. The mutuality of these exchanges puts the ESL learners on new ground in their English-speaking experience. Suddenly they are elevated to the level of confidante, and the medium is that elusive written English! My students have generally never had such a low-anxiety context for serious English production.

E-mail provides students with an enjoyable context for reading and writing, and students' enthusiasm for e-mail is a major factor in their progress. MacGowan-Gilhooly (1991) stresses the importance of enjoyable reading and writing for effective learning. Garner and Gillingham (1996) took it a step farther and quoted Dyment, who says that e-mail leads to improvements in students' "unity of expression, grammatical competence in a second language, and mechanical aspects of writing (spelling, capitalization, & punctuation) ..." (p. 68). Dyment mirrors my own experience as the authors quote him as saying, "[E-mail writing in the classroom] ... can be so immediate that my students love to write this way ... My students become extremely motivated in not making grammatical and spelling mistakes. It's absolutely amazing to watch this transformation" (1996, p. 69). I have seen the same transformation occur with my ESL students at CCNY; their sentences become longer, they don't shrink from detail, and they are not as afraid to attempt compound and complex sentences.

The process of writing e-mail is interesting. For native speakers, writing e-mail is generally a low-monitor affair. That is, even the most meticulous writers disregard capitalization and eschew proofreading in order to respond quickly to their peers. However, ESL learners take a different tack. My students will gaze at a message from their partners, determination furrowing their brows, laboring over the vocabulary, idiomatic usage, and unfamiliar sentence forms. Their motivation for understanding exactly what the message means is the social, emotional, pure joy of human contact. Krashen says that language learners learn by stretching and by seeking meaning (Krashen, 1987, pp. 30–32). He said, "We acquire by understanding language that contains structure a bit beyond our current level of competence .... This is done with the help of context or extra-linguistic information" (p. 31).

E-mail is "comprehensible input" in its most sublime form. My ESL students are transported over the abyss of language gaps by their desire to understand and to sustain their harmonious electronic relationship. Therefore, they will read and read and read again with dictionary at their elbows in order to understand. Then they will take the leap and write and edit and craft a message that continues the strand of their relationship. Often they will pick up and attempt to use bits and snatches of language that they have recently acquired. They do this not because they desire to regurgitate learning or to satisfy a teacher, but because they desperately and earnestly want to communicate with a partner that they are beginning to care about. That, in my opinion, is the purest form of language learning. This low-anxiety context coupled with the strong desire to communicate make an e-mail exchange the perfect medium for real language learning. This is why I use e-mail exchanges in my classes.

THE CCNY/TRI-COUNTY EXCHANGE

The e-mail exchange between David's ESL class and Lou's basic writing class began in the summer of 1994 and has continued through several terms. Intercultural E-Mail Classroom Connections (IECC),[4] an e-mail forum or "list"[5] devoted exclusively to helping teachers establish intercultural classroom partnerships, provided the forum needed for making the contact.

---

[4] To subscribe to IECC, send an e-mail message to: iecc-he-request@stolaf.edu, and, in the body of the message, type the word *subscribe*.

[5] A list is an automated e-mail distribution system that allows all subscribers to receive any message that is sent to the system. Thus, like-minded "members" of the list can send or post a message and reach everyone on the list.

Hoping to find someone interested in an e-mail exchange, Lou posted a message to IECC in March, 1994 requesting a partner class for a summer project. The message was transmitted to all members of the list (more than 300 at the time, in about 20 countries), and David answered. Below is Lou's message, followed by David's reply:

Date: Sat, 19 Mar 94 22:38:10 EST
From: "David Tillyer, CCNY" <DATCC@CUNYVM.CUNY.EDU>
Subject: Re: Seeking English-speaking College Basic Writing Class
To: LWOOD@tricty.tricounty.tec.sc.us
In-Reply-To: Your message of Fri, 18 Mar 1994 15:06:07–0500 (EST)
On Fri, 18 Mar 1994 15:06:07 -0500 (EST) you said:

My name is Louise Wood, and I teach developmental English at Tri-County Technical College in Pendleton, South Carolina, USA. The average age of our student body is 28, though individual classes may vary significantly from this average.

I am interested in having my basic writing class (15–20) correspond with a similar group during all or part of the summer term. Our summer term begins May 15 and goes through July 31, 1994.

Tri-County is a two-year technical college with an open door policy. I work with students who are admitted to the College but who are not yet ready to go into college English. I want my students to have as many "real world" writing experiences as possible, and I really think they would be very enthusiastic about using electronic mail. I look forward to hearing from some of you with similar interests.

Sincerely,

Louise Wood

Tri-County Technical College

Louise. I'm going to have an ESL class with a significant electronic component this summer +/- July 1–Aug. 5.

Their average age is probably around 24. It's hard to predict, but they will probably be largely Dominican, Chinese, Russian, and Haitian. I will have anywhere from 18 to 28. I always insist that both sides of the pen pal relationship have an assignment of significance to complete. Mine will likely have a five page paper to turn in describing the culture that their pen pal comes from based on their summer-long interview. City College is on 135th Street in Harlem. Most of my people are on financial aid and they will be about 85% freshmen. Do you want to talk further? Peace, David Tillyer City College of New York

City University of New York

DATCC@CUNYVM.CUNY.EDU

Once we determined that our classes would be compatible, we began working out the details for the project and corresponded for over 2 months before starting an intense 3-week exchange in June. We discussed our expectations, the weight of the e-mail assignment, the timing for the exchange, our computer-room access, and class size. As we planned, one problem we encountered was a marked difference in class size. Since the CCNY class was twice the size of the Tri-County class, we decided to have the Tri-County students double up and write to two partners. Before the exchange began, each student at both schools was given an individual computer account and was randomly assigned a partner for the project. Although we questioned the wisdom of random assignments at the onset, so many stimulating and entirely unpredictable relationships (several cross-generational) developed that we continued the practice in succeeding semesters. Typically, classes at CCNY and Tri-County have both traditional students who are recent high school graduates and nontraditional, returning students who are older; thus, the partnerships were rich with possibilities for unusual friendships.

Because most of the students were not computer literate and none were familiar with e-mail, teaching them to use e-mail was essential to the success of the project (Strickland & Strickland, 1993). We each devoted at least one class period to the process and distributed detailed instructions. To give encouragement as students came online, we made sure that each student had an e-mail message from us that both congratulated them on successfully logging in and gave them further instructions.

Although most of the students were able to send a message during the initial session, they needed further practice to become proficient, and some students continued to need support throughout the exchange. For both classes, it has been useful to have more technically oriented students help others. For ESL students, this interaction not only helps them learn the technology but also promotes a purposeful, task-based oral exchange in the target language, and, as Ur (1981) reminded us, task-based discussions are the most useful for developing language skills.

With our computer novices, we could not set up the exchange, leave our students to their own devices, and expect the project to work. Minor problems like miskeyed addresses (o for 0 and l for 1) or forgotten passwords became major daily obstacles to getting messages out, and we needed to be available to help and sometimes intervene. Often we found that the student who was disconsolate over not receiving answers from his partner was the very student who had a mailbox full of returned messages. Some students, with little grasp of the technology, would sit staring at a screen of error messages uncomprehendingly, yet deny utterly that there was a problem. Vigilance was necessary on our parts.

Also, our teacher-to-teacher communication did not end once the project was underway. Indeed, during the exchange we communicated daily and sometimes several times a day. Because the students depended on hearing from their partners and felt rejected when messages did not come, we could allay anxiety by informing each other when a student was sick for any length of time or was having unusual difficulty mastering the system and getting mail out. Students tended to wait patiently when they knew the partner was ill or was attempting to contact them but was having difficulty with the technology. Staying in close contact was important also because on several occasions we had to reassign partners when a student had a lengthy illness or had to withdraw for other reasons.

During the planning process, we both had agreed that having a significant assignment as a focus for the exchange was essential to its success. As Tillyer and Sokolik (1992) pointed out, "A project focuses on the end product and so gives students something tangible to show for their hard work" (p. 47) One of the difficulties lay in designing an assignment that could be an integral part of two different courses. We both wanted to stress intercultural awareness, so we decided to make an activity David had previously used successfully, the culture contact profile, the major assignment of the exchange. Students were to write culture contact profiles of their partners based on information gathered through their e-mail correspondence. We discussed the assignment and distributed a handout at the beginning of the semester so that students would understand the purpose of the exchange. To help them get started on the project, students brainstormed to think of appropriate questions and points that would give them insight into their partner's culture. The three-to-five-page typed paper was to include pertinent information about the partner—including family background, interests, religion, goals, and college major—and a discussion of the partner's culture. Tri-County students discussed both the urban culture of New York and the culture of their partner's country of origin. Both classes were encouraged to use appropriate quotes from their partners and to consult other sources for additional information. Culture contact profiles were graded like other assigned papers for the course but were given double weight to reflect the time and effort needed to complete the assignment.

The response to this short, 3-week exchange far exceeded our expectations. Most notably, students demonstrated a heightened interest in writing. One of the hallmarks of both the ESL classroom and the BW classroom is a near pathological reluctance to write; but, as mentioned before, in both New York and Tri-County we had students waiting by the computer room door for us to unlock it. Typically, in a writing classroom a student will go to his or her seat and wait for instructions, but in our classrooms, students hurried to their computers eagerly seeking word from their distant partners. Our experience is born out by Jaeglin (1998) in his survey of learners' and instructors' attitudes toward computer-assisted discussion. Our classes unanimously and enthusiastically endorsed the project. In fact, one Tri-County student shared her enthusiasm with the president of the college by sending him an electronic message that celebrated her newly found communication mode.

Chun (1998) noted that "… the types of sentences being written by students on the computer require not only comprehension of the preceding discourse but also coherent thought and use of cohesive linguistic references and expressions. These skills, which are important components of writing proficiency, are enhanced by [computer-assisted classroom discussion]" (p. 71). Again our experience supports Chun's point as we found that as students wrote frequently, engaging in real communication, writing became natural and written fluency improved. They were more willing to tackle the complexities of reading ideas and opinions and writing detailed responses.

Because the e-mail exchange we began in the summer of 1994 was so successful, we conducted a similar e-mail exchange during the fall of 1994. Then in the spring of 1995, we again paired our classes for an exchange that lasted approximately ten weeks, the length of time our schedules overlapped. This time, we took a different approach and orchestrated the beginning discussion by giving students in each class a set of questions to start the discussion. These were people who were unused to written dialogue, and the discussion starters were designed to provide "hooks" on which to hang a productive conversation. The thought was that students should get into meaningful dialogue before the questions were all answered and that was fine with us. We tried to select questions that would require more than a superficial answer, and we gave a different set of questions to each group so that the partners would not be responding to questions they had already seen.

CCNY's students were given these questions to ask:

- What qualities do you value in a friend and why are these important?
- Describe a typical day in your weekday life.
- Describe your town and tell me what your neighborhood is like.
- Tell me about a family member or another person who has had a big influence on your life.
- Why did you decide to go to college?
- What do you intend to do when you graduate?

Tri-County's students were given these questions to ask:

- How was your life in your native country different from your life in the U.S.?
- What problems have you encountered in adjusting to American life?
- What are your strengths?

- Tell me about a positive memory you have of your childhood.
- Who or what encouraged you the most to continue in school? Describe that influence.
- Where do you want to be and what do you hope to be doing 10 years from now?

In addition, partly to facilitate discussion, we arranged to have students in both classes read and write on several of the same topics: education, discrimination, the environment, family, and the role of women. Although we tried to synchronize our schedules so that our classes would be writing on the same topic during the same week, neither of us kept on schedule as we had planned. Therefore, while our classes were writing on similar topics, we might have one class finishing a topic before the other class started. Also, we had wanted the partners to discuss the topics and readings and use each other as resources while writing their papers, but we did not structure an assignment to ensure that this collaboration happened. Consequently, this arrangement did not generate as much discussion as we had hoped. This type of exchange, we discovered, is very difficult to monitor, and it is unrealistic to expect students to communicate effectively on so many different topics. Having two, or at most three, well defined collaborative projects is a much more manageable approach.

Somewhat more successful was our students' participation in a forum called THIRTY-L, a LISTSERV mail distribution list. David had used THIRTY-L for several semesters for full-class student exchange. In the spring of 1995, Lou's class joined the list, and the result was an enthusiastic exchange of ideas by a portion of each class. Such an asynchronous electronic discussion, as Doucette (1993) noted, is learner-centered, not teacher-centered, and "often richer and more complex—better—than almost any classroom discussion" (p. 23). Topics of discussion varied from religion, success, and the role of women to musical preferences and current events. Ideally, we had hoped that every student would participate actively, but in reality, approximately one half of the students actually posted messages to the list. Our disappointment that the exchange was not more general on THIRTY-L was softened by the fact that those students who became the "live-wires" on THIRTY-L were not necessarily the most active participants in class discussions.

This is not surprising; Markley (1998) noted that e-mail has an equalizing effect that allows students to establish relationships without regard to appearance. In an e-mail relationship, words, not attractiveness or dress or social status, are all-important. In spite of this, however, most e-mail correspondents sooner or later crave a glimpse of their partners. So it was with our students: The more they came to know their partners, the more they wanted to know. We found that exchanging photos and videos is an effective way to keep this natural curiosity piqued. Therefore, about two thirds of the way through the spring semester, at student urging, we exchanged videos of our classes. In addition to the video, Lou sent David individual photos of her class and some shots of the Tri-County campus. David taped them up on the wall in the computer center and was amazed at how often students got up and went to the wall to look at the faces of their partners.

PROBLEMS ENCOUNTERED

Although these successful exchanges added tremendous vitality to the class-room, they were not without problems. Students who lacked keyboarding skills struggled at first and had to spend more time at the computer. Unequal class sizes meant that some students had to double up and correspond with two partners. (Admittedly some welcomed the opportunity, but often they had difficulty finding the time.) Withdrawals were the most serious problem and necessitated making adjustments after the exchange had started; likewise, un-equally motivated or unresponsive partners created some frustration. (Once THIRTY-L was in place, however, concerned students handled the problem of the unresponsive partner themselves by making inquiries on the list. A partner could not be silent for very long without everyone in both classes wanting to know why). Although these difficulties required attention and flexibility, we were able to work through them, and they were not significant enough to un-dermine the project.

POSITIVE OUTCOMES

The e-mail partnership brought a number of positive results as we have high-lighted throughout this discussion. Most students wrote eagerly and fre-quently, thus overcoming a reluctance to write. Confidence increased and written fluency improved. In the fall and spring exchanges, students were ex-pected to write to their partners a minimum of once a week, but most wrote more frequently, and our more avid e-mailers could often be seen writing and checking their mail several times a day. Their writings, a sampling of which fol-low, served a variety of purposes from discussing an assignment or cultural dif-ferences to giving advice on personal matters or opinions on current issues or events.

In preparing for their culture contact profiles, students on both sides had the opportunity to view life from a different perspective and to explore their own roots as well. In the following message (her second to her partner), Mar-tha, a 36-year-old African American who so enthusiastically endorsed e-mail in the quote that opened this chapter, discussed her background and began to tell her partner about her community and state:

From: TRCADM::TCAXXXXXXX 14-Jun-1994 08:52:54.25
To: SMTP% "XXXXX@CUNYVM.CUNY.EDU"
Subj: response to your message

Hi, Mari I have lived in Anderson, South Carolina since I was born. My grand-
mother and grandfather' parents were slaves. They came to America on a
slaveship. They were sold to a plantation owner. They had to work in the fields
hoeing, planting and picking cotten. If you do know what cotten it is used to
make clothings and diffrent kinds of materials. In South, Carolina farming is
one of majority resoures in the state. The state has a vast number of dairy and
tobbac farms. The city has grown a lot with increase in factories and shopping
centres.

Mari, I will write tomorrow,

Love Big M

Martha, or "Big M" as she referred to herself, had never used a computer
and was unaccustomed to writing. As a result, she lacked keyboarding skills
and her messages were usually brief, even though she took a long time to craft
them. She tended toward simple sentences that moved from one thought to
another without benefit of transition, and, serious about her writing, she
struggled to produce standard English. Partly as a result of these factors, she
wrote haltingly and much less fluently than she spoke. In spite of these difficulties, however, the pull of a new friendship drew her to the keyboard, and she
eagerly communicated with her partner.

Martha became unusually candid in discussing her ancestry with her partner. This openness is typical of the response that comes naturally with the
anonymous intimacy in e-mail correspondence, but that can be difficult to
elicit in a classroom setting. For Martha, this correspondence was a beginning
that helped her gain confidence in her ability to communicate. Through perse-
verance and hard work, she has since gone on to earn an Associate Degree in
Accounting.

In addition to corresponding with partners, students used THIRTY-L to
exchange ideas on a number of academic, personal, and newsworthy topics.
The following are three responses to the Oklahoma City bombing that oc-
curred on April 19, 1995:

Sender: THIRTY-L Discussion List for CCNY
THIRTY-L@CUNYVM.BITNET>
From: R. McClain
<TCXXXXXXX@TRICTY.TRICOUNTY.TEC.SC.US>
Subj: The Bombing
I am appalled and angered by such an act which occured in Oklahoma City.
When President Clinton said that he didn't want the American people intimi-
dated, he is a bit late. Worring about people still trapped in the rubble, could
not sleep last night. How do you feel.
Your class mate
Robert McClain

Sender: THIRTY-L Discussion List for CCNY
<THIRTY-L@CUNYVM.BITNET>
From: lourde <XXXCC@CUNYVM.BITNET>
Subj: Re: The Bombing
Hi, McClain I feel the same way I couldn't sleep last night, about what happen to Okhoma city. I feel so sorried the victims and thier families. There is nothing we can do, but greif with them,up to this point. There are a lot of questions in my mind. Therefore I wonder if you can answer some of them. First why would somebody made a Bomb to kill insent people?

Sender: THIRTY-L Discussion List for CCNY
<THIRTY-L@CUNYVM.CUNY.EDU>
From: Lucien<XXXCC@CUNYVM.CUNY.EDU>
Subj: Justice!!!
Multiple recipients of list THIRTY-L
<THIRTY-L@CUNYVM.CUNY.EDU>
Dear friends,
Last wenesday I was in Canada watching news in french when I heard about the bombing in Oklahoma City. It is really sad to see so any people disappearing at the same time in this cahotic situation. This is really sad. Those bullies arecruel;they must be condemned according to the law established in this country.Those dogs don't even care about children.Oh this is sad! I don't think they are human beings.I wonder what kind of persons they are.I wonder if they have a heart to love,and a brain to think,and a mind to analyze things before they take actions. I wish F.B.I. members to do a good job by finding those dogs (bullies) and punish them as worst as possible. I have a great compassion for the american families who are sad today by losing one of their family's member in this terrific bombing caused by some bullies-dogs-humans. May God help the F.B.I. find them as prompt as possible. Be careful my friends.It is not safe any-more to continue living in this world. Let's pray God to save our life.
Your friend Lucien Charles

These three messages are indicative of a barrage of messages posted to THIRTY-L in the days after the horrific bombing in Oklahoma City. These messages illustrate what e-mail meant to students who rarely write anything more complicated than a grocery list. Writing about the Oklahoma City bombing represented more than a response to a theoretical exam prompt; it represented the expression of feelings about a very real, though incomprehensible event. Robert's response, that of an outraged citizen, is more like what we would see in the letters column of the local paper. However, it is unlikely that he, a basic writing student, would have sent such a letter as this or that the newspaper would have printed it. But here on the forum of THIRTY-L, he was able to express his frustration and anger.

Likewise Lourde, sensing in Robert's words a voice of authority, chose to ask a question. Another person would never have seen this unmonitored writing, unedited and heartfelt, if it were not for this forum. This kind of unfettered writing is essential to building writing confidence. Lourde would not have turned in a class essay with as many errors, but she felt safe sending this message to her classmates.

Lucien's plaint for "Justice!!!" shows his leadership abilities. A strong writer, Lucien could be counted on to jump into the fray on any issue. He, thus, became an anchor in the writing forum. However, in class, he was quiet and almost shy. Lucien's personality also did not show itself so prominently in carefully prepared essays, created for maximum grade-appeal. E-mail did this for Lucien and, months after the class, Lucien still contacts David occasionally via e-mail, demonstrating the writing confidence inspired by this exchange.

Kasper (1998) noted that "task anxiety and insufficient understanding of the writing process ... plague and inhibit the writing performance of ESL students" (p. 59). Lucien and Lourdes do not exhibit "task anxiety" as they rail against the kind of outrage that makes any human being want to communicate. They would not have turned these messages in as a class paper without revising, but the writing process was started in those who would not write without this forum. Kasper continued, " ... mechanical accuracy is not the means to achieving fluency and clarity of expression; rather, mechanical accuracy is the result of having worked to express ideas most fluently and clearly" (p. 59). Lucien and Lourde did not concern themselves with mechanical accuracy in their appeals for justice, but they brought themselves to the new threshold where it was a natural response to write a profoundly held belief. The polishing and shaping work of the editorial process came later. Lourde had the furthest to come and she indeed began to consciously and successfully edit her work over the period of that semester.

A REASON TO WRITE

Whether discussing an assignment, sharing life experiences, or expressing outrage over a criminal act, students had a reason to write and many did so eagerly. Students benefitted from the question–answer format of the e-mail discussion that stimulated thinking and the free exchange of ideas that encouraged students to develop those ideas.

Furthermore, as a result of the exchange, a number of mutually beneficial relationships developed that were not only cross-cultural but also cross-generational. One such partnership between Reyna and Nancy precipitated an unexpected and encouraging change of attitude. Nancy, a diligent, hard-working 50-year-old, had returned to school after a plant lay-off and seriously pursued her studies. Reyna, a young Dominican immigrant with a poor self-image, was a lackluster writer, not concerned enough to correct her errors. David had just about resigned himself to having her repeat her ESL course. However, about 3 weeks before the end of the course, she began revising work that she had not been willing to edit before, and David started receiving notes that Reyna was attending tutoring sessions. David complimented her on her newfound enthusiasm, and the praise seemed to add fuel to the fires of self-renewal. Not until the postsemester exit conference did Reyna confide that she was really inspired by Nancy, her long-distance study partner and her first and only American friend. Nancy had told Reyna to get herself organized and get past her ESL course because she had even bigger hurdles to cross if she wanted a college degree. Eliza Doolittle she was not, but Reyna did pass the course! (Reyna nearly has enough credits to graduate with a degree in education and is currently doing an internship, working with autistic children). For Nancy, the reward lay in knowing what a positive influence she had had on someone else's life.

USING THE COMPUTER: TURNING ANXIETY INTO CONFIDENCE

In addition to the cognitive and affective gains associated with the exchange of ideas and the forming of friendships, students also profited from the use of computers. Many, particularly older students with little or no exposure to computers, were highly apprehensive; thus, in the process of teaching e-mail, we witnessed a great deal of frustration, a few tears, and a record 76 unsuccessful log-in attempts at one sitting. With practice, however, every student learned to use e-mail, and anxiety was replaced by self-assurance. Robert, a middle-aged victim of a plant lay-off, made no secret of his anxiety and had to be pressed to go near a computer. After several days and a few successful exchanges with his partner, however, he became an eager user and announced at the end of the term that he had changed his major from surgical technology to computer technology. Other students with more prior exposure to computers gained in other ways. As Susan, a basic writing student, expressed, "I grew up in a home where the computer has been a mainstay … but never really understood how it could help me." As a result of her active participation in the exchange she saw the computer, for the first time, as a valuable communication tool to help her "gain access" to the outside world.

ASSESSMENT

Kasper (chap. 1, this volume) notes that "assessment is a critical component of any college course, and ideally … should derive from instructional practice." Kasper goes on to say that assessment should "simulate real-world tasks … (that) reflect a students' ability to interact with language and information." Because we agree that instructional practice and evaluative measures should be closely linked, we handled assessment in two different ways. Lou considered effort and consistency in writing e-mail, along with classroom participation, when assigning students a participation grade in the course that amounted to 10% of their final grade. David treated the e-mail interviews as research required to write the culture contact profile, and, throughout the semester, he emphasized to his students that they would need the information that their partners were providing for their culminating project.

Both Lou and David had eight assigned writing pieces for the semester (with appropriate second and third drafts), but both also gave more weight to the culture contact profiles. In the culture contact profile, we considered organization, development (emphasizing concrete examples), evidence of insight into the partner's culture, and correctness. The culture contact profiles reflected a new maturity of style overall. The fact that students were writing about a real person seemed to propel them to treat their subject matter seriously. Editing was sharper and the culture papers were more focused than the eight other written pieces. Not all students actually made it through several drafts of eight written assignments. This led David to reduce the number of graded submissions required in subsequent semesters when extensive e-mail writing was also expected. The results were quite promising. All but three students passed the courses. David was also happily surprised as about 70% of his class passed the City University of New York's rather demanding Writing Assessment Test[6] at the end of the semester. At the time of this class, all students were required to pass this test before their 61st credit. For this many freshman ESLers to pass was a significant gain.

GUIDELINES

Having participated in a number of successful exchanges and worked through the attendant pitfalls in the process, we have come to regard the following factors as essential to establishing and maintaining successful e-mail partnerships (Wood & Tillyer, 1997):

- Establish open communication with the partner teacher. Prompt responses are essential for planning and conducting the exchange. If the teachers cannot keep in touch, what hope do the students have?
- Before the onset of the classroom exchange, be sure that both instructors are committed to the exchange. Some questions to ask include: How much time each week will be devoted to the exchange? How much

---

[6]The CUNY WAT gives students 50 minutes to write an expository essay on their choice of one of two possible topics. The test is instructor-scored, with the score based on overall or holistic judgment of the writer's skills. These judgments are made according to the standard of the CUNY Evaluation Scale, a six-point scale aimed at defining "minimal readiness" for a college-level freshman composition course. To be considered as passing, the essay must be scored at four or higher by two independent readers.

credit will students get for the project that will result from the exchange? How would you handle students who refused to write to their partners? Students will recognize and reflect their instructor's level of dedication to the project, and without mutual commitment, the exchange has little chance to be successful.

- Determine that the arrangement is feasible for both groups. Students in both groups must have reasonable access to computers and the Internet. Having individual computer accounts and multiple computers is vastly preferable, but, with proper planning, students can stagger their time at the computer and all use the same account.

- Make sure that language levels are compatible. Students do not need to have identical skills, but they must be able to communicate. If in doubt, an exchange of writing samples would be helpful.

- Structure the exchange as a significant part of the course, and require a serious assignment based on the e-mail exchange. College students are extremely busy and to ask them to carry on an exchange without grade compensation is to ask for volunteerism. Students are willing to write until other academic pressures become too great. Then one side may quit, leaving the other side of the exchange without the wherewithal to complete the assignment!

- Be aware of cultural differences. Do not over-emphasize them or short-circuit the discovery process; however, you need to be alert to potential anger or confusion caused by cultural misunderstanding. If all of your partner class is from the same culture, it may be useful to have students discuss cultural differences they have noticed.

- Be flexible and prepare to make adjustments as necessary. Students get sick, have family problems, and occasionally withdraw from school. Also, the best-laid plans sometimes need adjustment. Most of the time there is a creative alternative.

Motivating BW and ESL students to write is a continuing challenge, and no strategy is 100% effective with every student. The e-mail exchange, however, is the most productive means we have found for achieving this goal. The lure of the technology creates interest and adds excitement, and the dynamic, never-predictable nature of the communication process sustains interest and prolongs excitement. Simply put, writing becomes a valid means of expression to our students when they have an eager audience and a reason to write.

REFERENCES

Brooks, J. G., & Brooks, M. G. (1993). *In search of understanding: The case for constructivist classrooms*. Alexandria, VA: Association for Supervision and Curriculum Development. (Synopsized in *Classroom Compass* [1:3])

Chun, D. M. (1998). Using computer-assisted class discussion to facilitate the acquisition of interactive competence. In J. Swaffar et al. (Eds.), *Language learning online* (pp. 57–80). Austin, TX: Labyrinth.

Daly, J. (1985). Writing Apprehension. In M. Rose (Ed.), *When a writer can't write* (pp. 43–82). New York: Guilford.

Doucette, D. (1993). Transforming teaching and learning using information technology. *The College Board Review, 167*, 18–25.

Dulay, H., & Burt, M. (1977). "Remarks on creativity in language acquisition." In M. Burt, H. Dulay, & M. Finnochiaro (Eds.), *Viewpoints on English as a second language* (pp. 95–126). New York: Regents.

Garner, R., & Gillingham, M. (1996). *Internet communication in six classrooms: Conversations across time, space, and culture.* Mahwah, NJ: Lawrence Erlbaum Associates.

Hilles, S., & Lynch, D. (1997). Culture as content. In M. A. Snow & D. M. Brinton (Eds.), *The content-based classroom: Perspectives on integrating language and content* (pp. 371–376). New York: Longman.

Jaeglin, C. (1998). Learners' and instructors' attitudes towards computer-assisted class discussion. In J. Swaffar et al. (Eds.), *Language learning online* (pp. 121–138). Austin, TX: Labyrinth.

Kasper, L. F. (1998). ESL writing and the principle of nonjudgmental awareness: Rationale and implementation. *Teaching English in the Two-Year College, 25*, 58–66.

Krashen, S. (1987). *Principles and practices in second language acquisition.* Herfortshire, UK: Prentice-Hall International.

MacGowan-Gilhooley, A. (1991). *Achieving fluency in English: A whole-language book.* Dubuque, IA: Kendall/Hunt.

Markley, P. (1998). Empowering students: The diverse roles of Asians and women in the ESL computer classroom. In J. Swaffar et al. (Eds.), *Language learning online* (pp. 81–96). Austin, TX: Labyrinth Publications.

Shaughnessy, M. (1977). *Errors and expectations: A guide for the teacher of basic writing.* New York: Oxford University Press.

Smilkstein, R. P. (1993). The natural human learning process. *Journal of Developmental Education, 17*(2), 2–10.

Strickland, K., & Strickland, J. (1993). *Uncovering the curriculum: Whole language in secondary and postsecondary classrooms.* Portsmouth, NH: Boynton/Cook.

Tillyer, A., & Sokolik, M. (1992). Beyond portfolios: Looking at student projects as teaching and evaluation devices. *College ESL, 2*(2), 47–51.

Ur, P. (1981), *Discussions that work: Task-centered fluency practice.* Cambridge, UK: Cambridge University Press.

Wood, L., & Tillyer, D. (1997). The intercultural e-mail partnership: Enhancing the writing classroom. *NADE's English/Writing SPIN Newsletter, 1*(2), 3–4.

11

The Internet and Content-Based College ESL Instruction

Reading, Writing, and Research

Loretta F. Kasper
Kingsborough Community College/CUNY

Modern computer applications, particularly the Internet, have expanded the body of instructional materials and opportunities available to faculty and students. The vast stores of information available on the Internet represent the largest body of interdisciplinary resources in history. These resources contain a wealth of information from archives, libraries, and databases all over the world, including texts, graphics, sound files, software, and full-motion video (Warschauer, 1996a). With its extensive collection of reading materials and numerous contexts for meaningful written communication, the Internet engenders a highly motivating learning environment that encourages students to interact with language in new and varied ways (Pennington, 1996). Consequently, the Internet has tremendous potential as a resource in content-based ESL instruction, where it may be used to teach students the language and research skills they will need in their mainstream college courses.

While the Internet can offer many benefits to content-based college ESL instruction, it is a dynamic educational medium that may present significant challenges to educators as they attempt to integrate Internet activities into existing or evolving pedagogical models (Lankes, 1997). However, we need to face and meet these challenges because computer technology in general, and the Internet in particular, are assuming an ever-greater role in education. This chapter describes the benefits of using the Internet in content-based courses, and it also offers caveats on Internet use in the language classroom. The chapter provides concrete guidelines for how to incorporate Internet technology into content-based ESL instruction and details specific content–Internet-based activities. Finally, it presents student achievement data that supports the use of the Internet as a CBI resource.

THE BENEFITS OF USING THE INTERNET IN THE CONTENT-BASED COLLEGE ESL COURSE

When incorporated into a content-based course, the Internet offers ESL students a number of significant educational benefits:

* The Internet helps increase English language literacy.
* The Internet encourages the development of critical literacy and academic research skills.
* The Internet promotes student-centered learning.
* The Internet fosters enhanced metacognition of specific linguistic and research skills, as well as of the overall process of acquiring knowledge.

Increasing English Language Literacy

Moll (1994) defined literacy as "a particular way of using language for a variety of purposes, as a sociocultural practice with intellectual significance" (p. 201). With the development of computer-mediated communication, this definition of literacy has taken on broader dimensions (Murray, 1991), and the computer may now be viewed as both a necessary component of literacy and a means to achieving that literacy. With its rich text-based environment, the Internet offers ESL students a powerful medium through which to develop and refine literacy skills.

The real potential of the Internet lies in its ability to provide both a foundation for language learning that is abundant with authentic textual material and, simultaneously, the means and motivation for this material to be used (Cobb & Stevens, 1996). Rather than being created precisely for the purpose of demonstrating points of language, as is the case with many print texts, Internet texts are written for native English speakers; thus, they are authentic materials (Higgins, 1991). Because much of the information presented on the Internet is in English, at the click of a mouse, ESL students have available a diverse collection of authentic English language texts dealing with a wide array of interdisciplinary themes. Furthermore, by allowing easy access to multiple cross-references on related topics across several documents, or screens, hypertext links contained on Internet pages provide a networked environment in which students are encouraged to read widely (Tierney et al., 1997). Reading widely is facilitated in a hypertext environment because simply by hitting the *back* or *forward* keys, students can easily return to reread or review any site visited during the computer session (Liu, 1998). As students engage in this type of extensive and extended reading, vocabulary and language structures become increasingly familiar, intertextual associations become clearer, and a broader base of schematic knowledge is developed.

In fact, Leipentre and Stephan (1995) maintained that a successful Internet search requires the use of critical reading skills (such as predicting content, categorizing, guessing meaning from context, skimming, and scanning) and that as students navigate through the large amounts of information on the Internet, they unconsciously practice these critical reading skills. To direct their search and to help make them aware of the critical reading skills being used, Leipentre and Stephan recommend giving students a set of questions, as illustrated in Appendix A.

The Internet supports the development of reading skills by creating a functional learning environment through access to a broad range of interesting, relevant, and interdisciplinary textual material that engages students in meaningful and authentic language processing (Shea, 1996). These rich textual resources are supported by abundant hypermedia that allows students to read and respond to text, view pictures, and hear audioclips, thus providing a natural opportunity for students to simultaneously practice listening, speaking, reading, and writing skills (Warschauer, 1996a). In addition, hypermedia consolidates and concretizes abstract content-based concepts because it encourages processing via multiple modalities. This multimodal processing results in a strong text representation that consists of the collaborative effects of both visual and verbal cues as presented on the Internet page (Chun & Plass, 1997). The result is increased comprehension and a higher level of reading skill.

Finally, the visually stimulating interactive learning experience supported by the Internet (Muehleisen, 1997) creates an educational environment favorable to students of different cognitive learning styles (Haley & Luton, 1998), labeled by Gardner (1983, 1993) *multiple intelligences.* Christison (1996) maintained that the most effective language learning activities actively engage the use of several of these multiple intelligences by presenting information through a multimedia approach, such as is present on the Internet.

As students build reading skills and increase their schematic knowledge base, they are better able to engage in the written articulation of this knowledge through various modes of discourse. Students read widely in their interactions with Internet texts, and these texts suggest many topics for expository writing requiring in-depth analysis of key intra- and interdisciplinary concepts. In this way, the Internet also becomes an ideal instructional resource for developing the writing skills so critical to ESL students' success in college. As students work individually and with peers, producing analytical responses to the course materials and to each other's writing, they refine critical thinking skills. By engaging in close reading and in-depth discussion of salient issues in science, psychology, business, and other academic disciplines, students acquire the linguistic and cognitive tools needed to compose written pieces spanning such rhetorical modes as description, definition, comparison–contrast, cause–effect, and argumentation.

Moreover, the Internet fosters exploration and production of words and ideas through computer networks that link writers with others in the same class or around the world, and so provides students with a real audience for their writing, along with peer interaction for revision and conferencing (see e.g., Tillyer & Wood, chap. 10, this volume). In fact, Warschauer (1998) maintained that computer-mediated communication contributes to written fluency. As he explained it, when ESL students write on the computer, they spend more time on and give greater attention to the task of composing. Warschauer (1996b) believes that ESL students perceive computer-mediated communication as less threatening than face-to-face communication, so they take greater risks in their writing, leading to writing that is more syntactically and lexically complex.

Thus, the Internet can be a powerful resource for building both language skills and content knowledge. In fact, my own research (Kasper, 1998a) demonstrates that an instructional approach that combines CBI and the Internet quickly raises students' skill levels, resulting in increased pass rates and higher levels of language proficiency.

Developing Critical Literacy and Research Skills

In addition to building English language literacy, the Internet can also be used to build critical literacy; that is, the ability to locate and evaluate information (Mather, 1996). Critical literacy is a skill that students need if they are to take full advantage of the multitude of valuable sources the Internet has to offer them. The Internet offers a powerful and useful resource for content-based instruction, but students must be made aware that Internet sources unfortunately are neither always credible nor valid. This is because information found on the Internet may be raw, unfiltered, and even contradictory. It is therefore crucial that students be taught how to discriminate between valid and invalid source material because in our electronic information age, evaluating the credibility and validity of resources is the responsibility of a critically literate reader (Farah, 1995). To guide them in determining whether an Internet source is reliable and credible students may be given a list of questions that ask them to consider factors such as the source and timeframe of the information.

A sample list of questions used to guide students' evaluation of online information is provided in Appendix B. Instructional activities that foster the development of critical literacy skills give students the tools they need to become information managers (Mann, 1994), able to evaluate the ever-increasing and often unmoderated sources and quantities of electronic information.

Strong critical literacy skills are key to the research papers that are a central component of many mainstream college courses. Conducting and writing up research requires the ability to gather and evaluate information drawn from a variety of sources, to present that information in an organized fashion in a report of some length, to critically analyze issues, and finally, to cite the sources used to prepare that report. Although research papers are a major component of many college courses, the development of academic research skills is an area that is often neglected in ESL courses. This is unfortunate because writing a research report is an especially frightening prospect for ESL students and presents them with an enormous challenge to their English language skills, one for which they are often unprepared (Horowitz, 1986). Preparing students to do research can yield benefits that extend beyond the ESL program since, as Mustafa (1995) reported, incorporating instruction that targets the development of research skills into ESL courses teaches students the rhetorical conventions of term papers and leads to better writing and higher performance levels in mainstream courses.

Promoting Student-Centered Learning

In addition to facilitating the development of literacy and research skills, the Internet benefits ESL instruction by promoting student-centered learning. When ESL students use the Internet as a content-based resource, they are provided with a context for individualized instruction as they search for information relevant to their own interests. The Internet then boosts comprehension of this information through multisensory stimulation that provides additional cues to aid students in the construction of meaning. Finally, the Internet puts students in control of their own learning as they proceed step by step in their search for information. The resulting self-directed exploration of topics chosen by students creates a learning experience that is personally meaningful and educationally beneficial and that engages students cognitively in the kind of information processing that is key to cultivating both the English language and the academic skills they need to succeed in college.

Finally, a content-based ESL course is the perfect context for developing the type of collaborative research projects that are a key component of a student-centered approach to learning. This collaborative research involves students in authentic academic tasks in which they must understand and use varied and creative language (Egbert & Jessup, 1996) and nurtures cognitive engagement by requiring that students rely on themselves and on their peers as resources for increased understanding of content-based concepts (Strommen & Lincoln, 1992). Both linguistic and content knowledge are strengthened as students must first negotiate meaning, and then formulate, communicate, and evaluate both their own ideas and those of their peers. (Bliss, 1998; Egbert & Jessup, 1996).

Crismore and Liu-Shing (1985) consider individualized instruction, multisensory stimulation, and student control to be essential components of a learning environment designed to prepare students to meet the challenges of college level work. Moreover, both Crismore and Liu-Shing (1985) and English (1996) believe that the educational environment created by instructional applications of Internet technology fosters the development of metacognitive skills necessary for more efficient learning.

Enhanced Metacognition

Metacognition refers to the knowledge we have about the way(s) in which we learn. Our metacognitive model for a given task consists of a cognitive map containing effective and ineffective strategies and procedures for performing that task. Developing and strengthening metacognition is key to improving students' performance because research has shown a significant positive correlation between the strength of the metacognitive model and successful task performance (Devine, Railey, & Boshoff, 1993; English, 1996; Kasper, 1997a; Raphael, 1989). Furthermore, as demonstrated in a number of recent studies (see e.g., Blakey & Spence, 1990; Collins, 1994; Garner, 1994; Kasper, 1997a; Sandman, 1993), the metacognitive model can be effectively developed and strengthened through explicit instruction.

Providing activities (see appendices) that guide students through the process of an Internet search and that ask them to describe in writing each of the steps they follow in that search can help to strengthen metacognition. By writing about the process of information gathering and knowledge acquisition, students are taken step by step back over that process. They must reflect on what they have done to acquire information and on how and what they have learned from that information. This helps to increase awareness of which steps lead to success and which to failure. As students complete this activity, they actively reflect on the process of knowledge acquisition, and they gradually learn more not only about how to conduct research, but also about how they acquire knowledge.

To continue building metacognition, students may be invited to write about what they have read, exploring meanings and making connections to other items in their knowledge base. To articulate their understanding of the texts they have encountered, students must think deeply about those texts and about discussions they have had with peers and teachers. Electronic correspondence creates archived logs that may be reread and reflected on and thereby empowers ESL students to become more aware of the learning process and helps to build metacognitive skills (English, 1998).

Finally, through their readings of Internet texts, students are exposed to different perspectives on issues of interest. As they discuss and write about these viewpoints, students are encouraged to reconsider issues from additional new perspectives. Thus, searching for, accessing, reading, and discussing information on the Internet becomes an effective means not only for developing linguistic and academic skills, but also for strengthening metacognitive awareness, leading to overall learning enhancement.

CAVEATS ON INTERNET USE
IN THE LANGUAGE CLASSROOM

As just described, the Internet provides a multitude of educational benefits to ESL students. However, although the Internet can be a powerful tool in the content-based classroom, instructors must be aware of and prepared to deal with some of the problems that may arise when they incorporate technology into their courses. Many of our ESL students come from societies or financial situations in which they had limited access to computer technology (Smoke, 1997). These students will almost certainly be unfamiliar, and may well be uncomfortable, with the Internet. Providing guidance through step-by-step instructions and questions designed to direct their Internet work can help to put these students at ease.

Instructors who incorporate the Internet into their ESL courses must themselves be comfortable with and competent users of computer technology. In this way, they will be able to teach students how to use that technology to improve language learning, and they will be able to develop interesting and valuable content-based lessons.

When instructors are able to arrange for time in a computer lab with Internet access, they must be sure to prepare carefully designed but flexible lessons. Students must be given specific activities to complete in the computer lab, and instructor's expectations must be realistic, for students come to the computer lab with very different skills and beliefs. Many students do not have basic keyboarding skills, and this makes accessing the materials on the Internet much more difficult because precise typing of the URL (Uniform Resource Locator, or Internet address) is essential. Others, particularly those having limited experience with computers, may be technophobic. Therefore, the instructor must provide both guidance and encouragement, as some students will catch on quickly, whereas others may lag behind in their development of technological skills.

Using a computer and accessing information on the Internet can at times be a frustrating experience. Although we may think of our society as technologically advanced, in colleges across the nation, the number of students is still generally greater than the number of available computers. In addition, many of the computers in use are old enough to be considered obsolete by current standards (Reilly, 1996). Even if there are enough computers, students may sometimes experience difficulty logging onto the college's computer network. If many students attempt to log on at the same time, system overloads and slowdowns may result or the system may crash entirely. When this happens, lessons will go unfinished in spite of the most careful planning. This means that instructors using the Internet must always prepare back-up activities, perhaps in the form of printed worksheets or texts that students can complete offline.

In spite of these potential difficulties, the Internet is a useful and highly motivating resource that should, whenever possible, be incorporated into content-based college ESL courses. When students learn how to use the Internet, it becomes a vehicle for meaningful learning and can offer a multitude of educational benefits, both linguistic and cognitive.

DESIGNING EFFECTIVE COURSE ACTIVITIES

As stated in the previous sections, the Internet can be an effective tool for building both English language and critical literacy skills, as it promotes student-centered learning and enhances metacognition. For the Internet to be used most effectively in CBI, course activities must take advantage of the Internet's potential to develop ESL students' linguistic and academic skills by putting them in charge of their own learning. Activities that promote students' choice of and responsibility for course content result in active engagement in a learning experience that is perceived by students as relevant to their linguistic and academic goals. As reported by Brinton in chapter 3 of this volume, perceived relevance appears to be a critical factor in the effectiveness of CBI. Therefore, activities that engage students in study that is personally meaningful should be promoted in content-based courses.

I believe that to maximize the acquisition of language and academic skills, content-based activities should require students to read widely on subject areas that they have chosen to study in depth, should encourage collaborative learning, and should provide extensive practice in conducting and reporting on academic research. I developed an activity that I call *focus discipline research* to meet each of these goals. Focus discipline research provides ESL students with the opportunity to develop and refine reading, writing, and critical literacy skills as they build a strong knowledge base through sustained research in a discipline they have *chosen* to study over time. Focus discipline research provides the context for what Pally (1997) referred to as *sustained content study* (p. 293), which benefits ESL instruction by engaging students in extended practice with both linguistic structures and disciplinary content and enabling them to become "content experts" in a subject area of their own choosing.

Students should be encouraged to choose their focus discipline based on personal interest and/or college major. In my course, students may choose a focus discipline from among the 10 content areas covered in their textbook, *Interdisciplinary English* (Kasper, 1998b).[1] Because they have *chosen* to do extensive research in that discipline, they are invested in a learning experience that is personally meaningful, important, and relevant.

Students are engaged in extended study of their chosen subject area through a series of progressive focus discipline papers. They are required to use the Internet as an informational resource in preparing these papers. Students are taught research skills, are given questions to guide their research, and work in collaborative groups with other students who have chosen to focus their study on the same discipline. Students in each of these *focus discipline groups* work as a team to gather and discuss information for their projects. Through these groups, learning becomes not only an individual endeavor, but also a social one as students work together to construct knowledge. Moreover, because peers become resources for furthering knowledge and understanding of content area and linguistic information (Strommen & Lincoln, 1992), common group goals are created and students are encouraged to cooperate to achieve these goals (Bracey, 1994). Thus, students become responsible not only for promoting their own learning, but also for contributing to the knowledge of the group.

COURSE DESCRIPTION

My pedagogical approach is illustrated by describing activities that I use in my high intermediate content-based ESL courses.[2] The high-intermediate level at my college translates into an entry TOEFL score of approximately 400. The activities described are used in a content-based unit on environmental science. The sciences are a popular area of study for ESL students in American higher education (*Open Doors*, 1996/97), and issues in the field of environmental science are often in the news and may impact other disciplines. For these reasons, many students choose environmental science as a focus discipline, and all students are motivated to learn more about this content area.

Among the topics studied by the entire class as part of the environmental science unit is the greenhouse effect, its immediate and possible future impact on our weather, and the resulting effects on issues in disciplines such as business and nutrition. The greenhouse effect is a timely topic these days and one for which there is a great deal of information to be found on the Internet.

---

[1] The 10 disciplines represented in the text, *Interdisciplinary English*, are: linguistics, environmental science, computer science, mathematics, business and marketing, psychology, sociology, physical anthropology, biology, and diet and nutrition.

[2] All page citations refer to readings contained in the book, *Interdisciplinary English* (Kasper, 1998b).

Prereading Activity

The lesson on the greenhouse effect begins with a prereading exercise that asks students to consider how the climate of the earth has changed over the past 10 years. They are asked if they have experienced or heard about unusual storms, floods, drought, famine, or heat waves. They are asked to explain how they think these events are related to global warming. These questions prime students for the reading by activating preexisting schemata, or background knowledge.

The greenhouse effect is a somewhat abstract topic and one that requires some understanding of complex chemical principles. The global warming link from the web page of the Environmental Protection Agency (*http://www.epa.gov/globalwarming/*) contains additional hyperlinks to visual resources that may be used as a prereading activity to concretize these abstract scientific concepts and thereby facilitate comprehension. I direct students to one of these hyperlinks (*http://www.epa.gov/globalwarming/reports/slides/cc&i/b-ghouse.html*), which illustrates the greenhouse effect through a diagram depicting the earth, the sun, and the ozone layer. While viewing this visual, students go step by step through an analysis of what happens when the sun's ultraviolet radiation mixes with man-made pollutants. This web page facilitates comprehension in two ways—it serves as a visual prereading exercise, and it provides students with an imagery link that they can later access to clarify the complex scientific concepts that will be presented in the textbook reading, "The Greenhouse Effect" (Kasper, 1998b, pp. 35–39).

Interaction With Text

This reading defines the greenhouse effect and explains the cause–effect relationship between greenhouse gases and global warming. The text details the environmental, chemical, and political implications of ozone depletion and global warming. Thus the textbook chapter provides a general description of the Greenhouse Effect and discusses the many areas of everyday life that are affected by environmental factors. The chapter also offers a general view of what may happen if the greenhouse problem is not solved in the near future. As students read the textbook chapter, they engage in vocabulary building and express their understanding of the text through written answers to open-ended comprehension questions. We then discuss the contents of the chapter in class to check comprehension and clarify any questions students may have.

Furthering Knowledge Through an Internet Search

Now students are asked to search the Internet to find additional information on the greenhouse effect. To direct their Internet search and to help make them aware of the critical reading skills being used, students are given the set of questions provided in Appendix 1.

The lesson described in this chapter asks students to access web sites that deal with the greenhouse effect and its potential impact on business, nutrition, and governmental issues, to name just a few. For example, an article published on the web page of the Washington Post (*http://www.washingtonpost.com/ wp-srv/Wplate/1997-11/12/1691-111297-idx.html*) describes some of the potential consequences of global warming (Warrick, 1997); while an article on the web page of the *New Scientist* (*http://global.newscientist.com/970719/features.html*) dismisses the greenhouse effect as a hoax (*New Scientist*, 1997). As students read these essays, they are exposed to contrasting opinions on this issue. This provides a wonderful opportunity to teach students the discourses of comparison–contrast and argumentation in which they describe and evaluate differing viewpoints in an essay. To prepare students to write this essay, we list the arguments for treating the Greenhouse Effect as a genuine problem versus those for viewing it as simply a hoax, and we analyze the strengths and weaknesses of each argument. Because climate plays such a major role in everyday life, students become very involved in researching this topic, and almost all of them, even those typically shy and quiet, express an opinion. Thus, Internet research becomes a highly motivating vehicle to developing linguistic and academic skills, as students actively practice the four basic language skills—reading, writing, listening, and speaking—and the critical thinking and analytical skills necessary for college-level work.

Synthesis of Concepts Through Writing

The final Internet search activity of the overall course lesson directs students to narrow the focus of their search to the impact of global warming on the world's economy and food supplies. This search prepares them for the final writing activity, which requires them to do an interdisciplinary analysis. In the final writing activity, students must put together all of the information they have gathered through the textbook reading and the Internet research to write an essay on the following topic:

> Considering all the information you have gained from this unit, what are the potential effects of global warming on world nutrition? How may what we eat be affected by our changing global climate? What other areas of our lives will be affected by nutritional changes caused by the greenhouse effect?

Again, the instructional paradigm described here makes use of both print and electronic media to develop and enhance linguistic and content knowledge bases. As students acquire information, they link new knowledge to what they already know, creating a network of associations within the newly formed knowledge base that may then be used to facilitate performance on future linguistic and academic tasks.

Focus Discipline Research

While the entire class studies the greenhouse effect and uses the Internet for additional research as part of the environmental science unit, students in the environmental science focus discipline group continue to research other topics related to this subject area throughout the semester. These students complete a series of three progressive papers in which they report on the additional information they have gathered through their extended research. The information in these three papers is then put together into a research project that culls all of the information acquired. Students must cite both the print and the electronic sources they have used to prepare this research project.

Students who choose environmental science as a focus discipline are asked to use both print and electronic media as sources for information on the following topics: recent changes in global climate, recent changes in geographical patterns due to climate, and the effects of a weather phenomenon known as El Niño.

They are asked to write three papers, due at regular intervals over the course of the semester, in which they describe and discuss each of these topics.

In the first paper, students describe recent changes in global climate, answering the following questions in the essay: Have the predictions of scientists been correct? Has there been a gradual increase in global temperature over the past several years? Has there been an increase in storms and in unstable weather patterns?

In the second paper, students describe recent changes in geographical patterns as a result of the changing global climate. They search for information on beach and land erosion resulting from severe storms. They are asked to address the following questions in their essay: How have storms, floods, and other weather phenomena reshaped the coastlines and the appearance of the earth?

In the third paper, students describe the weather phenomenon known as El Niño, addressing the following questions in their essay: What environmental changes result from this weather system? How often does El Niño occur? What causes El Niño? What are the effects of El Niño on global climate?

Finally, students are required to synthesize the information gathered for the three progressive focus discipline projects into a final research project. The final research project described here is a five- to seven-page paper that requires students to draw interdisciplinary connections between environmental science and another content area as follows:

In a final research project of five to seven pages, bring together all of the information you have gathered and discuss the effects of a changing climate on either business or government. Choose to focus on *only one* of these areas in your project, and answer the following questions: What are the specific effects of climate changes on <your chosen area>? How serious are these effects? What can be done to deal with problems caused by climate in <your chosen area>? What predictions have been made for the future in <your chosen area> in light of a continually changing climate? Please be sure to include a bibliography in which you cite each of the sources you have used to prepare your research project.

STUDENT ACCOMPLISHMENTS

Overall, the results of the focus discipline activity have been quite positive, and students have produced some very thoughtful responses in their research projects. The following excerpt from a focus discipline project on environmental science (reprinted with permission) is indicative of student accomplishments in this course. This paper, written by a high intermediate level student, presents a powerful analysis of the effects of a changing climate on the behavior of the world's governments. This student researched both print sources (books and magazines) and Internet sources (electronic newspapers and articles) to prepare the paper that follows:

About 150 years ago, the earth's atmosphere had remained unchanged for several thousand years. Since the mid-1900's, people's actions have been changing the heat ability of the atmosphere. Scientists who study the earth's atmosphere and climate have been talking about the greenhouse effect and finally about "global warming" ...

Politicians, who for years have ignored the warnings of scientists and environmental protection movements, are becoming alarmed. They are announcing and making decisions on an international scale ... In 1988, in order to protect the stratospheric ozone layer, 120 countries agreed to limit their use of CFCs and signed the Montreal Convention. In 1989, several heads of state and heads of government of the industrialized nations signed the Hague Appeal to turn public opinion to threats to the environment. Government authorities realized that climatic change is one of the questions on which the planet's future depends. The United States and Sweden had already prohibited the use of CFCs in aerosol cans towards the end of the 1980s; Germany has announced that it will have reduced its use by 95%. ...

The International community has a serious problem, which has direct relation to global climate change. This is the problem of ozone depletion. Ten years ago the nations of the world came together in Montreal to take wise steps toward protecting the Earth's stratospheric ozone layer. These efforts were expanded in the scientific discovery—a hole in the ozone layer above Antarctica, which was the size of the North American continent.

After that discovery was confirmed the world's political system began to sign any agreement much easier than before. Copenhagen Agreement was signed in 1990. Nations have agreed on the nature of the climate change threat, and we have taken the first initial steps to destroy that threat. All the nations of the world will need to work together to develop our steps after the year 2000. So we must achieve a new aim for the future.

The great poet William Butter Yeats wrote, "I have spread my dreams under your feet. Tread softly because you tread on my dreams." Unless we tread softly, our dreams for the future will be nothing but dreams. Let us make sure that our next steps are the right ones.

This is a strong indication of the type of work students can produce when they are engaged in cognitively demanding tasks that foster the development of language skills through the exploration and analysis of content-based academic material. The ESL writer expressed both pride and amazement in an e-mail message (reprinted with permission):

"My DEAR TEACHER:

As you noticed, I tried to put as much efforts on my project as I could. If you remember from our first lessons, this topic attracted me. To be honest, I was scared by your first lessons, when you were telling us about our future assignments. I could never imagine before that I, ESL student, would read, understand, and discuss by writing of global warming, greenhouse effect, and El Niño. I am very proud of myself that I could reach it" (19 June, 1998).

Both overall performance and the quality of the projects produced in this course were very impressive. The pass rates in this high intermediate course, ESL 91, were significantly higher than those in the overall ESL program at my college. From ESL 91, students may move on to either ENG 92 or ENG 93, depending on their performance on departmental reading and writing examinations. On the basis of their scores on these examinations, 73.3% of the students in this course were able to skip a level, and move from ESL 91 to ENG 93. This is significantly better (Chi-squared $= 28.47; p < .001$) than performance in the ESL program overall, where only 21.4% of students were able to skip a level and move from ESL 91 to ENG 93. In addition, the percentage of my students who needed to repeat the ESL 91 course was significantly lower (Chi-squared $= 5.64; p < .02$), at only 8.3%, as compared with 21.2% of students in the overall program.

STUDENT FEEDBACK

In addition to higher pass rates, the benefits of incorporating the Internet into content-based ESL instruction are supported by students' enthusiastic feedback. Students have said that they love using the computer and are fascinated by the amount of information available on the Internet. At first the computer intimidates some of them, but with practice most of them acquire the skills they need to explore its vast potential as a research and language learning tool. Many of the less computer literate students view developing these skills as a challenge and excitedly report their successes to the class. I have found, and students' feedback verifies, that the Internet never fails to engage them in learning and that it helps to increase their understanding of even complex interdisciplinary concepts.

Students report that this type of instruction is not only very motivating, but also very useful. They say that Internet resources help them develop and refine their English language skills, enabling them to study and practice various points of grammar, vocabulary, and mechanics on their own. In addition, they appreciate the opportunity to learn how to do research and how to present that research in a written format. After completing the focus discipline projects in my ESL course, students feel more confident about their ability to prepare research reports for their mainstream courses.

Working with the focus discipline groups has had several wonderful benefits. The focus discipline groups have resulted in strong multicultural friendships. Students bond with each other because they are involved in a common task. They support each other in their search for information and work to be sure each person in the group understands the topic. The social discourse afforded by the group encourages students to elaborate and reflect on both their own ideas and those of their peers, helping to build a strong personal and group knowledge base. Students enjoy the opportunity to build and to share knowledge with group members, and even those students who are typically shy and quiet become more confident about presenting their knowledge to their classmates.

CONCLUSION

The focus discipline activities described in this chapter actively engage students in sustained content study, require that they work through complex texts and use English as a means of increasing knowledge, and encourage students to network with each other as they discuss the information they each have gathered. Through activities that guide their Internet research projects (see appendices), students learn how to be critical readers and thinkers and how to evaluate the validity and reliability of research sources. As my own research has shown, these skills, developed in content-based ESL courses, benefit students long after they leave the ESL program and lead them to perform better in subsequent college courses (Kasper, 1997b).

At times there have been computers that did not work, Internet pages that loaded slowly, and system crashes on the college computer network. Yet, since I incorporated the Internet into my content-based college ESL courses, students arrive early for class, go to the computer lab on their free periods, and are excited about using English to acquire knowledge. I have seen their faces light up when they discover a web page that answers a question they are researching or one that gives them some new information they might never have considered before. I have watched them engage in animated discussions on a topic under study. I have seen different focus discipline groups working together and debating how an issue would be viewed in the different disciplines.

As ESL students use their new language to learn academic content, they come to regard English as a means to acquiring knowledge, not just as a collection of grammar, vocabulary, reading, and writing exercises. The language-learning experience becomes more meaningful and is thus enriched. This is the greatest rationale for content-based college ESL instruction. When the Internet is incorporated into a content-based college ESL course, this experience becomes richer still and offers students personal and educational benefits that will reach far beyond the ESL course.

REFERENCES

Blakey, E., & Spence, S. (1990). Developing metacognition. *ERIC Digest (ED 327 218)*. [Online]. Available: http://ericps.ed.uiuc.edu/npin/respar/texts/home/metacog.html

Bliss, A. (1998). Collaborative writing using research on the World Wide Web. *Paper presented at the TCC 98 Online Conference*. April 7–9, 1998. Available: http://leahi.kcc.hawaii.edu/org/tcon98/paper/bliss.html

Bracey, B. (1994). Emergent learning technologies/Common themes. *Institute for Alternative Futures Report*. [Online]. Available: gopher://unix5.nysed.gov/ [1998, March 10].

Christison, M. A. (1996). Multiple intelligences and second language learners. *Journal of the Imagination in Language Learning, 3*, 8–13.

Chun, D. M., & Plass, J. L. (1997). Research on text comprehension in multimedia environments. *Language Learning and Technology, 1*(1), 60–81.

Cobb, T., & Stevens, V. (1996). A principled consideration of computers and reading in a second language. In M. C. Pennington (Ed.), *The power of CALL* (pp. 115–136). Houston: Athelstan.

Collins, N. D. (1994). Metacognition and reading to learn. *ERIC Digest (ED 376 427)*. [Online]. Available: http://www.ed.gov/databases/ERIC_Digests/ed376427.html

Crismore, A., & Liu-Shing, W. (1985). A computer-assisted reading component for reading reflectively and rhetorically in a college composition program. *ERIC Digest, (ED 264515)*, 1–45.

Devine, J., Railey, K., & Boshoff, P. (1993). The implications of cognitive models in L1 and L2 writing. *Journal of Second Language Writing, 2*(3), 203–225.

Egbert, J. L., & Jessup, L. M. (1996). Analytic and systemic analyses of computer-supported language learning environments. *TESL-EJ, 2*(2). [Online]. Available: http://www-writing.berkeley.edu/TESL-EJ/ej06/ai.html

English, J. A. (1996). Metacognition in the computer-mediated classroom: A new advantage. *Computers & Texts, 13* (Dec.). [Online]. Available: http://info.ox.ac.uk/ctitext/publish/comtxt/ct13/english.html

English, J. A. (1998). MOO-based metacognition: Incorporating online and offline reflection into the writing process. *KAIROS: A Journal for Teachers of Writing in Webbed Environments, 3*(1). [Online]. Available: http://english.ttu.edu/kairos/3.1/features/english

Farah, B. D. (1995). Information literacy: Retooling evaluation skills in the electronic information environment. *Journal of Educational Technology Systems, 24*(2), 127–133.

Gardner, H. (1983). *Frames of mind: The theory of multiple intelligences.* New York: Basic Books.

Gardner, H. (1993). *Multiple intelligences: The theory in practice.* New York: Basic Books.

Garner, R. (1994). Metacognition and executive control. In R. B. Ruddell, M. R. Ruddell, & H. Singer (Eds.), *Models and processes of reading (4th edition),* (pp. 715–732). Newark, DE: International Reading Association.

Haley, M. H., & Luton, K. (1998, July). Taking new directions on the multimedia highway. (Presentation abstract). *CALICO 98.* San Diego, CA.

Higgins, J. (1991). Fuel for learning: The neglected element of textbooks and CALL. *CAELL Journal, 2*(2), 3–7.

Horowitz, D. (1986). What professors actually require: Academic tasks for the ESL classroom. *TESOL Quarterly, 20*(3), 445–462.

Kasper, L. F. (1997a). Assessing the metacognitive growth of ESL student writers. *TESL-EJ, 3*(1). [Online]. Available: http://www-writing.berkeley.edu/TESL-EJ/ej09/a1.html

Kasper, L. F. (1997b). The impact of content-based instructional programs on the academic progress of ESL students. *English for Specific Purposes, 16*(4), 309–320.

Kasper, L. F. (1998a, April 7–9). Interdisciplinary English and the Internet: Technology meets content in the ESL course. *Paper presented at the TCC '98 Online Conference.* Available: http://leahi.kcc.hawaii.edu/org/tcon98/paper/kasper.html

Kasper, L. F. (1998b). *Interdisciplinary English (2nd ed.).* New York: McGraw-Hill.

Lankes, R. D. (1997). The bread and butter of the Internet. *ERIC Digest (EDO-IR-97-02).* [Online]. Available: http://ericir.syr.edu/ithome/digests/David.html

Leipentre, S., & Stephan, L. (1995). Telnet treasure hunts: Learning to read (on) the Internet. In M. Warschauer (Ed.), *Virtual connections* (pp. 331–335). Honolulu: University of Hawaii Press.

Liu, K. (1998). Electronic communication, new technology, and the ESL student. In T. Smoke (Ed.), *Adult ESL: Politics, pedagogy, and participation in school and community programs* (pp. 289–311). Hillsdale, NJ: Lawrence Erlbaum Associates.

Mann, C. (1994). New technologies and gifted education. *Roeper Review, 16*(3), 172–176.

Mather, P. (1996). *World Wide Web: Beyond the basics* (chap. 6). [Online]. Available: http://ei.cs.vt.edu/~wwwbtb/book/chap6/critical.html

Moll, L. C. (1994). Literacy research in community and classrooms: A sociocultural approach. In R. B. Ruddell, M. R. Ruddell, & H. Singer (Eds.), *Theoretical models and processes of reading.* 4th ed. (pp. 179–207). Newark, DE: International Reading Association.

Muehleisen, V. (1997). Projects using the Internet in college English classes. *The Internet TESL Journal, 3*(6). [Online]. Available: http://www.aitech.ac.jp/~iteslj/Lessons/Muehleisen-Projects.html

Murray, D. E. (1991). *Conversation for action: The computer terminal as a medium of communication.* Amsterdam: John Benjamins.

Mustafa, Z. (1995). The effect of genre awareness on linguistic transfer. *English for Specific Purposes, 14*(3), 247–256.

New Scientist (19 July 1997). Features. [Online]. Available: http://global.newscientist.com/ns/970719/features.html

Open Doors (1996/97). New York: Institute of International Education. [Online]. Available: http://www.ne.org/opendoors/forstud.htm

Pally, M. (1997). Critical thinking in ESL: An argument for sustained content. *Journal of Second Language Writing, 6*(3), 293–311.

Pennington, M. C. (1996). The power of the computer in language education. In M. C. Pennington (Ed.), *The power of CALL* (pp. 1–14). Houston: Athelstan.

Raphael, T. E. (1989). Students' metacognitive knowledge about writing. *Research in the Teaching of English, 23*(4), 343–379.

Reilly, B. (1996). New technologies, new literacies, new problems. In C. Fisher, D. C. Dwyer, & K. Yocam (Eds.), *Education and technology: Reflections on computing in classrooms* (pp. 203–220). San Francisco: Jossey-Bass.

Sandman, J. (1993). Self-evaluation exit essays in freshman composition: "Now I have new weaknesses." *Teaching English in the Two-Year College, 20*, 18–22.

Shea, P. (1996). Media, multimedia, and meaningful language learning: A review of the literature. *WebNet 96*. October 15–19. San Francisco, CA. [Online]. Available: http://aace.virginia.edu/aace/conf/webnet/html/159.htm

Smoke, T. (1997). The challenges of technology in ESL. *Selected papers from ESL for the 21st Century*. A New Jersey Statewide Higher Education Conference. October 18, 1997. Elizabeth, NJ: Union County College.

Strommen, E. F., & Lincoln, B. (1992). Constructivism, technology, and the future of classroom learning. *ILTweb*. [Online]. Available: http://www.ilt.columbia.edu/k12/livetext/docs/construct.html

Tierney, R. J., Kieffer, R., Whalin, K., Desai, L., Moss, A. G., Harris, J. E., & Hopper, J. (1997, May). Assessing the impact of hypertext on learners' architecture of literacy learning spaces in different disciplines: Follow-up studies. *Reading Online*. Available: http://www.readingonline.org/research/impact/index.html

Warrick, J. (1997). Consensus emerges earth is warming—Now what? *Washington Post, November 12, 1997*, A01. [Online]. Available: http://www.washingtonpost.com/wp-srv/Wplate/1997-11/12/1691-111297-idx.html

Warschauer, M. (1996a). Computer-assisted language learning: An introduction. In S. Fotos (Ed.), *Multimedia language teaching* (pp. 3–20). Tokyo: Logos International.

Warschauer, M. (1996b). Comparing face-to-face and electronic communication in the second language classroom. *CALICO Journal, 13*(2), 7–26.

Warschauer, M. (1998). Interaction, negotiation, and computer-mediated learning. *INSA de LYON*. [Online]. Available: http://www.insa-lyon.fr/Departements/CDRL/interaction.html

APPENDIX A:
INTERNET SEARCH ACTIVITY

Directions: Answer the following questions as you search for information on the greenhouse effect on the Internet. Try to make your answers as specific and as descriptive as possible.

Step One: Get into Netscape, and enter the following URL in the line marked *Location*: http://www.epa.gov/greenhouse/. This URL will take you to a web site on global warming. Be sure that you type the URL *exactly* as it is written on this sheet.

Step Two: Now follow the hypertext links to access each of the web pages contained on this site on the greenhouse effect by clicking on the underlined words.

Step Three: Now you will practice accessing sites on your own. Answer the following questions to help guide you in your search:

1. Which keyword should you enter into the search engine to find information on the greenhouse effect?
2. What do you have to do to access a web file on *the greenhouse effect?*
3. Once you have accessed this file, how do you get information on *the greenhouse effect?*
4. After reading the article that you accessed on the Web, write *two new things* you have learned about the greenhouse effect using this Web site.

Step Four: Now, narrow the focus of your search to information on *the effect of the greenhouse effect on water and food supplies*. Do a new search and answer the above four questions to guide you in this new search.

APPENDIX B:
QUESTIONS TO GUIDE YOU
IN EVALUATING INTERNET RESOURCES

Does the information add anything to what you already know about the topic?

Who is providing the information contained on the Internet page?

Where did the information come from?

Do they provide evidence to support the points they are making?

How old is the information?

When was the Internet page last updated?

How broad is the topic?

Is the information provided in a WWW or gopher document, a text file, a newsgroup posting, or an e-mail message?

Is the information clear and well organized?

Who recommended this site as a good source of information?

12

The Role of Information Technology in the Future of Content-Based ESL Instruction

Loretta F. Kasper
Kingsborough Community College/CUNY

The college ESL population has been steadily increasing for a number of years (Crandall, 1993), and it has been predicted that by the 21st century, approximately 50% of all undergraduates in U.S. colleges and universities will come from homes where English is a second or foreign language (City University of New York, 1994). Given this prediction, what does the future hold for ESL instruction in general and for content-based instruction in particular? What skills will ESL students need to be successful in the academic and workforce environments of the 21st century?

The essays in this volume have described how a content-based pedagogy may be used to develop the linguistic and academic skills that students must have if they are to pass institutional assessment examinations and handle the requirements of college courses. Although these skills have been and still are necessary, they are no longer sufficient to meet the demands of today's academic and workforce environments. Due to the spread of online communication, knowledge of information technology has joined the basic skills deemed requisite for all college students (Hooker, 1997; Twigg, 1998). In fact, Rossetti (1998) noted that the ones who succeed in all walks of life today are those who are able to use new technologies to access, adapt, and make intelligent use of information and knowledge.

The basic goal of a CBI paradigm is to give ESL students the tools they need to succeed in college courses, and if we are to continue to meet this goal, we must make information technology a key component of content-based courses. Thus the question becomes not *whether* to use information technology in the ESL classroom, but rather *how* to use it most effectively to enable students to develop the skills and competencies they will need to succeed in the present and future age of information. Both Oblinger (1998) and Warschauer (1998) asserted that information technology is most effective when used to promote a problem-based and collaborative learning model. Content-based courses support a learning environment that is both task-based and student-centered; therefore, these courses provide the ideal context in which to introduce students to information technology, using this technology both to support traditional classroom methodology and curricular goals and to explore new possibilities for teaching and learning.

This chapter discusses some of the issues that must be considered in order for information technology to become an integral component of the design of content-based courses. Some of these issues are practical in nature and concern whether faculty and administrators are willing and able to incorporate technology into the ESL classroom and whether students have adequate access to computers and the Internet. Others are pedagogical in nature and concern how information technology can best be used to strengthen a content-based pedagogy of critical collaborative inquiry and problem solving.

THE ROLE OF FACULTY AND ADMINISTRATORS

Before information technology can be made part of a content-based curriculum, faculty and college administrators must be both willing and able to use it. Some college faculty are already exploring innovative ways to present instruction; however, many others remain reluctant to integrate information technology into the classroom. According to Cummings (1995), this reluctance may stem from a variety of reasons. Equipment may be unavailable, incompatible, or obsolete, and technical support may be unreliable or lacking. Instructors may not be trained nor feel comfortable using technology in their teaching. They may have insufficient time and/or little incentive for developing materials or instructional innovations. Still others may fear that technology will depersonalize instruction, replacing face-to-face contact with machine interfaces.

Increasing ESL instructors' comfort level with technology is critical to assuring that it is used successfully in content-based courses. According to Harapnuik (1998), many adults are fearful and apprehensive toward new learning experiences with technology. This is true of ESL instructors as well as of their students. Faculty must be provided with access to computers, as well as with training in how to use them most effectively to enhance instruction.

Olivier and Shapiro (1993) note that observing others can alleviate fear of technology and that comfort and confidence increases with computer use. Therefore faculty should be provided with workshops that both allow them to observe how others use technology and give them personal hands-on experience with that technology.

Faculty development workshops can benefit instructors in-service; however, to insure that all ESL faculty enter the profession equipped with the skills needed for technology integration, graduate teacher education courses should provide extensive training in the educational uses of Internet technology (Borras, 1996). Borras asserts that graduate courses should include hands-on experience in how to use major Internet tools for communication, information research, and site evaluation as well as how to author basic educational Web projects. In this way, from the beginning of their careers, ESL faculty will be equipped to make information technology an integral component of instruction.

Although faculty training is important, without administrative support it may be difficult, if not impossible, to integrate technology into instruction (Mecklenburger, 1989; Raven Lee & Johnson, 1998). Administrative support is critical to implementing the faculty development programs needed to promote the skills required to create technology enhanced learning contexts. Seeking support for technology integration often involves persuading administrators that technology will benefit not only instruction, but also enrollment. Administrators who believe that a technology enhanced program will lead to increased student enrollment are more likely to tie technology based innovations to the curriculum and goals of the institution and to support faculty in their use of technology (Sachs, Winther, Decker, & O'Connor, 1996). In the final analysis, the full potential of technology will be realized only if faculty and administrators work together to adopt an educational philosophy that makes use of the unique capabilities of technology.

STUDENTS' ACCESS TO TECHNOLOGY

Access to and training in technology is an issue not just for ESL instructors, but for their students as well. Although technological literacy has now joined the basic skills required in college, many ESL students suffer from inequity in their access to technology. In his plenary address to the 1999 Teachers of English to Speakers of Other Languages (TESOL) Pre-Conference Online Workshop *"Language Teaching in the Age of Information,"* Warschauer (1998) said that many of our ESL students encounter "unequal access to the ... technological ... skills needed for success in today's world" (p. 11). He went on to advise that the college classroom may be the only place where ESL students have access to technology. Dusick (1998) agreed, stating that, "without technology in the schools, the gap between the technologically elite and the technologically disadvantaged will only widen and put our students at a greater disadvantage" (p. 12). Yet, if ESL students are to derive maximum benefits from technologically enhanced instruction, they need not only access to technology, but also training in how to use technology to its best advantage.

Training is a must so that users become empowered, and not disillusioned or disenfranchised by the technology (Sachs et al., 1996). Many ESL students are computer novices who must develop an adequate comfort level when using computers. As novice computer users, these students are likely to make a number of errors, experiencing frustration as they spend a large portion of their computer time trying to recover from these errors (Lazar & Norcio, 1998). Because the probability for error increases in a networked environment, as exists on the Internet, students must be trained to deal appropriately with errors if they are to derive any educational benefits from information technology use.

According to Lazar and Norcio (1998), instructors should spend some time teaching effective error management techniques to make students aware that errors are a normal part of computer use, and that they can recover and learn from the errors they make. Each small success that students experience with technology helps to increase confidence and empowers them to take control of their own learning. Increased learner control enhances feelings of self-efficacy, self-determination, and motivation (Kinzie & Sullivan, 1989; Lawless & Brown, 1997). Furthermore, when students begin to view errors as challenges that promote better learning, they acquire a skill that generalizes to learning contexts both within and outside of the computer lab and gain confidence to explore and take risks in the overall learning environment (Kasper, 1998).

THE EDUCATIONAL BENEFITS OF INFORMATION TECHNOLOGY IN ESL INSTRUCTION

According to *The President's Educational Technology Initiative* (1998), when technology is used as part of a pedagogical model that involves students in complex, authentic tasks, the results are student-centered cooperative learning, increased teacher–student and peer interaction, and more positive attitudes toward learning. Additionally, research (Berger, 1992; Raven Lee & Johnson, 1998) has found that technology strengthens attention and concentration and therefore provides motivation for students to spend more time on task. Furthermore, technology delivers content that meets the needs of students with diverse learning styles (Lewis, 1998), creating a context for individualized and lifelong learning, both proven factors in academic and professional achievements (*The President's Educational Technology Initiative*, 1998).

This research suggests that technology should become a key component of content-based ESL instruction; however, Warschauer (1998) advises that we need to consider both the question of how to use information technology to teach language and that of how to teach language so that ESL learners can make effective use of available technology. As Sachs et al. (1996) caution, "The integration of [technology] into the ESL course is not something to be entered into without a clear idea of what will be accomplished using that technology" (p. 3). Research conducted during the 1990s (see Cradler & Bridgforth, 1996) suggests that to be most effective, the use of information technology should be suited to well-planned curricular goals and should involve carefully designed activities that provide students with meaningful educational experiences and opportunities for individualized instruction.

Recently, colleges have begun to tighten standards and to demand more and more of their student population, and all students today are faced with increasingly stringent time limitations on developmental education (Yamasaki, 1998). ESL students, in particular, need to earn their place as members of the academic community more quickly than ever before. As these students are given less time to meet institutional standards for language proficiency, their rapid acquisition of strong grammar, reading, and writing skills becomes ever more important. Information technology resources offer a powerful context for developing basic language skills because when ESL students get online, they immediately have many more opportunities to use English as they read Internet texts, compose e-mail, and listen to sound clips on Web pages. Moreover, Internet resources provide an abundance of interactive exercises through which ESL students can develop linguistic proficiency.

Grammar instruction often presents a significant challenge to ESL faculty because each student in a class may have specific and distinct grammatical problems. Because grammatical needs can vary so widely in a single class, it is difficult, if not impossible, to cover the full range of grammatical systems sufficiently for all students during class time. However, to articulate knowledge clearly and intelligently, students must learn to use grammar accurately, meaningfully, and appropriately (Larsen-Freeman, 1997; Master, chap. 5, this volume). It is here that information technology resources available on the Internet may be used to facilitate and enhance grammar instruction and meet student needs through exercises that target a variety of linguistic forms and functions and provide many opportunities for self-study and extra practice. Sites like *Dave's ESL Café* (located at *http://www.eslcafe.com/*) and various college and university Online Writing Labs (e.g., the Purdue Online Writing Lab located at *http://owl.english.purdue.edu/*), which may be accessed at any time of the day or night, provide a large body of interactive exercises that enable students to target and work on the specific forms and structures that give them problems.

My ESL students have found computer-based grammar exercises to be both beneficial and useful, and they prefer them to print exercises because of the greater range of items with which to practice, the immediate feedback provided, and the chance to return to tackle difficult or confusing items again and again. For these students, using computer-based exercises has helped to create a more individualized learning situation. To illustrate, in one case a student was having problems recognizing sentence boundaries, and as a result, his writing was plagued with run-on sentences and sentence fragments. On the Internet, he located a number of exercises that focused on sentence boundaries. He was able to access and return to practice with these exercises as often as he needed to and he received immediate feedback on his responses. Through this extended and independent practice, he achieved greater awareness of how to construct complete and coherent sentences. His grammatical accuracy improved quite rapidly, his self-confidence increased, and his writing became more correct and better developed.

In addition to facilitating grammatical proficiency, the Internet helps to develop reading skills by providing ready access to a broad range of media and links to remote information resources that might otherwise be unavailable to ESL students. Content-based textual material abounds on the Internet, and the nonlinear nature of hypertext offers ESL students a highly interactive and innovative reading experience that quickly builds skills both in meaning construction and critical literacy. Hypertext technology enables readers to pick and choose blocks of text by interacting with the machine (Barnes, 1994). In the process of exploring hypertext links, students learn to make intertextual connections and to identify relevant information (Lepeintre & Stephan, 1995). Warschauer (1998) notes that reading online also develops critical literacy because those who cannot make critical evaluations cannot even find what they need to read on the Internet. As they learn text navigational skills and are able to control the direction of their reading and research, ESL students are transformed from passive receivers of knowledge to active explorers of information using hypertext links to connect information in an intuitive, associative manner. This transformation paves the way for students to explore the reading–writing connection through in-depth analysis of and written response to text.

Writing tasks that promote this reading–writing connection foster intertextual analysis of themes and issues and provide students with a powerful tool to enhance text comprehension by encouraging them to integrate key ideas with background knowledge and personal experience (Kasper, 1996; Kennedy, 1994; Leki, 1993; Zamel, 1992). Computer-mediated communication, or CMC, offers students a conversational and text-based electronic learning environment through which they may acquire, share, and discuss these ideas as they communicate in an asynchronous (e.g., via e-mail) or a synchronous (e.g., in MOOs) mode with peers and instructors. The result is a self-directed, collaborative learning context that can be used to develop linguistic proficiency through various types of content-based research projects in which students gather and share resources electronically with those in their class, in other parts of the country, or across the world (see e.g., Bliss, 1998; Egbert, chap. 9, this volume; Tillyer & Wood, chap. 10, this volume; Kasper, chap. 11, this volume). By requiring students to actively set and then regulate and monitor their own progress, these computer-mediated collaborations encourage self-directed learning, a skill that will be critical in the academic and workforce environments of the 21st century (Twigg, 1998). Finally, because CMC results in archived logs that may be reread and reflected on, it empowers ESL students to become more aware of the learning process. Thus, it helps to build metacognitive skills (English, 1998), which have been found to correlate with improved performance on various linguistic and academic tasks (Devine, 1993; Kasper, 1997).

In addition to the linguistic benefits it provides, CMC also helps to facilitate the socioaffective aspects of learning by stressing the importance of strategic, transactional writing and greater peer interaction and collaboration. The ability to network with others across the room, the city, the country, or even the world offers ESL students the potential for social contexts that satisfy affiliation needs through connections with others who share their interests and experiences. As students interact with each other posting, reading, and responding to electronic messages, they learn community norms and develop a sense of personal efficacy and social affiliation (Sproull, 1998). Once again, these are skills that will serve them well in the academic and workforce environments.

Finally, distance learning is fast becoming part of the mainstream college curriculum, as colleges and universities strive to increase access to educational opportunities for students within and beyond the institution. Online course offerings are more flexible and learner-centered, free students from scheduling restrictions, and expand the physical college classroom to meet the needs of an increasingly diverse student population (Angiello & Caruso-Deane, 1998). Distance education programs also provide access to lifelong learning for everyone as students anywhere with access to a computer may take courses online (Gates, 1998). Because many institutions are expanding their online course offerings, when ESL students enter the college mainstream, they may elect to take courses offered through distance learning programs at their own or at another institution. Successful distance education requires skill in self-directed learning (Oblinger, 1998; Twigg, 1998), which students can acquire through their experiences using information technology in their ESL courses. Therefore, content-based ESL courses that incorporate information technology give ESL students the skills they need to participate in these new course formats and thereby provide them with more extensive educational options.

CONCLUSION

It is the role of educators to give students the knowledge they need to succeed, and knowledge today goes beyond rote learning and test performance. It includes the ability to search for information with all available media and to utilize technological tools to accomplish a variety of tasks (Dusick, 1998). Warschauer (1998) asserted that to prepare ESL students to succeed in the age of information, "We have to teach [them] to use English to carry out the kinds of complex critical inquiry, investigation, analysis, experimentation, and collaboration needed for success in today's world" (p. 9). Through instructional activities that make language learning the context for "significant investigation, individual application, and personal reflection" (LALAC, 1997, p. 4) of content-based issues, we can encourage students to view English as a means of constructing and expanding knowledge. As an integral component of content-based courses, information technology encourages students to become self-directed learners able to solve problems independently and offers them a powerful context for developing the metacognitive and critical thinking skills necessary for success in today's world.

As information technology continues to develop in the future, new avenues will open for the design and implementation of content-based ESL courses, and the possibilities for using technology to enhance instruction will grow and be limited only by the imagination and creativity of educators. The use of information technology can bring many educational benefits to ESL instruction; however, one caveat must be noted. As information technology use increases, students will be required to assume a more active, more responsible role in their own learning process. Although some students will embrace this increased independence, not all will. Baynton (1992) suggested that in our efforts to help students become autonomous, critical learners, a balance must be struck between independence, competence, and support to achieve control of the learning process. Warschauer (1998) suggested that this balance may be struck through guided and structured collaborative projects involving social investigation, exploration of cultural themes, and critical analysis. Warschauer believes that these types of projects are key to helping students develop not only technological literacy, but also linguistic and academic skills, including fluency, syntactic, lexical, and pragmatic competence and the ability for sophisticated communication, abstract, critical thinking, and complex negotiation.

Thus, as the role of computers grows in the future, it is critical that instructors be sure to use available technology to enhance, but never to replace personal interaction between students and teachers. Technology benefits content-based ESL instruction only insofar as it is used to afford students increased opportunities and support for self-directed learning and to build communicative competence along with linguistic accuracy.

In concluding this chapter and this volume of essays, I would like to leave readers, from the ranks of both faculty and administration, with a call to action. This call asks that readers continue to develop and expand content-based programs that will enable ESL students to acquire the linguistic and academic skills they need to enter and to succeed in mainstream courses. It also asks that readers recognize that technological literacy now counts among the basic skills required for college-level work. Finally, this call to action asks that educators devote attention to gaining the expertise *they* need to effectively incorporate information technology into ESL courses. In this way, we can help to insure that students leave our ESL courses prepared to meet the challenges of the academic and the workforce environments of the 21st century.

REFERENCES

Angiello, R., & Caruso-Deane, L. (1998, November). *Re-educating educators to rethink the way we teach*. Paper presented at CIT '98, Miami Beach, FL.

Barnes, S. (1994). Hypertext literacy. *Interpersonal Computing and Technology: An Electronic Journal for the 21st Century, 2*(4), 24–36. [Online.] Available: http://www.helsinki.fi/science/optek/1994/n4/barnes.txt

Baynton, M. (1992). Dimensions of "control" in distance education: A factor analysis. *American Journal of Distance Education, 6*(2), 17–31.

Berger, C. (1992). Ann Jackson and the four methods of integrating technology into teaching. *Syllabus, 21*, 2–4.

Bliss, A. (1998). *Collaborative writing using research on the World Wide Web*. Paper presented at the TCC 98 Online Conference. 7-9 April 1998. [Online]. Available: http://leahi.kcc.hawaii.edu/org/tcon98/paper/bliss.html

Borras, I. (1996, November). Internet for teachers: Case study of a graduate course. In *Proceedings of WebNet 98* Orlando, Florida (CD-ROM). Charlottesville, VA: Association for the Advancement of Computing in Education.

Cradler, J., & Bridgforth, E. (1996). *Recent research on the effects of technology on teaching and learning*. [Online]. Available: http://www.fwl.org/techpolicy/research.html

Crandall, J. (1993). Diversity as challenge and resource. In *Proceedings on the conference on ESL students in the CUNY classroom: Faculty strategies for success* (pp. 4–19). New York: CUNY.

Cummings, L. E. (1995). Educational technology—A faculty resistance view; Part 1: Incentives and understanding. *Educational Technology Review, 4*, 13–18.

City University of New York (1994). *Report of the CUNY ESL Task Force*. New York: The Instructional Resource Center, CUNY.

Devine, J. (1993). The role of metacognition in second language reading and writing. In J. G. Carson & I. Leki (Eds.), *Reading in the composition classroom: Second language perspectives* (pp. 105–127). Boston: Heinle & Heinle.

Dusick, D. M. (1998). The learning effectiveness of educational technology: What does that *really* mean? *Educational Technology Review, 10*, 10–12.

English, J. A. (1998). MOO-based metacognition: Incorporating online and offline reflection into the writing process. *KAIROS: A Journal for Teachers of Writing in Webbed Environments, 3*(1). [Online]. Available: http://english.ttu.edu/Kairos/3.1/features/english

Gates, B. (1998). *Conversations on community colleges, technology, and tomorrow*. Keynote address presented at the Conference on Information Technology (CIT) '98. Miami Beach, FL, 3 November.

Harapnuik, D. (1998, November). Inquisitivism or "The HHHMMM??? What does this button do?" approach to learning: The synthesis of cognitive theories into a novel approach to adult education. In *Proceedings of WebNet 98*. Orlando, Florida (CD-ROM). Charlottesville, VA: Association for the Advancement of Computing in Education.

Hooker, M. (1997). The transformation of higher education. In D. G. Oblinger & S. C. Rush (Eds.), *The learning revolution: The challenge of information technology in the academy* (pp. 20–34). Bolton, MA: Anker.

Kasper, L. F. (1996). Writing to read: Enhancing ESL students' reading proficiency through written response to text. *Teaching English in the Two-Year College, 23*(1), 25–33.

Kasper, L. F. (1997). Assessing the metacognitive growth of ESL student writers. *TESL-EJ, 3*(1). [Online]. Available: http://www-writing.berkeley.edu/TESL-EJ/ej09/a1.html

Kasper, L. F. (1998). ESL writing and the principle of nonjudgmental awareness: Rationale and implementation. *Teaching English in the Two-Year College, 25*(1), 58–66.

Kennedy, B. (1994). The role of topic and the reading/writing connection. *TESL-EJ, 1*(1). [Online]. Available: http://www-writing.berkeley.edu/TESL-EJ/ej01/a3.html

Kinzie, M. B., & Sullivan, H. J. (1989). Continuing motivation, learner control, and CAI. *Educational Technology Research and Development, 37*(2), 5–14.

LALAC. (1997). *Learning through language: A call for action in all disciplines.* [Online]. Available: http://www.sfasu.edu/lalac/brochure.html

Larsen-Freeman, D. (1997). Grammar and its teaching: Challenging the myths. *ERIC Digest (March).* [Online]. Available: http://www.cal.org/ericcll/digest/Larsen01.htm

Lawless, K. A., & Brown, S. W. (1997). Multimedia learning environments: Issues of learner control and navigation. *Instructional Science, 25*, 117–131.

Lazar, J., & Norcio, A. (1998). The effects of error management, exploration, and conceptual models on learning to use the Internet. In *Proceedings of WebNet 98* Orlando, FL. November 7–12. (CD-ROM). Charlottesville, VA: Association for the Advancement of Computing in Education.

Lepeintre, S., & Stephan, L. (1995). Telnet treasure hunts: Learning to read (on) the Internet. In M. Warschauer (Ed.), *Virtual connections* (pp. 331–335). Honolulu: University of Hawaii Press.

Leki, I. (1993). Reciprocal themes in ESL reading and writing. In J. G. Carson & I. Leki (Eds.), *Reading in the composition classroom: Second language perspectives* (pp. 9–32). Boston: Heinle & Heinle.

Lewis, B. (1998). Designing web courses for different learning styles. In *Proceedings of WebNet 98* Orlando, Florida. 7–12 November. (CD-ROM). Charlottesville, VA: Association for the Advancement of Computing in Education.

Mecklenburger, J. (1989). Technology in the 1990's: Ten secrets for success. *Principal, 69*(2), 6–8.

Oblinger, D. (1998). *Global education in the twenty-first century.* Keynote Address presented at CIT '98. Miami Beach, FL. 4 November 1998.

Olivier, T. A., & Shapiro, F. (1993). Self-efficacy and computers. *Journal of Computer-Based Instruction, 20*(3), 81–84.

Raven Lee, J., & Johnson, C. (1998). Helping higher education faculty clear instructional technology hurdles. *Educational Technology Review, 10*, 15–17.

Rossetti, M. (1998). E-mail communication. *LTAI-L* list—TESOL 99 Preconference Online Workshop: *Language Teaching in the Age of Information.* October 28, 1998. Available: http://www.internetsmart.com/ltai/logs/index.html

Sachs, C., Winther, D., Decker, S., & O'Connor, R. (1996). Challenges and opportunities: management and use of technology in IEP programs. Panel presentation at Tri-TESOL '96. Seattle, WA. [Online]. Available: http://www.wsu.edu/~sachs/Academia/Present/challenges/Challenges.html

Sproull, L. (1998). *A database is not a community: Important social dynamics in online groups*. Keynote address presented at WebNet '98. Orlando, FL. 12 November 1998.

The President's Educational Technology Initiative. (1998). [Online]. Available: http://www.whitehouse.gov/WH/EOP/OP/html/edtech/html/edtech.html

Twigg, C. A. (1998). What we know about information technology and learning. Keynote Address presented at the Conference on Information Technology (CIT) '98. Miami Beach, FL. 1 November, 1998.

Warschauer, M. (1998). New media, new literacies: Challenges for the next century. *Language Teaching in the Age of Information*. TESOL 99 Preconference Online Workshop. [Online]. Available: http://www.internetsmart.com/ltai/ltai.html

Yamasaki, E. (1998). Effective policies for remedial education. *ERIC Digest*. [Online]. Available: http://www.gseis.ucla.edu/ERIC/digests/dig9806.html

Zamel, V. (1992). Writing one's way into reading. *TESOL Quarterly, 26*, 463–485.

About The Authors

Loretta F. Kasper is associate professor of English at Kingsborough Community College/CUNY. She received a PhD in cognitive psychology with a specialization in psycholinguistics from Rutgers University in 1985. Dr. Kasper has been developing and teaching content-based college ESL courses since 1985. She has published numerous scholarly articles and book chapters on her work in the field. Her most recent research focuses on the use of multimedia and the Internet in content-based instruction. Dr. Kasper is the owner and moderator of Content-ESL, an e-mail discussion list devoted to issues in content-based instruction. In addition to this volume, she is the author of two content-based textbooks—*Teaching English through the Disciplines: Psychology* and *Interdisciplinary English*.

Marcia Babbitt has been codirector, with Rebecca Mlynarczyk, of the ESL Program at Kingsborough Community College/CUNY since June 1996. She is also director of Kingsborough's Intensive ESL Program and coordinator of ESL for Kingsborough's College Now Program. Before assuming her post as codirector of ESL, she supervised ESL in Kingsborough's Reading and Writing Center. Professor Babbitt holds a PhD in linguistics from the Graduate Center of the City University of New York and a master's degree in Spanish language and literature from the State University of Iowa.

Rebecca Williams Mlynarczyk has taught developmental writing and reading at the City University of New York since 1974 and is currently associate professor of English at Kingsborough Community College. In her role as codirector of the ESL program, she has been actively involved in many aspects of the college's content-based Intensive ESL Program. She received her PhD in applied linguistics from New York University in 1993. She is the author of *Conversations of the Mind: The Uses of Journal Writing for Second-Language Learners* and co-author, with Steven Haber, of *In Our Own Words: A Guide With Readings for Student Writers*. She has published numerous articles on the teaching of writing and reading to second-language learners.

Donna M. Brinton is a Lecturer in the Department of Applied Linguistics and TESL at UCLA and academic coordinator of the UCLA ESL Service Courses. She is co-author of the books *Content-Based Second Language Instruction* (with Marguerite Ann Snow & Marjorie Wesche), *The Content-Based Classroom* (with Marguerite Ann Snow), and *New Ways in Content-Based Instruction* (with Peter Master). In addition to her work in content-based instruction, Ms. Brinton is interested in the area of materials and curriculum development, the use of instructional technology in second and foreign language learning, the teaching of pronunciation, and novice teacher development. She has published in all the above areas and also enjoys doing short-term international teacher training in these same areas.

Judith W. Rosenthal received her BA in human biology and her PhD in physiological chemistry from Brown University (Providence, Rhode Island). Twenty-five years later, she earned a master's degree in bilingual/bicultural education from Kean College of New Jersey. Dr. Rosenthal is the author of *Teaching Science to Language Minority Students* as well as of numerous articles. She has been on the faculty of Kean University since 1974 and teaches biology courses in both English and Spanish.

Peter Master is associate professor in the Department of Linguistics and Language Development at San Jose State University. He is the author of *Systems in English Grammar: An Introduction for Language Teachers* and co-editor, with Donna Brinton, of the books, *New Ways in Content-Based Instruction* and *New Ways in English for Specific Purposes*. Peter Master also serves as co-editor of the journal, *English for Specific Purposes*.

Sharon Myers is associate professor in the Department of Classical and Modern Languages at Texas Tech University in Lubbock, Texas. She is also director of the International Teaching Assistant Training Program and the Academic ESL Program. Dr. Myers has 8 years cumulative experience working overseas, 6 years in Peru and 2 years in Mexico. Dr. Myers has published reports of her work in a number of print and online journals, including *English for Specific Purposes* and *TESL-EJ*. Dr. Myers received her PhD in multilingual/multicultural education from Florida State University, Tallahassee in 1992.

Joy Egbert is an assistant professor in the School of Education at Indiana University. Dr. Egbert received her PhD in higher education teaching/ESL from the University of Arizona in 1993. Her area of specialization is computer-assisted language learning (CALL), and she has published numerous articles and book chapters in the field. Dr. Egbert is co-editor, with Elizabeth Hanson-Smith, of the volume *CALL Environments: Research, Practice, and Critical*

Issues. Dr. Egbert is on the steering committee of TESOL's CALL Interest Section and is the Editor of the INTESOL newsletter, *TESOLIN*. Dr. Egbert's latest work has been developing a distance CALL course for graduate level MATESOL students, available at: http://www.indiana.edu/~cell/main.htm

David A. Tillyer is an adjunct instructor at the City College of New York (CUNY) and Westchester Community College (SUNY). He has taught English as a second language since 1977—using computers since 1983 and using the Internet since 1990. From 1983 to 1987, he was general manager of the Regents/ALA Company, the first commercial supplier of computer assisted English language learning materials. Professor Tillyer started the online writing lab for the U.S. Information Agency, an online writing course for foreign nationals in U.S. consulates. He has conducted teacher-training seminars in the U.S. and in Europe, mostly on uses of the Internet in language teaching and has supervised more than 20 online collaborative projects linking two or more schools. His publications include articles in journals from TESOL and IATEFL to online journals.

Louise S. Wood is currently developmental English department head at Tri-County Technical College in Pendleton, South Carolina, a position she has held since 1986. She received a BA from Columbia College, Columbia, South Carolina, and an MEd from the University of Virginia. In 1997 she attended the Kellogg Institute at the National Center for Developmental Education, Appalachian State University. Her professional affiliations include the National Association of Developmental Education, South Carolina Association of Developmental Education, North Carolina Association of Developmental Education, National Council of Teachers of English, and South Carolina Technical Education Association. In 1995, she received a Partners in Technology Award from Sixth Floor Media of Houghton Mifflin for her use of e-mail with basic writers.

AUTHOR INDEX

217

SUBJECT INDEX

A

Accessibility of content-based materials, 9
Administration,
  of content-based programs, 26–45
    addressing student needs, 28
    budgeting, 35–36
    choosing a director, 29–30
    course design, 27–28
    recruiting students, 38–40
    scheduling courses, 37
    support from college, 29
Assessment, 19–22, 114–115, 144–145,
    179–180
  alternative forms of, 21
  and instructional practice, 19–20
  and standardized tests, 19–20
  as a multifaceted construct, 20
  as an interactive process, 21
  frequency of, 20
  goals of, 19
  in lower level courses, 114–115
  of language and content, 19–22
  perceptions of, 19, 21–22
Associative stage (of learning), 5
Audiotapes, 109, 114, 121, 137–142
  as content-based resources, 137–138
  production of, 138–141
  use of, 141–142
Authenticity, 58–60
Autonomous stage (of learning), 5

B

Basic interpersonal language skills, 5

C

Cognitive academic language learning ap-
    proach (CALLA), 6
Cognitive academic language proficiency, 5
Cognitive construct, 6
  reading as a, 6–7
  writing as a, 7–8
Cognitive learning theory, 5–8
Cognitive map, 7
Cognitive stage (of learning), 5
Collaborative learning (see, Learning com-
    munity)
Comprehensible input
  CBI and, 4
  definition of, 4
  e-mail as, 169
Comprehensible input hypothesis, 4
Computer,
  as content, 151–163
  benefits of using, 159–160
  culture and, 154–155
  slideshows, 160–161
Computer mediated communication
    (CMC), 186, 207–208
Content,
  instruction versus language instruction,
    19–20, 93–94, 102–104
  language instructor's need to master, 18
  relevance to student needs, 18
  selection of, 18, 57–58
Content area knowledge, 18, 60
Content-based instruction
  definition of, 93
  lower level students and, 107–121
  models of, 10–17
  program design in, 26–38

223